Food in the United States, 1820s–1890

Recent Titles in
Food in American History

American Indian Food
Linda Murray Berzok

Food in Colonial and Federal America
Sandra L. Oliver

FOOD IN THE UNITED STATES, 1820S–1890

SUSAN WILLIAMS

Food in American History

Greenwood Press
Westport, Connecticut • London

Library of Congress Cataloging-in-Publication Data

Williams, Susan.
    Food in the United States, 1820s–1890/Susan Williams.
      p. cm. — (Food in American history, ISSN 1552-8200)
    Includes bibliographical references and index.
    ISBN 0–313–33245–2 (alk. paper)
    1. Food—History—19th century.   2. Food habits—United States—
History—19th century.   3. Cookery, American—History—19th century.   I. Title.
II. Series.
  TX355.W55   2006
  641.30973′ 09034–dc22   2006015156

British Library Cataloguing in Publication Data is available.

Copyright © 2006 by Susan Williams

Library of Congress Catalog Card Number: 2006015156
ISBN: 0–313–33245–2
ISSN: 1552-8200

First published in 2006

Greenwood Press, 88 Post Road West, Westport, CT 06881
An imprint of Greenwood Publishing Group, Inc.
www.greenwood.com

Printed in the United States of America

The paper used in this book complies with the
Permanent Paper Standard issued by the National
Information Standards Organization (Z39.48–1984).

10 9 8 7 6 5 4 3 2 1

The publisher has done its best to make sure the instructions and/or recipes in this
book are correct. However, users should apply judgment and experience when
preparing recipes, especially parents and teachers working with young people. The
publisher accepts no responsibility for the outcome of any recipe included in this
volume.

To my mother, who first taught me the joys of eating and the importance of dinner

CONTENTS

SERIES FOREWORD

This series focuses on food culture as a way to illuminate the societal mores and daily life of Americans throughout our history. These volumes are meant to complement history studies at the high school level on up. In addition, Food Studies is a burgeoning field, and foodies and food scholars will find much to mine here. The series is comprehensive, with the first volume covering American Indian food and the following volumes each covering an era or eras from Colonial times until today. Regional and group differences are discussed as appropriate.

Each volume is written by a food historian who is an expert on the period. Each volume contains the following:

- Chronology of food-related dates
- Narrative chapters, including
  Introduction (brief overview of period as it relates to food)
  Foodstuffs (staples, agricultural developments, etc.)
  Food Preparation
  Eating Habits (manners, customs, mealtimes, special occasions)
  Concepts of Diet and Nutrition (including religious strictures)
- Recipes
- Period illustrations
- Glossary, if needed
- Bibliography
- Index

ACKNOWLEDGMENTS

Writing a book is a lonely task, but one which an author does not complete alone. Many people assisted me in the preparation of this manuscript. Some offered research assistance, others writing assistance, still others emotional and culinary sustenance. My scholarly interest in the history of food and its culture is thirty years old this year. I remain indebted to the many people who sparked that interest and have helped me along the way, especially my dear friend and former editor, Wendy Wolf. For research assistance on this project, I thank Bob Foley, Simone Blake, Linda LeBlanc, Sara Marks, and Janice Ouellette at Fitchburg State College. Additional thanks to my colleagues in the Social Science Department at Fitchburg State, who were continually supportive and gave me much needed reprieves from departmental duties for writing. My undergraduate Writing History seminar was dubious about food-centered research projects, but their seminar papers helped me to sift through a great deal of literature, and some of them even offered fresh ways of thinking about the culture of food. Thanks to the Ruth Butler Grant committee at Fitchburg State College for their financial support of my research, and to Karen Valeri for the many ways that she has helped me on this and other projects.

I want to thank Wendi Schnaufer, my editor at Greenwood Press and the inspiration behind this series, for her enthusiasm, guidance, and patience, as well as Vivek Sood at Techbooks for his careful editing of my manuscript. I could not have written this new food book without the existence of "Feeding America: The Historic American Cook Project," an online digital archive of most of the important cookery sources any American food scholar would require, housed at the Michigan State University Library. This is a model project, making accessible seventy-six fully digitalized and searchable cookbooks from the late eighteenth to the early twentieth centuries. I am also grateful to the librarians and curators at the Library of Congress for the rich availability of food-related materials on the "American Memory" Web site. Friend, colleague, and archivist extraordinaire Sandra Markham at the Library Company of Philadelphia offered me prompt, inventive, and thorough ways of solving research dilemmas. She is indeed "Miss Information." Sandra Oliver, fellow author in this series, was another important source of assistance, comfort, and knowledge.

Finally, thanks to my friends and family for their support during the ups and downs of this project. The women of the Waterloom Center and my Saturday morning walking group, as well as my other friends in New Ipswich offered me great affection, entertainment, food, drink, sympathy, and healthful exercise to ward off the stresses of writing. Thanks for tolerating all of those foodie films I made you watch. My Northway friends gave me renewed energy to push on and finish the job at a time when I really needed it. Thanks especially to Mary Susanne Lamont for being such a devoted organizer and loyal friend. *Vive la canadienne*. My sisters, Mary McLaughlin and Ann Chiara, sang with me, laughed, cried, praised my cooking, or just hung out with me. You are the best. My mother, Helen Williams, the only one of us who ever formally studied cooking, taught me from a young age to appreciate food and cookery. I hope she understands how great an impact she has had on my scholarly path through the world of food history. And last, but certainly not least, thanks to Charlie, Dudley, and Emmy (my canine family) and to my husband, Harvey Green. Harvey has always given me both intellectual and edible support, even when immersed in his own writing projects. Our partnership has made this journey rich and deeply satisfying.

TIMELINE OF FOOD-RELATED EVENTS

1824	Mary Randolph, *The Virginia House-wife* published in Washington, DC.
1825	First tin can patented in United States by Thomas Kensett. Jean Anthelme Brillat-Savarin published *Physiologie du goût (The Physiology of Taste)* in Paris.
1826	American Temperance Society founded in Boston.
1828	Eliza Leslie, *Seventy-Five Receipts for Pastry, Cakes and Sweetmeats* published in Boston.
	The French Cook by Louis Eustache Ude published in Philadelphia.
1829	Lydia Maria Child's *The American Frugal Housewife* published in Boston.
	Yuengling Brewery opened in Pottsville, Pennsylvania.
1830	*Godey's Lady's Book* began publication in Philadelphia.
1833	Sylvester Graham began preaching the gospel of vegetarianism in Philadelphia.
1837	Queen Victoria ascended the throne of England.
1839	Sarah Josepha Hale published her first cookbook, *The Good Housekeeper*.
1840	Americans drank 3.1 gallons of alcoholic spirits per capita and 1.3 gallons of beer.
1841	Catharine Beecher published *A Treatise on Domestic Economy*.

1843	First patent issued for an ice cream freezer.
1845	Irish Potato Famine began.
1848	U.S.-Mexican War ended, bringing California and the Southwest into the Union.
1849	California Gold Rush began.
1850	American Vegetarian Society founded in New York City.
1851	Crystal Palace Exhibition opened in London, followed by New York Crystal Palace a year later.
1853	Gale Borden invented a process for producing condensed milk. Potato chips invented in Saratoga, New York.
1858	John Landis Mason patented a glass canning jar with a zinc screw cap.
	First patented can opener, by Ezra Warner, Waterbury, CT.
	Joseph Schlitz Brewing Company founded in Milwaukee.
1859	The Great American Tea Company (later A&P) opened a store on Vesey Street in New York City.
1861	First commercial pretzel factory opened in Lititz, Pennsylvania.
1861–1865	American Civil War.
1862	Homestead Act passed by Congress, luring settlers into the Midwest and West.
1863	Thanksgiving declared a national holiday by President Abraham Lincoln.
	Timothy Earle of Smithfield, Rhode Island, was awarded patent for the first rotary eggbeater.
1865	Beer magnate Matthew Vassar founded Vassar College, the first privately funded woman's college.
1866	Cadwallader C. Washburn opened his first flour mill in Minneapolis, Minnesota, which ultimately became General Mills. Charles Pillsbury opened his first mill there three years later.
1868	Edmund McIlhenny began producing Tabasco Sauce.

1869	Transcontinental railroad completed.
	H. J. Heinz and L. Clarence Noble began manufacturing bottled horseradish sauce.
1872	White Mountain Ice Cream Freezer patented in Laconia, New Hampshire.
1873	Dover cast-iron egg beater patented in Boston.
1876	Root Beer exhibited by Charles E. Hires at Philadelphia Centennial Exhibition.
	Juliet Corson opened the New York Cooking School.
1877	Charles Elmé Francatelli's *The Modern Cook: A Practical Guide to the Culinary Art in All Its Branches* published in Philadelphia.
1879	Boston Cooking School opened.
1880	Philadelphia Brand Cream Cheese introduced by the Phoenix Cheese Company (acquired by Kraft in 1928).
1882	Meadow Springs Distilling Company in Milwaukee, Wisconsin, began selling Red Star Yeast.
1884	Mrs. D. A. Lincoln's *Boston Cooking School Cook Book* published.
1885	Americans drank 1.4 gallons of spirits per capita and 11.4 gallons of beer.
1886	Coca Cola invented by Dr. John S. Pemberton in Atlanta, Georgia.
1888	*Miss Parloa's New Cook Book and Marketing Guide* published in Boston.

CHAPTER 1

INTRODUCTION

What foods did nineteenth-century Americans eat? How and why did those foodways change over time? How did they vary from region to region, from class to class? How did large-scale demographic and material forces reshape American ideas about diet and culinary tastes? How and why did certain foods and eating rituals acquire ideological dimensions during the so-called Victorian period? These are the fundamental questions of this book. In order to answer these questions, we must first deconstruct them a bit. First, for purposes of this book, "Victorian" will be used loosely to identify a period of time that ranges between the 1820s and 1890, despite the fact that Queen Victoria actually reigned over the British Empire between 1837 and 1901. I have selected the 1820s as a starting point in order to coincide with the beginning of the Industrial Revolution in the United States. The textile mills at Lowell began operation during that decade, as did many other fledgling factories that ultimately transformed the way Americans worked, lived, and ate.

The designation "American" raises another set of questions. During this time, Americans identified themselves in increasingly varied ways, whether as part of a particular region, class, race, gender, or ethnicity. I will try to address those areas of difference throughout the book, to offer a picture that represents the social and cultural diversity of the United States during this period. What Americans ate depended on where they lived and what was locally available to them, as well as on where they came from. Local conditions shaped food choices, whether "local" was defined by geopolitical region, climate, topography, or even by the area merchants who sold groceries and the neighbors who lived nearby.

Cultural origins also determined food preferences, as did socioeconomic status, and literacy. Taste—the physical and sensory attributes of foods—played as large a role in shaping Victorian foodways as it does today. Taste can be affected by novelty, by ideology, by social and even political aspirations, as well as by the extent to which certain foods resonate with deeply ingrained cultural memories. Anthropologists have argued that food has deep semiotic significance, grounded both in experiential and metaphysical judgments: "Goods that minister to physical needs—food or drink—are no less carriers of meaning than ballet or poetry." In other words, food and drink can be as culturally expressive as any other human artifact. Moreover, goods, including food and drink, do not operate outside a context. "All goods carry meaning, but none by itself," they argued. "The meaning is in the relation between all the goods."[1]

Regarding the intersection between taste and experience, scholars have looked to the work of nineteenth-century French food writer Jean Anthelme Brillat-Savarin, whose book *The Physiology of Taste* (1825) was an early attempt to analyze the deeper meanings of food and drink. Brillat-Savarin himself described three different sensations that characterized the experience of tasting: direct, complete, and reflective. He illustrated this theory by using the experience of eating a peach:

> He who eats a peach, for instance, is first of all agreeably struck by the perfume which it exhales; he puts a piece of it into his mouth, and enjoys a sensation of tart freshness which invites him to continue; but it is not until the instant of swallowing, when the mouthful passes under his nasal channel, that the full aroma is revealed to him; and this completes the sensation which a peach can cause. Finally, it is not until is has been swallowed that the man, considering what he has just experienced, will say to himself, "Now there is something really delicious!"[2]

In an age that increasingly was characterized by self-reflection and post-enlightenment intellectual pursuits, ideas about appropriate food and drink would have been subjected to the same scrutiny, whether scientific or metaphysical, as other aspects of American life.

Between 1820 and 1890, American foodways changed in part because the country itself expanded dramatically. What had once been a cluster of colonies clinging to the Atlantic coast became, by 1848, a continental nation that stretched from sea to sea and from Canada to Mexico. In 1820, the United States had a population of just over 10 million people, 1.5 million of them enslaved. Only 55,000 people lived in Illinois, the western edge of civilization in 1820. By 1840, the population of the country had grown to almost 17 million, and Illinois had almost half a million residents. Iowa had become the new frontier. Expansion meant that the majority of Americans were constantly on the move during their lifetimes. They moved west, whether on wagon trains to Oregon or in pursuit of gold in California, or to any of the territories in between. Along the way, they encountered new, often strange, foodways. Some of these were foodways of necessity—survival en route depended on a family's ability to adapt to the local conditions. Others were the result of new, blended American communities—where people exchanged ideas about eating as readily as ideas about politics, religion, and how to get rich. In this frontier context, food helped to normalize life. On the Kentucky frontier, for example, "re-creating aspects of the culture they left behind, whether through dress, food, or furnishings, may well have made the dislocations of frontier life more bearable for homesick pioneers."[3] Other historians of the frontier have noticed the role of the civilizing process, especially among women, as an important strategy for countering the deprivations of frontier life. Civilizing activities certainly included the restoration of pre-migration food and dining rituals.[4]

At the same time as thousands of Americans were moving westward, other Americans moved inward, from their rural villages and farms into the rapidly growing industrial cities. There, they found themselves surrounded by people unlike their old neighbors in the countryside. When Harriet Hanson Robinson and her husband, William, married in 1848, they moved into a boarding house in Boston so that William could pursue his career in journalism. Boarding house life must have been quite different for the Robinsons, who were accustomed to a close-knit world of family and community. In their wedding "Outfit," Harriet listed furniture, lamps, and numerous items for housekeeping, but no cooking utensils—since the family ate in a common boarding house dining room instead of in their own quarters. The young family subsequently moved to Lowell, where they occupied a house on Abbott Street. There, courtesy of William's mother, who sent them a wagonload of old furniture, they had a table and four straight-backed chairs for dining in their sitting room. Harriet supplemented her family's diet with produce from her garden—lettuce, tomatoes, rhubarb, and grapes.[5]

In addition to in-migrants like the Robinsons, the lure of America's opportunities drew thousands of immigrants, carrying their ideas about cooking and eating with them, into the United States. Traveling by wagon, steamship, and railroad, these new Americans crisscrossed the countryside in pursuit of a new life. After Congress passed the

Homestead Act in 1862, which guaranteed settlers 160 acres of land in return for a five-year residency commitment, the Minnesota Territory filled up with hundreds of thousands of Germans, Norwegians, Swedes, Irish, English, Scots, Welsh, Swiss, Czechs, Bohemians, Danes, and Hollanders.[6] For many of these immigrants, especially those in cities, employment in some part of the food-provisioning sector became a strategy for making it in the new world. As grocers, bakers, confectioners, butchers, chefs, domestic cooks, and even operatives in canning factories and meat-packing plants, these immigrants helped to internationalize American cuisine.

Food, like other aspects of cultural life in the growing American republic, reflected an ongoing tension between the persistence of traditional ingredients and cookery, albeit reshaped in an American context, and the appeal of new "modern" possibilities. Between 1820 and 1890, American foodways became increasingly specialized, far more diverse, and in some ways more homogenized. The regionalism that had characterized American food customs since the beginnings of European settlement gradually began to give way to a new, national food culture. By the end of the Victorian era, Americans could have fixed expectations about that which they consumed at the table.

Foreign observers can provide one picture of what American food customs might have looked like at the beginning of this period. Frances Trollope, the intrepid English traveler who journeyed all over the United States in the late 1820s, described what must have been a common scene in rural America: a self-sufficient farmstead. "We visited one farm, which interested us particularly from its wild and lonely situation, and from the entire dependence of the inhabitants upon their own resources," she wrote in her popular book *Domestic Manners of the Americans.*

> It was a partial clearing in the very heart of the forest. The house was built on the side of a hill, so steep that a high ladder was necessary to enter the front door, while the back one opened against the hill side; at the foot of this sudden eminence ran a clear stream, whose bed had been deepened into a little reservoir, just opposite the house. A noble field of Indian-corn stretched away into the forest on one side, and a few half-cleared acres, with a shed or two upon them, occupied the other, giving accommodations to cows, horses, pigs, and chickens innumerable. Immediately before the house was a small potato garden, with a few peach and apple trees.

Trollope's description of the family's crops and livestock suggested a traditional diet of cornbread or cornmeal mush, potatoes, and stewed, grilled, fried, or roasted meat and poultry, enlivened by pickled peaches, apple sauce, and, of course, pie. The family, an Ohio farmer, his wife, and their three young children, lived in a two-room log house with a lean-to kitchen. Trollope saw only beds and chests of drawers in the two sparsely furnished main rooms. She reported that the woman of the household, with help from her sister, spun and wove all textiles, sewed the family's clothing, and knitted stockings for all family members. The farmer manufactured shoes for his family, although he was "not a shoemaker by trade." The farmwife also made soap, candles, and, "from the sugar-trees on their farm," maple syrup and maple sugar. Like many rural women, she also translated her excess into cash "by sending a batch of butter and chicken to market." The money enabled her to purchase coffee, tea, and whiskey for her family. Trollope commented that although their corn crop seemed large, they did not appear to have a surplus: "They used no wheat, nor sold any of their corn, which, though it appeared a very large quantity, was not more than they required to make their bread and cakes of various kinds, and to feed all their live-stock during the winter."[7]

For Trollope, the self-sufficiency of this Ohio family seemed distinctly American. She, like Thomas Jefferson before her, equated independence and an agrarian lifestyle with virtue and freedom from decadence. The simple foodways implied by the family's farmstead merited approval from Mrs. Trollope. These people were not "living beyond their means." They respected tradition and honored the natural rhythms of the agricultural calendar. By contrast, Trollope, and other foreign observers of American habits during this era, adopted an entirely different tone when describing the eating customs of Americans who were more urbane, more upscale, and more well off. While in Cincinnati, one of the fastest-growing cities in the Ohio Valley, Trollope attended a tea party. She characterized the food served as a "massive meal," including "tea, coffee, hot cake and custard, hoe cake, johnny cake, waffle cake, and dodger cake, pickled peaches, and preserved cucumbers, ham, turkey, hung beef, apple sauce, and pickled oysters."[8] Her choice of the word "massive" suggested that, for Trollope and other genteel observers, Americans seemed lacking in social graces, and even worse, they were all too prone to gluttony. Moreover, she felt that the partygoers consciously resorted to food as a strategy to avoid having to converse with one another, especially with those of the opposite sex. What Trollope failed to recognize about this tea party and its "massive" quantities of food was the degree to which food signified hospitality, and that abundance was a matter of national pride. For the partygoers, ample food was evidence of the success of their new country, something European observers frequently had difficulty understanding.

The food served at this event, however, suggests a persistence of traditional American foodways, albeit enhanced by a growing array of new ingredients. The cakes, for example, were almost all corn-based. Early American settlers had inherited from their Native American fore-runners a local diet grounded in corn, squash, and beans, fleshed out by fish and game. To this basic assembly of New World foods, Europeans brought their own imported preferences for beef, lamb, pork, wheat, rye, barley, peas, cabbages, and various herbs and spices.[9] Throughout the eighteenth century, continued immigration into North America by newer groups of Europeans further expanded American food options. Those options, however, although more ethnically diverse than in the seventeenth century, continued to be limited by climate, topography, and proximity to markets, limitations that persisted well into the nineteenth century.

In contrast to Trollope's observations of American food customs in 1831, etiquette writer Elizabeth Ellet depicted a more modern family in the frontispiece of her 1873 *New Cyclopedia of Domestic Economy and Practical Housekeeper*. The family, which included a father, mother, and three children, sat around a table enjoying their evening meal. A tall vase of flowers graced the center of the table, surrounded by a caster set, a bread rack, and a water pitcher and four glasses on a tray. A platter containing both a roast leg of lamb and a small turkey sat before the father, along with a carving fork and knife—which rested on a knife rest. Other items on the table included a divided salt dish, a small bowl with a spoon, a butter dish, and a covered entrée dish. A black female servant stood behind the family holding a tray with a covered bowl and a tumbler. A gilt-bronze French garniture set, centered around a clock, sat on the mantelpiece, further enhancing the overall material elegance of dining room. As final confirmation of this family's social position and gentility, the hands of the clock rested on five, the newly fashionable dining hour for urban-dwelling Victorian Americans.[10]

These two depictions of American foodways reflect the dramatic changes going on in the United States between 1820 and 1890. American society and, consequently, its cuisine were transformed, not only by territorial expansion and new technologies but also by an economic transformation, which changed class structure, consumer possibilities, and social relations. Moreover, the gradual movement of Americans from their traditional homes in the rural countryside, or small-scale towns and villages, into large metropolitan centers generated new ways of operating socially, as well as new solutions to the more practical necessity of finding food in a non-agricultural setting. For the majority of Americans by 1890, markets had replaced gardens, farm-yards, and fields as the sources of their daily bread. Finally, American culture, while never homogeneous, was itself transformed during the Victorian era, as it absorbed the multiple new cultures of newly arrived Americans. During the 1880s, more immigrants arrived in the United States than the total number of all immigrants recorded in the Federal Censuses of 1790 through 1880. A country that had once been a mélange of English, French, Spanish, Dutch, Swedish, African, and German cultural customs became, by 1890, a country characterized by diversity on a large scale.

Along with demographic diversity came economic diversity. During the nineteenth century, a market revolution transformed the American economy from one that was primarily local and farm based, with the beginnings of a manufacturing sector and the continuation of traditional artisanal production, to one firmly grounded in large-scale, national industrial capitalism. By the 1830s, transportation enhancements—roads, canals, steam-powered ships, and railroads—ensured that American consumers could have fixed expectations about their food choices. The availability of fresh produce from California, oysters from the Chesapeake Bay, lobsters from New England, and oranges from Florida offset the seasonality that had determined menu and dietary choices from the beginning of European settlement in North America.

The growth of the American economy was accompanied by a redistribution of wealth and the emergence of a large body of middle-class consumers. These middle-class artisans, factory managers, merchants, office workers, and other "new" professionals defined themselves, in part, by their consumer choices. As members of the middle class, they deemed it important to express gentility and cosmopolitan taste in their daily lives, attributes traditionally equated with those above them on "the social ladder." Food, and the whole realm of artifacts associated with its preparation, presentation, and consumption, became increasingly important as a measure of class distinction.

Within this new social context, food must be considered both from a supply-side perspective—that of changing agriculture and animal husbandry practices, new preserving and food-processing techniques, and mass distribution of the products to American consumers—and through a demand-side analysis. On the supply side, modern machinery—metal plows, seed drills, the revolving horse-drawn hay rake, reapers, mechanical threshers, mowers, corn planters—transformed agricultural productivity.[11] Illinois farmer Eddin Lewis had become a large-scale purveyor of hogs, barreled pork, lard, butchered beef, and corn to markets in St. Louis by 1848. Lewis, a wealthy resident of Sugar Creek, was part of an agricultural revolution. Between 1838 and 1858, farm sizes in Sugar Creek, as elsewhere, increased significantly: the more land under cultivation, the greater the output.[12] Refinements in milling, slaughtering, and packaging food, as well as the advent of refrigeration, completed the process, improving American food options in terms of both quantity and variety.

The changes in American foodways during the Victorian era, however, were linked just as much to buying power and social aspirations as to availability. Food producers and distributors learned to employ sophisticated marketing techniques to shape and manipulate consumer expectations, thus creating a demand for new kinds of goods, including foodstuffs and the tools to prepare and serve them. This "created demand" worked through a multitude of new urban shopping venues, as well as new or newly available literary avenues, including cookbooks, domestic advice books, women's magazines, and newspapers.

Food, and the rituals that supported its preparation and consumption, formed an integral part of the social capital of community in Victorian America.[13] Neighbors, male and female, helped one another to get in the crops, make the hay, husk the corn, pare and dry apples, and complete the dozens of other tasks that made their lives both more secure and more pleasant. An elaborate system of communal labor, visiting, and other forms of social and economic exchange shaped community life. Food was frequently a central part of those exchanges, whether the participants lived in traditional towns and villages or in urban neighborhoods.[14] In fact, what was served during those social interactions offered important social cues about the nature of the social relationship. Women who called on other women expected that tea might be part of their reception. Men, too, had expectations about social visits. William J. Brown, an African American living in Providence, Rhode Island, wrote in his diary about those expectations:

> If a person went out to make a call or spend the evening and was not treated to something to drink, they would feel insulted. You might as well tell a man in plain words not to come again, for he surely would go off and spread it, how mean they were treated—not even so much as to ask them to have something to drink; and you would not again be troubled with their company.[15]

As ordinary Americans came to enjoy the luxury of a certain amount of discretionary income, they began to expand their horizons beyond the boundaries of local community. They consumed the outside world vicariously through literary outlets, but they also experienced new places and palates directly through travel, tourism, and vacationing. In 1835, Sarah Josepha Hale, a published writer and subsequently the editor of the popular women's magazine *Godey's Lady's Book*, wrote an essay titled "The Romance of Travelling" as part of her book *Traits of American Life*. "We must travel, if we would be in fashion," she began. "Men, women, and even children, are abroad to see the wonders of the grand canal, and the grander cataract. There is nothing like change, for enlarging the mind, and furnishing subjects for conversation." Moreover, she continued, "we should be acquainted with our own country and people. It is only by such means, that errors will be corrected, prejudices removed, and that good feeling and liberality of sentiment cultivated, which are indispensable to the perpetuity of the Union."[16]

Although Europeans had been traveling in America since the seventeenth century, and many seafaring Americans had been traveling the world equally as long, the nineteenth century became the great age of tourism in the United States. "Fashionable tourists," whether European or American, sought to experience the wonders of the Catskills, the White Mountains, Saratoga Springs, and the Niagara frontier in western New York. Along the way, they encountered fashionable hotels, inns, restaurants, and other tourist attractions, all of which exposed them to new experiences in food as well as scenery. Tourism and consumerism were inextricably linked, according to one travel historian, who argued,

> Tourism played a key role in *creating* a consumer-oriented society and economy. The tourist experience was crucial to the transformation of old-fashioned middling artisans, shopkeepers, and professionals into a new middle class, converting them from a tradition of self-denying soberness and frugality to a consumer ethic that sought liberation and fulfillment in purchases.[17]

This new, consumer mentality carried over into all realms of middle-class life, including menus and meals at home. Reading, which may be construed as a sort of intellectual tourism, opened women's eyes to innumerable possibilities for expanding their domestic repertoires and, subsequently, their gentility. The burgeoning American publishing industry began to produce new, American-authored cookbooks and domestic advice books. Lydia Maria Child's well-loved *American Frugal Housewife*, first published in 1829, was one such book. With Child and numerous other domestic advisors at their side, American women no longer had to rely on oral traditions, handed down from mother to daughter, for their cookery instruction. Nor were they limited to derivative works, copied almost word for word from British cookery texts. Child directed her advice "to those who are not ashamed of economy," and she proclaimed proudly that her book was truly "American" in its origin and its practicality. With regard to traveling, however, Child issued a stern warning to her readers. In a chapter titled "Hints to Persons of Moderate Fortune," she wrote, "There is one kind of extravagance rapidly increasing in this country, which, in its effects on our purses and our habits, is one of the worst kinds of extravagance; I mean the rage for travelling." She chastised those who went into debt over "luxurious and idle" pursuits, especially mothers, "who have left the children at home with Betsey, while they go to improve their minds at the Mountain House, or the Springs." She feared that the lure of travel might cause too many of her readers to "sacrifice permanent respectability and comfort to present gentility and love of excitement."[18] Child's concerns suggest, however, that the horse was already out of the barn by the late 1820s. Americans, those of means and those of more ordinary circumstances, were already hooked on the pleasures and cultural benefits of travel. The impact on American food customs paralleled that of the other great transformations of the Victorian era.

During the Victorian age, Americans north and south and east and west experienced profound changes in their diets and food rituals. The growth of the country, both territorially and economically, brought a world of new options—new ingredients, new ways of cooking, new technologies for commercial food processing, and new accoutrements for serving and eating food. As the population became increasingly diverse, conflicts arose that sometimes generated new ideologies about food and eating—vegetarianism, water cures, and temperance, for example. Traditional ideas about foodways and diet, however, did not disappear. They persisted in the face of all of these changes, maintained by a growing middle class who found comfort and stability in familiar things at the same time as they were celebrating the new and different as evidence of their newly acquired market power.

NOTES

1. Mary Douglas and Baron Isherwood, *The World of Goods* (New York: Basic Books, 1979), 72.

2. Jean Anthelme Brillat-Savarin, *The Physiology of Taste*, trans. M. F. K. Fisher (1826; San Francisco: North Point Press, 1986), 40.

3. See Elizabeth A. Perkins, "The Consumer Frontier: Household Consumption in Early Kentucky," *Journal of American History* 78 (September 1991): 509. Although Perkins focuses on the late-eighteenth century, many

of her observations about frontier experiences are applicable to the nineteenth century as well.

4. See Julie Roy Jeffrey, *Frontier Women: Civilizing the West? 1840–1880*, rev. ed. (New York: Hill and Wang, 1998), especially chapter 7, "Will She Not Overstep the Bounds of Propriety If She Ventures into the Arena of Action?"

5. Claudia L. Bushman, *"A Good Poor Man's Wife": Being a Chronicle of Harriet Hanson Robinson and Her Family in Nineteenth Century New England* (Hanover: University Press of New England, 1981), 106–108.

6. Marjorie Kreidberg, *Food on the Frontier: Minnesota Cooking from 1850 to 1900, With Selected Recipes* (St. Paul: Minnesota Historical Society Press, 1975), 9.

7. Frances Milton Trollope, *Domestic Manners of the Americans*, 4th ed. (London: Whittaker, Treacher, & Co, 1832), 58–59. For a more detailed analysis of women's economic contributions to rural households via butter and egg money, see Joan M. Jensen, *Loosening the Bonds: Mid-Atlantic Farm Women, 1750–1850* (New Haven: Yale University Press, 1986).

8. Trollope, 66.

9. For a survey of the food preferences and food culture of the earliest American immigrants, see Ken Albala, *Food in Early Modern Europe* (Westport, CT: Greenwood Press, 2003) especially chapter 2, "Ingredients," 21–79. See also Waverly Root and Richard de Rochemont, *Eating in America: A History* (New York: Ecco Press, 1981), 60–73.

10. Elizabeth F. Ellet, ed., *The New Cyclopaedia of Domestic Economy, and Practical Housekeeper* (Norwich, CT: Henry Bill Publishing Co., 1873), Frontispiece.

11. For a quick survey of the technological changes in farming, see Brooke Hindle and Steven Lubar, *Engines of Change: The American Industrial Revolution, 1790–1860* (Washington, DC: Smithsonian Institution Press, 1986), 94–99.

12. John Mack Faragher, *Sugar Creek: Life on the Illinois Prairie* (New Haven: Yale University Press, 1986), 199–203.

13. For a discussion of social capital and the importance of community during this period, see Karen V. Hansen, *A Very Social Time: Crafting Community in Antebellum New England* (Berkeley: University of California Press, 1994).

14. See Christine Stansell's discussion of the exchange networks among urban, working- and middle-class women in *City of Women: Sex and Class in New York, 1790–1860* (Urbana: University of Illinois Press, 1987), 41–62.

15. William J. Brown, *The Life of William J. Brown, of Providence, R.I., with Personal Recollections of Incidents in Rhode Island* (1883; reprint Freeport, NY: Books for Libraries Press, 1971), 93, quoted in Hansen, 86.

16. Sarah Josepha Hale, "The Romance of Travelling," from *Traits of American Life* (1835), in *A Tourist's New England: Travel Fiction,*

1820–1920, ed. Dona Brown (Hanover, NH: University Press of New England, 1999), 41.

17. Dona Brown, *Inventing New England: Regional Tourism in the Nineteenth Century* (Washington, DC: Smithsonian Institution Press, 1995), 6, 39.

18. Lydia Maria Child, *The American Frugal Housewife* (1832; reprint Worthington, OH: Worthington Historical Society, 1965.), 99–103. Sarah A. Leavitt has surveyed American domestic advice literature in *From Catharine Beecher to Martha Stewart: A Cultural History of Domestic Advice* (Chapel Hill: University of North Carolina Press, 2002).

CHAPTER 2
FOODSTUFFS

The food options available for planning menus and serving meals changed dramatically during the nineteenth century. At the outset of the Victorian era, a world where most Americans lived on farms and in small towns and villages, many families grew much of their own food and processed it at home. What they did not grow themselves, they were generally able to purchase from local shops or trade for with neighbors. Exchange networks were much as they had been in the eighteenth century—local or regional, and often informal—but were also beginning to reach outward in new ways as the American economy matured. Families that were able to produce a surplus of anything, whether it was meat, crops, orchard fruit, pickles, preserves, or butter and cheese from the dairy, had traditionally traded those goods informally with their neighbors. By the nineteenth century, trading had become more systemized and was generally conducted through the auspices of a country store, a grocer, or a meat market.[1] Local shops in American towns and cities advertised a variety of goods including groceries, seafood, meats, fruit, vegetables, bread, pastries, ice creams, and confections. These advertisements offer a likely snapshot of eating patterns, as well as marketing practices.

Prescriptive literature also suggests changes, both in the methods of acquiring food and in the food itself. Thomas De Voe, a New York butcher and observer of the market scene, published a guide to the marketplace in 1867. He noticed significant changes in the manner in which New Yorkers acquired their food, particularly a

Shoppers rich and poor at New York City's Washington Market in 1873, as depicted in *Frank Leslie's Illustrated Newspaper*. (Courtesy of the Library of Congress Prints and Photographs Division, Washington, D.C.)

loss of direct contact with the purveyors of the foods that they were purchasing:

> Some fifty years ago it was the common custom for the thrifty "old New Yorker," when going to market, to start with the break of day, and carry along with him the large "market-basket," then considered a very necessary appendage for this occasion. His early visit gave him the desired opportunity to select the *cuts* of meat wanted from the best animals; to meet the farmer's choice productions,

either poultry, vegetables, or fruit, and *catch* the lively, jumping fish, which ten minutes before, were swimming in the fish-cars.[2]

De Voe lamented that, at present, heads of families rarely even visit public markets; they do all of their purchasing through agents from their shops—butchers, confectioners, grocers, and others.

By the end of the Victorian era, at least half of all Americans lived in large towns and cities, and they had to acquire everything they ate from a food distribution network that had become international in scope and governed by an industrial capitalist economy. Corn, oats, and barley—traditional staples of the Anglo-American diet—were now supplemented by a massive wheat enterprise, produced by large agribusinesses in the Midwest. Bread, once a homemade or locally produced commodity, poured out of the ovens of General Mills and Pillsbury, as did the white flour now used by American cooks to produce the muffins, cakes, biscuits, and other baked goods enumerated in American cookbooks.

Pork, sheep, and cattle, raised by agribusinesses in the West and Midwest, were transported to stockyards, where they were slaughtered, packaged, and transported around the country. De Voe noted, "The producer is often hundreds of miles in one direction, while the consumer may be as many hundred in another, from the mart at which the productions were sold and purchased. Through the course of the year, the products of the North, South, East, and West, are to be found in our large public market-places." These goods, whether meat, bread, flour, vegetables, fruits, or other edibles, were then redistributed all over the United States, as well as sent to foreign countries.[3]

Commercially produced canned goods emerged during this period as well. Canning and preserving foods, primarily by smoking, drying, or salting, had been widely practiced previously—but many of the techniques were hit or miss. Until people understood the relationship between bacteria and spoilage, many of the assumptions about preserving food derived from custom rather than science. By 1819, one of the earliest canners, the William Underwood Company in Boston, was producing oysters, lobsters, fish, meat, soup, fruits, and even some vegetables, both for export and domestic consumption. Another canning pioneer, the New York City firm of Ezra Daggett and Thomas Kensett, also began packing salmon, oysters, and lobsters in 1819, and in 1825, it received a patent for a tin can. Packing in tin had advantages over glass, especially for shipping, but the resulting product was expensive and not reliably safe for consumption. Gradually

Sargent & Company, a New Haven hardware manufacturer, advertised their Sprague Patent Can Opener in 1884. (Courtesy of Dover Publications.)

over the next thirty years, two food-processing industries grew, side by side: one that packed in tin and one that bottled in glass. The invention of the can opener in 1858 confirmed a growing demand for this modern food product, but canned goods were still a luxury for most people until after the Civil War. The canning industry received a major boost from the war itself, jumping from 5 million cans in 1860 to 30 million by 1870. As the idea of food in tin cans gained acceptance, the types of foods canned diversified and led to the popularity of such new, exotic products as pineapple and grapefruit, and especially, canned soups.[4] During the last quarter of the nineteenth century, a wide variety of commercially canned vegetables, fruits, meats, and fish were introduced to American consumers, as canned goods became an ordinary part of American life, widely available in grocery stores for all to purchase.

Americans themselves had become much more diverse by the late nineteenth century—and new immigrant groups brought with them new foodways that permeated and sometimes transformed traditional American dietary assumptions. The Germans, who flocked to the United States throughout the nineteenth century and especially after the European political disruptions of 1848, taught Americans how to brew lager beer and wine, make pickles and canned relishes, and other foreign delicacies. Many foreigners, especially those of northern European origin, found their ethnic foods becoming Americanized and absorbed into the local "American" cuisine.

A COOKBOOK OF VICTORIAN INGREDIENTS

In writing on cooking, the main topics should be first, bread; second, butter; third, meat; fourth, vegetables; and fifth, tea—by which last is meant, generically, all sorts of warm, comfortable drinks served out in tea-cups, whether they be called tea, coffee, chocolate, broma, or what not.

Catharine E. Beecher and Harriet Beecher Stowe, 1874

Cookbooks offer conflicting pictures of what Victorian Americans ate—and those pictures changed over time. Catharine Beecher and her sister, Harriet Beecher Stowe, whose best-selling book *The American Woman's Home* appeared in 1870, took a rather austere view of what constituted the proper categories for discussion of food. Their topics—bread, butter, meat, vegetables, and "tea"—totally disregarded the American sweet tooth, which had been a forceful presence in cookery literature from the beginning. They neglected the mountains of pastries, puddings, cakes, ice creams, and other sweet dishes that filled whole chapters of many nineteenth-century cookbooks. Nor did they mention newly fashionable "French" salads, the increasing variety of available fruits, or the wide range of flavoring, seasonings, and condiments that enhanced a Victorian dinner table.

Despite the Beecher sisters' austere notions about diet, most other American cookery writers offered a much fuller palette of food items. Mary Randolph's *The Virginia House Wife* (1824) divided the contents of her book into thirteen categories, including Soup, Beef, Veal, Lamb, Mutton, Pork, Fish, Poultry, Sauces, Vegetables, Pickling, Cordials, and "Dishes for Lent." She also wove in recipes for desserts, puddings, cakes, jellies, preserves, and bread.[5] Miss Prudence Smith followed much the same pattern in *Modern American Cookery*, published in 1831. She included "directions for making soups, roasting, boiling, baking, dressing vegetables, poultry, fish, made dishes, pies, gravies, pickles, puddings, pastry, sick cookery, &c."[6] By 1851, Eliza Leslie had added "Venison, Hares, Rabbits &c." to this list, as well as "Store Fish Sauces" and "Catchups," an assortment of egg dishes, and a chapter on syllabubs and ice creams.[7]

These changes seem rather small, however, compared with the table of contents of Maria Parloa's *New Cook Book and Marketing Guide* (1888). Parloa's language and organization sounded thoroughly modern, as did her offerings—although her nineteenty-century roots were also clear. She, like her predecessors, began with soups, fish, meats, poultry and game, but then she inserted chapters on "entrées" and salads. She continued with "Meat and Fish Sauces," "Force-Meat and

Garnishes," and then vegetables, pies and puddings, dessert, cake, preserving, pickles and ketchup, potting, and concluded with bread. She also offered hints on "Breakfast and Tea," "Economical Dishes," "Bills of Fare," "Drinks," and "How to Do Various Things." Overall, by the end of the Victorian era, American cookery preferences and the foodstuffs required to support them reflected a newly cosmopolitan outlook, which was in keeping with the international complexion of the nation.

BREADS AND PLAIN CAKES

> The old saying, "bread is the staff of life," has sound reason in it. Flour made from wheat, and meal from oats and Indian corn, are rich in the waste-repairing elements, starch and albumen, and head the list of articles of food for man. Good bread makes the homeliest meal acceptable, and the coarsest fare appetizing, while the most luxurious table is not even tolerable without it. Light crisp rolls for breakfast, spongy, sweet bread for dinner, and flaky biscuit for supper, cover a multitude of culinary sins; and there is no one thing on which the health and comfort of a family so much depends as the quality of its home-made loaves.[8]
>
> Estelle Woods Wilcox, *Buckeye Cookery*, 1880

For Victorian cooks, as for generations of homemakers before and after them, bread presided as a daily staple. The task of obtaining bread had two tracks: one could bake or one could buy. At the beginning of the nineteenth century, home baking was common for all except those who lived in large cities and could afford to purchase their daily bread. By the end of the 1880s, however, the number of Americans who lived in cities was roughly equal to those who lived on farms and "in the country." Elizabeth Lea, a Maryland Quaker and cookbook author, had a bake oven installed in her kitchen at Walnut Hill. In her cookbook, she described the processes for creating a variety of baked goods, including homemade bread. She began by heating her oven early in the morning—hers was a brick oven with cast iron front, trimmed with brass. Once the oven had reached temperature, Lea baked bread, pies, biscuits, and puddings.[9] By the 1880s, many women, especially those who lived in cities, purchased their bread, although some continued to make home-baked bread, albeit in freestanding, cast-iron ranges.

Perhaps the greatest difference between the early and late Victorian era, however, was in the bread itself. Early cookbooks included numerous recipes for breads that were made from "Indian meal"—cornmeal—as well as rye flour or rice flour. Lydia Maria Child

This built-in Magee Range, made by the Magee Furnace Company, Chelsea, Massachusetts in 1865, is located in the Chamberlin-Taft family homestead in Greenville, New Hampshire. The stove, with its double ovens and six-burner cooktop, made it possible to prepare complicated meals for this prosperous family. (Collection of Robert Taft. Photo by author.)

included recipes for four types of bread in her *Frugal Housewife* in 1833: brown bread, dyspepsia bread, rice bread, and what she termed "flour bread."[10] Brown bread required six quarts of meal to make two "good sized loaves," according to Child. The meal, or flour, might have been all "Indian," which was cornmeal, or half Indian and half rye meal. Women experimented with proportions, both to obtain the desired taste and in response to availability of ingredients.

By the end of the century, bread had become white, made from wheat flour and grown and ground in large-scale mills in western New York State or the upper Midwest. White bread had been transformed from a luxury item for the wealthy into an everyday expectation for all Americans.

BUTTER AND CHEESE

Butter

Butter, one of the most traditional of women's crafts, began the nineteenth century as a product hand-churned by women and ended the century as the factory-made product of a commercial marketplace. For much of the century, and especially in rural communities, butter remained an important part of a women's economy—produced from surplus milk and sold or exchanged at a local marketplace for other necessary family goods. "Farm" butter was stamped with wooden butter prints, which designated the maker. As late as 1851, Eliza Leslie's *Directions for Cookery* provided four pages of directions about making butter, beginning with the milk pans ("Scale your milk pans every day after washing them; and let them set till the water gets cold. Then wipe them with a clean cloth. Unless all utensils are kept perfectly sweet and nice, the cream and butter will never be good. Empty milk pans should stand all day in the sun."). The cream had to be skimmed by hand from the top of the milk and put into "a large deep earthen jar, commonly called a crock." It had to be stirred twice a day to prevent the formation of a skin on top of the cream, which would damage the butter. Housewives would continue to add fresh cream as they obtained it, until they were ready to churn.

Churning was to be done at least twice a week to prevent the butter from becoming rancid. According to Leslie, "Butter of only two or three days gathering is the best. With four or five good cows, you may easily manage to have a churning every three days. If your dairy is on a large scale, churn every two days." It was important to keep the

Butter molds or butter "prints" came in various sizes and were used to mold a quantity of butter (generally a pound) and then mark it with a distinctive design to identify the producer. (Collection of Harvey Green.)

churn clean and to fill it with cold water to cool it before churning. When ready, the cream was strained into the churn, the lid put on, and churning commenced. "Move the handle slowly in warm weather, as churning too fast will make the butter soft," advised Leslie. When the handle became hard to turn, the cream had turned to butter. This was a crucial point in the butter-making process.

> Take it out with a wooden ladle, and put it into a small tub or pail. Squeeze and press it hard with the ladle, to get out all that remains of the milk. Add a little salt and then squeeze and work it for a long time. If any of the milk is allowed to remain in, it will speedily turn sour and spoil the butter.

After allowing the butter to rest for three hours, it was worked again, ideally on a marble slab or table. To finish the butter, it was washed in cold water, weighed into one pound units, smoothed and shaped, and then printed: "clap each pound on your wooden butter print, dipping the print every time in cold water." After printing, the butter rounds were spread on a clean linen cloth in the springhouse until hard, and then wrapped individually in linen pieces that had been wetted with cool water. Leslie wrote, "This receipt for making butter is according to the method in use at the best farm-houses in Pennsylvania."[11]

Two technologies helped to reshape the economy of butter manufacture. First, improvements in churns made it possible to convert cream to butter faster and more efficiently. Patents for churns increased significantly during the first half of the nineteenth century, peaking in 1848 with the issuance of fifty. Improved churning increased the scale of farm butter production, necessitating the use of butter prints to differentiate one woman's butter from another. These began to appear in the late 1820s and persisted as long as farm butter survived.[12]

The invention of the mechanical cream separator further contributed to the demise of dairy butter production. Around 1850, farm families began to sell their cream to larger, centralized creameries, rather than making butter in their home dairies. As churns improved, this part of the process could be accomplished in factories (called creameries) rather than home dairies. Thomas De Voe noted that butter was brought to the New York market from almost every county in New York State, although he had heard that the best, as well as the largest quantity of New York butter came from Orange, Chemung, and Cortland counties. He also mentioned Pennsylvania butter with admiration, particularly because it arrived at market "neatly done up in nice clean packages."[13] The DeLaval cream separator, introduced in the late 1870s, made it possible for farmers to take their milk to a central location, where the milk and cream would be separated mechanically instead of through gravity. At that point, the buttermaking process had become fully mechanized and the individual craft aspect disappeared in many parts of the country.[14]

Cheese

Cheese, a traditional means of preserving milk to forestall hunger during periods of scarcity, became an important commercial product in the United States during the nineteenth century. Although Eliza Leslie felt it necessary to provide directions for cheesemaking in 1851, increasingly by that date, the cheese consumed by American families was factory made, as dairy farmers banded together to pool their resources and maximize labor and profits. The first factory-made cheddar cheese was produced in 1851, in Rome, New York, and was the work of a farmer's milk cooperative.[15] De Voe noted that the best cheeses in New York State came from Herkimer and Jefferson counties, and

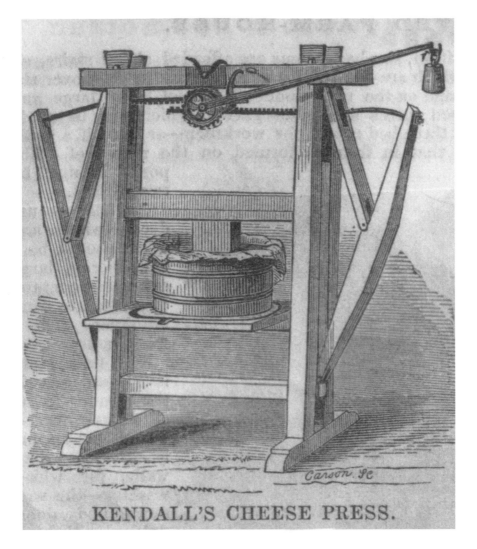

KENDALL'S CHEESE PRESS.

Various patented devices began to appear during the first half of the nine-
teenth century to make it easier to process larger quantities of cheese, including
"Kendall's Cheese Press," illustrated in *The Pictorial Cultivator Almanac for the
United States for the Year 1851.* (Collection of the author.)

that a Colonel Meacham, of Oswego, had a dairy herd of 154 cows—
so many that he was able to produce three hundred wheels of cheese
weighing 125 pounds each.[16]

Many of America's cheese preferences were determined by
ethnicity—thus, cheddar, the most prevalent British cheese, was also
dominant in the United States throughout its early history. De Voe

particularly admired "English dairy cheese." The arrival of new immigrant groups in the nineteenth century brought new cheesemaking skills and tastes. In Wisconsin, German artisanal cheesemakers made that state a center of cheese production, introducing brick cheese in 1871. Annie Pickett had started Wisconsin's first cheese factory in 1841, but by the post–Civil War era, large-scale cheese production had taken hold.[17]

American affluence after the Civil War also brought with it a taste for imported cheeses. European cheeses began to appear in upscale marketplaces, as well as on restaurant menus. The Parker House, one of Boston's finest restaurants, listed five different cheeses on its dessert menu in 1874, including Roquefort, Neufchatel, Gruyere, American, and Sage—the last two being traditional American cheddars.[18]

SOUP

> In making soup, allow yourself plenty of time. Dumplings should be put in about half an hour before the soup is done, and herbs a quarter of an hour:— vegetables, about an hour,—rice, twenty minutes. If herbs are put in too soon, the flavor will fly off and be lost.[19]
>
> Elizabeth Ellicott Lea, *Domestic Cookery*, 1853

Quaker housewife Elizabeth Ellicott Lea's description of making soup essentially defined prevailing notions about this most basic menu item. It required a long period of simmering over a hot fire before it was ready to eat. It generally contained some sort of carbohydrate—in this case, dumplings—but rice, noodles, peas, beans, barley, or other grains and legumes were commonly substituted. Other ingredients— vegetables, herbs, spices, or other flavorings—were up to the cook's discretion, although the flavor of herbs, as Lea knew, was fragile and would disappear if they were added too early. Lea did not even mention meat or fish, but these items were the defining elements for most soups. Soups had been around for centuries—they were not new to the world of Victorian America, but it was during this period that soups became gentrified, "Frenchified," canned, and, to some extent, homogenized.

Early nineteenth-century cookbooks certainly included soups, but only a limited array. Lydia Child's cookbook of 1833 did not even have a separate section for soup. She included soup directions as an afterthought in her discussions of other cookery. In a general discussion of fish, for example, she noted, "Four or five pounds of fish are enough to make a chowder for four or five people." She then told her readers who wished to make chowder to use a deep kettle, fry up some salt pork in the bottom, and then layer fish, crackers, sliced onions and potatoes, and "a whole bowl-ful of flour and water" to cover. For seasonings, Child added sliced lemon, salt, pepper, a bit of tomato catsup, and even a cup of beer, if desired. "A few clams are a pleasant addition," she concluded. The whole was then covered tightly and steamed until done.[20]

Child's recipes for making meat soups were comparably abbreviated. She included them in a larger section called "Common Cooking," where she discussed general cooking methods for veal, calf's head, beef, mutton and lamb, and poultry. Regarding beef soup, Child advised "stewing" over a slow fire for four hours. She recommended adding any leftover bones from a roast to the batch, but did not even mention the possibility of adding vegetables. The resulting product was a flavorful broth, thickened with flour, and seasoned with lemon, catsup, salt, and pepper. For variety, "some people put in crackers," or possibly dumplings made with eggs, flour, and water and dropped into the soup with a spoon.[21] Mutton or lamb soup was never mentioned as such, but Child commented that when stewing mutton, "if your family like broth, throw in some clear rice when you put in the meat," and season with summer savory or sage.

Chicken broth merited an actual recipe in Childs' *American Frugal Housewife* (1833), but the directions, as with her other soups, were very lean.

Chicken Broth

Cut a chicken in quarters; put it into three or four quarts of water; put in a cup of rice while the water is cold; season it with pepper and salt; some use nutmeg. Let it stew gently, until the chicken falls apart. A little parsley, shred fine, is an improvement. Some slice up a small onion and stew with it. A few pieces of cracker may be thrown in if you like.[22]

Although Child did not discuss soup in great detail, soup was undoubtedly on the tables of many families during the early nineteenth century. For those of lesser means, soup was an important way of stretching meat, by means of grains, legumes, root vegetables, and liquid. Child, writing for those of frugal means, recognized soup's economy, but did not feel compelled to cater to fashionable taste. Wealthier families ate soup as they had observed their counterparts in Europe doing. Soup on fashionable tables dated from the Renaissance, when Italian, French, and other European cooks had devised recipes for consommés, broths, potages, and soups.[23] Mary Randolph, writing

No. 0575.   Five Quarts.

Silver-plated soup tureen, made by the Meriden Britannia Company, Meriden, Connecticut. Tureens were commonly available as part of earthenware and ironstone dinner sets by the 1840s; a silver tureen, however, would have been used only for special occasions, and this particular tureen reflects the Victorian fascination with visual puns. Its bovine finial and handles suggest that it was designed for beef stew, consommé, or some other beef-based soup. (Courtesy of Dover Publications.)

for a more upscale readership, offered sixteen different soup recipes, many of which required more elaborate preparations than had Child's recipes. In Randolph's social circle, soup had become a fashionable first course at any dinner party.[24] Her recipes evidenced a concern not only with soup's flavor but also with its presentation. In her Beef Soup recipe, for example, Randolph assumed that her readers would be serving their soup from a tureen: "put the nicest pieces of meat in your tureen," she wrote, "and pour on the soup and vegetables, put in some toasted bread cut in dice, and serve it up."[25]

By 1851, when Eliza Leslie published her cookbook, soup offerings had expanded substantially and reflected a considerable degree of gentrification. Leslie began her book with a collection of thirty-two different soup recipes, including Family, Fine Beef, Mutton Veal, Rich Veal, Clear Gravy, *Soupe à la Julienne*, Maccaroni Soup, Rich Maccaroni Soup, Vermicelli Soup, Milk Soup, Rich Brown, Rich

White, Meg Merrilies' Soup (the recipe began with four pounds of venison), Venison, Hare or Rabbit, Mullagatawny ("as made in India"), Mock Turtle/Calf's Head, Ox Tail, Okra, Bean, Peas, Green Peas, Asparagus, Friar's Chicken, Cat-Fish, Lobster, Oyster (two kinds), Clam (two kinds), and Water *Souchy* (Dutch) Soup. The most prevalent ingredient in Leslie's soup recipes was veal, followed by beef, fowl, ham, oysters, and clams. Her soups were seasoned with almonds, cayenne, cloves, onions, bacon, pepper, parsley, nutmeg, celery, sweet marjoram, coriander seeds, mint, mace, sugar, salt, mace, lemon, vinegar, and butter. The basic meat or fish stock was augmented with potatoes, cabbage, spinach, egg yolks, turnips, okra, tomatoes, carrots, parsley root, and toasted bread cubes.[26]

The growing taste in Victorian America for diverse soups coincided with the rise of mechanized food processing, specifically canning. James H. W. Huckins began producing canned soup in Boston sometime around the time of the Civil War, advertising canned tomato soup in 1876. His advertisement in the 1882 Boston City Directory offered not only tomato but also "Hermetically Sealed" mock turtle, oxtail, julienne, pea, beef, chicken, macaroni, vermicelli, consommé, mutton broth, okra or gumbo, mulligatawny, green turtle, and terrapin soup. A competitor, the Franco-American Food Company, started by an immigrant French canner and soup maker, was selling much the same array, as were other soup makers around the country. The convenience of canned soups added to their appeal. Franco-American soups were advertised as being useful for feeding unexpected guests: quick, delicious, and "French."[27]

FISH AND SHELLFISH

Since colonial times, fish have been an important foodstuff for Americans. The taste for certain kinds of fish and shellfish persisted into the nineteenth century, especially among those living near the coasts and along the great rivers and inland lakes. Lydia Child discussed cod, haddock, mackerel, salt fish, salted mackerel, salted shad, smoked salmon, lobsters, and clams in her *Frugal Housewife*.[28] Fish dealers existed as a specialty trade in most Eastern cities and towns. In Fitchburg, Massachusetts, J. C. Stimpson advertised in 1848 that he could provide "Fresh fish of every variety, wholesale and retail, on reasonable terms."[29] For the next thirty years, the city directories of Fitchburg listed only one specialty fish dealer, presumably reflecting a limited demand for fish. By 1876, however, the number of fish dealers had increased to four, all of whom advertised a variety of offerings.[30] Four years later, Fitchburg had seven different fish dealers.[31] One of them, A. O. Carter, sold "Fresh and Salt Fish, Oyster, Clams, Lobsters, &c. in their season." This was typical of the rest of the advertisers. Most of these also sold "provisions" or "family groceries" in addition to fish, including flour, salt, eggs, butter, cheese, lard, poultry, dried apples, and beans. R. M. Huntley, for example, advertised in 1854 that he "Keeps constantly on hand Family Groceries, such as Flour, Salt, Lard, Pork, Mackerel, Fish, Sugars, Molasses, Tea, Coffee, Rice, Soap, Pearlash, Spices, &c. Also Camphene and Burning Fluid."[32]

Two things changed dramatically with regard to fish and shellfish consumption during the nineteenth century. Mass transportation made it possible for fish to be in markets around the country, regardless of proximity to a water body. The second change was partly related to the first. Shellfish, especially oysters and lobster, which had been considered "trash" by Europeans during the early colonial era, attained a high social value for Victorian Americans. The first lobster was shipped from New York City to Chicago in 1842. It died en route, but was cooked in Cleveland and, according to the Chicago *Daily American*, was "as fresh as could be desired" when it finally arrived in Chicago.[33] By the 1850s, lobsters graced the tables of the rich and powerful, usually taken from the shell and made into a variety of delectable entrees. Eliza Leslie, writing in 1864, discussed the etiquette of eating a lobster in a hotel. "Novices in lobster sometimes eat it simply with salt, or with vinegar only, or with black pepper," she said, "This betrays great ignorance of the article."

> To prepare it according to the usual custom,—cut up, very small, the pieces of lobster, and, on another plate, make the dressing. First, mash together some hard-boiled yolk of egg, and some of the red coral of the lobster, with a little salt and cayenne. Mix in, with a ford, mustard to your taste; and then a liberal allowance of salad-oil finishing with vinegar. Transfer the bits of lobster to the plate that has the dressing, and combine the whole with a fork.[34]

Leslie's directions corresponded to a general preference for lobster salad at fashionable tables. Housewives could either prepare this delicacy using fresh lobster or they could rely on canned lobster meat.

In her popular cookbook and guide to marketing, Maria Parloa discussed fish and how to shop for them. She discussed codfish, haddock, cusk, pollock, halibut, flounder, turbot, salmon, shad, blue-fish, blackfish or "tautog," whitefish or lake shad, sea bass, rock bass, swordfish, sturgeon, weakfish, small or "pan"fish, smelts, mullet, mackerel, Spanish mackerel, eels, lobsters, hard-shell crabs, soft-shell crabs, shrimp, terrapin, oysters, clams, and scallops. Of oysters, Parloa commented, "no other shellfish is as highly prized as this."[35] Oysters had become the most fashionable way to begin a dinner party by then, as well as a popular ingredient in numerous recipes. Whether washed down with beer, wine, or champagne, oysters were consumed almost to extinction during the last quarter of the nineteenth century. In 1880, oysters had become so desirable that the advertising section of the Fitchburg Directory included a new category for "Oyster Dealers," with three listings. All of these were in actually fish dealers, but had chosen to capitalize on the prestige of oysters and bill themselves as oyster specialists.[36]

The index of *Buckeye Cookery* (1880) listed twenty-three entries for "Oysters," despite the fact that the book was published in Marysville, Ohio—far from any ocean. This was testament as much to the success of refrigerated transportation as to the widespread popularity of oysters. "The delicious bivalves furnish an important, and, in most localities, a not expensive article of food," the authors noted, "and the ease with which they are prepared for the table, and the great variety of ways in which they may be cooked and served, make them a great favorite with housekeepers." They advised their readers, "The small shelled oysters have the finest flavor." The list of oyster recipes included "Boiled, Broiled, Broiled with Pork, Croquettes, Curried, Deviled, Escaloped, For soups, Fried, Fricasseed, Fritters, Omelet, Panned, Pickles, Pie, Raw, Roll, Shell, Stew, Steamed, To fry, and Walled." "Walled" oysters were cooked briefly, and then served on a plate, contained by a wall of mashed potatoes.[37]

MEAT

American consumption of meat changed during the nineteenth century as a result of advances in meat processing, as well as in the distribution of meat. At the outset of the Victorian era, pigs, sheep, and steers were typically grown and butchered at home, or close to home, and exchanged among neighbors. By the 1880s, meat was produced far from home and either driven overland or conveyed by railroad to large, centralized stockyards and slaughterhouses, where it was transformed into packages to be consumed far away from its place of origin. An 1892 article in *New England Grocer* described the hog business, as conducted by John P. Squire of Somerville and Cambridge, Massachusetts, in detail:

> The old method of conducting the business was to buy the slaughtered hogs, cut them up into the different parts, and sell them both as fresh and cured or

New York City butcher Thomas Farrington DeVoe, as he appeared
on the frontispiece of *The Market Assistant* in 1867. The traditional craft-based skills of butchering increasingly had to be combined with marketing skills as the meat industry grew in scale and
scope. (Courtesy of Special Collections, Michigan State University
Libraries.)

salted meats. Today the method, as is well known, is to purchase the hogs in the West, transport them to the packing house in Somerville and Cambridge, where they are slaughtered and then distributed to the trade. By the old way of doing business, the carcasses of the hogs were hung up until the animal heat had all left the body, and the sides were then packed in ice boxes until chilled through. In 1881 a large refrigerator, the largest one in the country at that time, was built. It took 30,000 tons of ice into its chamber at one time, had three floors, and a basement, and a total of about three acres of cooling space.[38]

Cookbooks suggest that nineteenth-century families consumed a variety of meat, although most families probably ate a less diverse array than what was proposed by the cookbook authors. Lydia Child mentioned beef (chuck steak), pork (shoulder), lamb, mutton (breast, shoulder), veal (breast, loin, shoulder), the hearts of bullock, pig, and lamb, calf's head, neat's tongue (also buffalo's and pig's tongues), ham, veal and beef liver, bacon, cured mutton, salt and corned beef, mince meat, ox flank, sweetbread, sausage, pickled pork, beef, and mutton. Rural families might have kept a pig or steer at home and slaughtered it in the fall, while town and city dwellers would have had to rely on local butchers, who solicited goods from the "country trade." As the meat industry developed and became concentrated, butchers and meat dealers increasingly served as gathering points, redistributing meat back to the hinterlands.

In most cities, selling meat became a specialized trade, where butchers would offer beef, pork, tripe, lard, butter, hams, lamb, veal, sausage, and other meat products. One butcher advertised himself in 1854 as a "Dealer in Beef, Pork, Lard, Hams, Vegetables, &c." He also offered "Fresh and Corn Beef of the very best quality, always on hand and at the lowest cash prices." Other butchers advertised that they dealt in beef, pork, lamb, and veal, as well as tripe, sausages, pig's feet, ham, lard, and country produce. They also produced specialty items, such as sausages. "Sausage meat cut and made to order" would have appealed strongly to new populations of ethnic consumers, Germans in particular.[39] Thomas De Voe commented in 1867 on the availability of "Country Sausages" in the New York City markets.[40]

Beef, according to Maria Parloa, "is one of the most nutritious, and, in the end, the most economical, kinds of meat, for there is not a scrap of it which a good housekeeper will not utilize for food." She gave her readers hints about selecting meat, diagrams depicting the types of cuts, as well as information regarding regional variations in cuts between Boston, Philadelphia, and New York. She offered pricing information for top round, rump cut across the grain, rump cut with the grain, sirloin, porterhouse, and tenderloin, and in doing so, she suggested the most popular cuts among her constituents in 1880.[41]

Pork included hams, sausages, ribs, bacon. According to Parloa, pork was not used in its fresh state as much as beef and mutton, but was commonly salted, smoked, and made into sausages. Corn fed pork, Parloa believed to be of the best quality: "after pork has been salted, if it is corn-fed, the fat will be of a delicate pinkish shade." The parts of the hog consumed included the leg, loin, ribs, shoulder, neck, flank, brisket, head, and feet. The loin, which consisted of the leg and shoulder, was often salted and smoked. "The loin of a large hog has about two or three inches of the fat cut with the rind," explained Parloa. "This is used for salting, and the loin flesh for roasting." Removing the rind and fat from the ribs resulted in spareribs, which, Parloa noted, "makes a sweet roast." The loin and ribs were also used for steaks and chops. All parts of the pig were consumed in one manner or another: the flanks and brisket were corned, and the head sold for head cheese, the feet pickled, and even the fat was used. It was cooked slowly (tried) until dissolved, resulting in lard, an important cooking and baking ingredient. If they did not purchase their lard ready-made, according to Parloa, "many cooks try their own from purchased leaf or clear fat."[42]

Veal was a seasonal meat; Parloa urged her readers to purchase only that available between April and September, when the prices were lower. She also gave its uses:

> The loin, breast, and shoulder are used for roasting. Chops are cut from the loin and neck, those from the neck being called rib chops or cotelettes. The neck itself is used for stews, pies, fricassees, etc. The leg is used for cutlets, fricandeaux, stews and roasts, and for braising. The fillet of veal is a solid piece cut from the leg—not like the tenderloin in beef, but used in much the same way. The lower part of the leg is called a knuckle, and is particularly nice for soups and sauces.

Parloa considered veal to be highly useful, although she believed it to be "not nutritious nor easily digested. Many people cannot eat it in any form," she continued, "but such a number of nice dishes can be made from it, and when in season the price is so low, that it will always be used for made dishes and soups."[43]

"Organ Meats," Parloa's final meat category, included liver, hearts, kidneys, and tongues. She felt that calf's liver was the best of the organ meats, whereas beef liver was stronger flavored and not as tender. For her more frugal readers, she advised that pig's liver was almost as good, but cheaper. Calf or beef hearts, when roasted, she noted, proved "delicious, but not easily digested." Kidneys, she explained, enhanced "stews, broils, sautés, curries, and fricassees." "Veal are the best," she added. Finally, she discussed tongues (beef and lamb) at some length, considering them "very delicate." They could be used for *bouilli* (beef boiled with root vegetables, sweet herbs, and seasonings), in mince pies, or jellied. Sometimes they were also salted and smoked, then served cold.[44]

POULTRY

Poultry, according to *The Frugal Housewife,* consisted of chicken, duck, goose, partridge, pigeon, and turkey. As with other animal-based food, poultry was frequently grown at home, or obtained locally in the early nineteenth century. By midcentury, poultry, like other meats, was grown commercially and distributed across a wide area. According to butcher Thomas De Voe, the poultry for the New York City market was imported from Long Island, Connecticut, Rhode Island, Massachusetts, Vermont, New Jersey, and Pennsylvania (the largest supplier).[45]

Poultry formed the basis of a great deal of Victorian cookery. It was relatively inexpensive, easy to digest, and lent itself to many culinary interpretations. Eliza Leslie's twenty-five recipes for poultry and game in 1851 revealed that Americans were consuming (or would have liked to consume) a variety of game birds as well as the usual domestic birds. The birds she mentioned in recipes included chicken, duck, fowl, goose, partridge, pigeon, reed-bird or ortolan, snipe, wood cock, plover, quail, grouse, and turkey. Chicken recipes were the most common, including baked chicken pie, broiled chickens, chicken croquettes and rissoles, chicken curry, chicken salad, fricasseed chickens, pilau, and pot pie. Leslie assumed that her readers would want to know how to stew, roast, and hash duck, as well as how to boil and roast fowl. She offered special occasion recipes, for Christmas goose pie, plain goose pie, roast goose, fine partridge pie, roast pheasant, partridge, quails, or grouse, pigeon pie, roast pigeon, roast reed-birds or ortolans, roast snipes, woodcocks, or plovers, boiled turkey, and roast turkey.[46] These recipe offerings suggest that by midcentury, American cooks were using a variety of poultry in many different ways, both for family meals and for company dinners, as well as holiday meals.

SALADS

Salad, according to one scholar of food, was looked upon with suspicion in Victorian America. "Well into the nineteenth century," he argued, "English writers were saying that cold salads needed pepper to warm the blood, or that they 'contain little nourishment, and are not much to be recommended.' "[47] Fannie Merritt Farmer, the esteemed cooking instructor and cookbook author, concurred, stating, "Salads, which constitute a course in almost every dinner, but a few years since seldom appeared on any table."[48] Salad was not, however, a new menu item in the nineteenth century. A manuscript cookbook from the fourteenth century described salad as an assortment of greens and herbs, including parsley, sage, garlic, chives, onions, leeks, mint, fennel, rue, rosemary, and purslain. These were washed and broken into small bits, then mixed with oil. "Lay on vinegar and salt, and serve it forth," concluded the recipe.[49]

Wealthier Americans were certainly aware of salads during the antebellum era. As early as 1827, Robert Roberts discussed the serving of salad in his *House Servant's Directory*, a guide for servants and other staff. Salad followed the second course, accompanied by cheese, according to Roberts:

> When you see that they are finished with the second course, then put round your small cheese plates as you take the others off, with a small knife; if there is salad, you must put on a fork likewise. Have your salad, butter, cheese, and cucumbers ready against the second course comes off; but there are many families that have the salad, butter, cheese, radishes, &c., all put on with the second course.[50]

Thirty years later, "A Practical Housekeeper" discussed salads and their position in the dinner menu, stating that salad, a part of the second course, "should be given with the roast meat; it should be placed fresh upon the table, then removed and dressed by a waiter."[51] This latter description implied that salad was not an everyday item. Roast meat appeared on middle-class menus fairly regularly, but not daily. The second direction, that the salad be dressed by a servant, implies a ritual that would not have been part of an ordinary family's dinner—unless company were present. This notion changed as a result of the rise of vegetarianism and other dietary reforms of the third quarter of the nineteenth century, when salad was increasingly perceived as "healthy," and therefore essential to the daily diet.

Horticulturist Robert Buist described some salad greens in *The Family Kitchen Gardener* in 1855, including nasturtium, which he claimed was used frequently in salads. He also mentioned a number of other salad ingredients, beginning with lettuce, which he discussed in detail. "It is unquestionably the best of the salading vegetables," he wrote.

"Many varieties are cultivated in Europe, and not a few in this country," he added.[52] Also mentioned by Buist with reference to salad were basil, burnet, celery, chervil, chive, corn salad or mache, cress, cucumber, endive, garlic, mint, mustard greens, radish, tarragon, and tomatoes.

HERBS, SPICES, VINEGARS, AND CONDIMENTS

Herbs and Spices

By the middle of the nineteenth century, American cooks were beginning to explore French cookery, which relied on a wide variety of herbs and spices. According to Lydia Maria Child, herbs were widely used during the earlier nineteenth century for medicinal purposes and for dyestuffs, as well as for cooking. She identified sweet marjoram, parsley, summer savory, sage, hyssop, and horseradish as the primary cooking herbs.[53] Many of the herbs used by American cooks during the nineteenth century were grown commercially by the Shakers. As early as 1800, Shaker communities were growing, drying, and selling medicinal herbs as one of their major economic occupations. By the time of the Civil War, a Shaker herb catalog listed 354 different herbs, barks, roots, seeds, and flowers.[54]

Buist's *Kitchen Gardener* did not separate out culinary herbs from culinary vegetables, although some herbs were cross-listed as medicinal. He identified many herbs as having associations with French cookery, beginning with basil: "The French are very partial to the flavor of this plant; its leaves enter into the composition of many of their soups and sauces; and, on account of their strong flavor of cloves, are used in all highly-seasoned dishes, and even introduced into salads." The French, also used borage flowers, according to Buist, putting them into salads for decoration. Chervil was "much cultivated by the French and Dutch, who use the tender leaves in soups and salads as frequently as we use Parlsey." Of garlic, Buist commented that it would be more commonly used in America except for its unpleasant odor, although "the French use it in sauces and salads." He felt that shallots, another item used frequently in France, were underrated in America: "Many epicures consider them the best seasoning for a good old-fashioned dish of beef-steaks," he wrote. "Though it has been two hundred years in cultivation, very little of the article is used in this country, unless by the French." In addition to these French-associated herbs and spices, Buist mentioned caraway, celery, chive, coriander ("commonly sold by confectioners, encrusted with sugar"), dill ("put into pickles to heighten the flavor, particularly of Cucumbers"), horseradish, marjoram, mint, mustard, parsley, rosemary, sage, tarragon, thyme, and cayenne pepper.[55] As cookery itself grew in complexity and sophistication, a thorough command of the "science" of seasoning was expected of ambitious cooks.

Although spices, in particular, came under attack from health reformers during the second half of the nineteenth century as "stimulants," mainstream cooks doubtless used them. Maria Parloa recommended a general assortment of culinary spices to her readers. "A small wooden or tin box should be partly filled with whole mace, cloves, allspice and cinnamon, and a smaller paste-board box, full of peppercorns, should be placed in it," she advised. "By this plan you will have all your spices together when you season a soup or sauce."[56]

Vinegars and Condiments

"The flavor of other sweet or savoury herbs may be preserved . . . by infusing them with wine or vinegar," wrote cookbook author James Sanderson. Sanderson, who had been chef at the Franklin House, one of Philadelphia's premier eating establishments, was fully versed in the most fashionable cuisine of the day. He knew that flavored vinegars could add a degree of subtlety to the taste of a dish, and offered recipes for ten different varieties. "Vinegar," he explained, "is employed in extracting flavours as well as spirits and wine. But such extracts are prinicipally used with salads, or as relishes to cold meats, and in a few instances to flavour sauces and soups; but, in English cookery, flavours extracted by sherry wines are preferred for soup." Sanderson recommended basil vinegar as a flavoring for soups, burnet vinegar as "a nice relish to cold meat," horseradish vinegar for cold beef, garlic vinegar to flavor gravy, green mint vinegar as a dressing for lamb, as well as vinegars made from celery, cress, tarragon, elder flower, and capsicum, cayenne, or chili peppers.[57]

The basis for any of these flavored vinegars was plain vinegar, which cooks could purchase or make themselves. Lydia Child advised her readers to purchase a barrel of "really strong vinegar" when they first set up housekeeping, and then to replenish it continually with leftover cider, wine, sour beer, anything left behind in pitchers, glasses, or tumblers, and even weak tea. "Nothing is hurtful," she wrote, "which has a tolerable portion of spirit, or acidity." The vinegar had to be nurtured, however, and it was possible to weaken it by adding too much. In that case, "a few white beans dropped in, or white paper

Caster sets, which often adorned the center of a family's dinner table during the late nineteenth century, offered a variety of condiments, including flavored vinegars, pepper sauces, Worcestershire sauce, red and black pepper, and mustard. This caster set, illustrated in the 1886–1887 catalog of the Meriden Britannia Company, revolved so that diners could easily select a seasoning of their choice. (Courtesy of Dover Publications.)

dipped in molasses, is said to be useful."[58] As the century progressed, more and more families purchased their vinegar in glass bottles, rather than keeping a vinegar barrel at home. In 1869 Henry J. Heinz and L. Clarence Noble formed a company to manufacture Heinz's mother's pickled horseradish, which they marked in glass bottles so that consumers could be assured of purity. By 1876, the company was also producing ketchup, celery sauce, pickled cucumbers, sauerkraut, and vinegar.[59]

Heinz products fell into the broad classification of "condiments." Since the beginning of the century, cookery literature had included recipes for piquant sauces, catsups, relishes, chutneys, and mustards, all of which added flavor and zest to foods. Marion Harland devoted an entire section of her popular cookbook, *Common Sense in the Household*, to catsups and vinegars. She began with a recipe for making mustard, about which she testified,

> Having used this mustard for years in my own family, I can safely advise my friends to undertake the trifling labor of preparing it in consideration of the satisfaction to be derived from the condiment. I mix in a Wedgwood mortar, with pestle of the same; but a bowl is nearly as good. It will keep for weeks.[60]

Harland published recipes for seven catsups and four flavored vinegars. She also offered her readers recipes for "store" sauces, to compete with the array of bottled sauces imported largely from England that tempted American consumers. "A Good Store Sauce" contained horseradish, allspice, nutmeg, pickled onions, whole black peppers, cayenne, salt, sugar and vinegar. Once this mixture had rested for two weeks, it would be "an excellent seasoning for any kind of gravy, sauce, or stew." She also attempted to replicate the most famous of the store-bought sauces, Worcestershire sauce. Her "Imitation" Worcestershire sauce had walnut or tomato catsup as its base, flavored with cayenne, shallots, anchovies, vinegar, and powdered clove. This recipe is from Harland's *Common Sense in the Household: A Manual of Practical Housewifery* (1871).

Imitation Worcestershire Sauce

3 teaspoonfuls cayenne pepper.
2 tablespoonfuls walnut or tomato catsup (strained through muslin).
3 shallots minced fine.
3 anchovies chopped into bits.
1 quart of vinegar.

Half-teaspoonful powdered cloves.

Mix and rub through a sieve. Put in a stone jar, set in a pot of boiling water, and heat until the liquid is so hot you cannot bear your finger in it. Strain, and let it stand in the jar, closely covered, two days, then bottle for use.[61]

VEGETABLES

Vegetables, at the beginning of the Victorian era, consisted mainly of cabbages, corn, salad greens, root vegetables, onion, and squash. Lydia Child mentioned asparagus, beet tops, cabbages, celery, dandelions, green peas, lettuce, onions, parsnips, potatoes, squash (winter and "green"), tomatoes, and vegetable oyster. Most of these were indigenous to New England, where Child lived, and easy to cultivate. Potatoes, a staple of the European peasant diet by the nineteenth century, had traveled across the Atlantic to America during the late seventeenth century and became widely accepted during the eighteenth. In 1796, Amelia Simmons, author of the first American cookbook, had praised potatoes as being superior "for universal use, profit and easy acquirement."[62] Potatoes persisted as a dietary staple for Americans during the nineteenth century for the very reasons Simmons had given. They were easy to grow, easy to keep, and easy to cook. For a nation of people on the move, potatoes were an ideal food.

By the later nineteenth century, American tastes for vegetables were expanding. This was partly due to the general expansion of the economy and an ensuing social demand for more status foods, as well as the ready availability of new kinds of vegetables grown by market farmers and in greenhouses, and exotic vegetables from California and the South, now shipped across the continent by rail. Thomas De Voe commented on the growth of the market gardeners in New Jersey, Connecticut, and upstate New York who supplied the New York City markets. New York City had previously been supplied by its suburbs—Long Island, Westchester and the New York counties, and New Jersey. But as the city grew, the suburbs could not meet the demand:

Upon Connecticut, Massachusetts, Western New York, New Jersey, and Pennsylvania, requisitions were made, and now the Southern States, Bermuda Islands, etc., send their early supplies to our markets—not only vegetables, but fruits, fish, nuts, etc.—for months anticipating our native supply. From Charleston, Norfolk, Savannah, and the Bermudas, tomatoes, potatoes, peas, cabbage, onions, strawberries, cherries, are brought at least twice a week during their seasons. Some of these articles are brought by hundreds of barrels at a time.

Early in the spring from the South, and still later from the North, many rare vegetables and other edibles are brought to market by the facilities afforded by the railcars and steamboats, thus inducing, as it were, in these latitudes, artificial seasons.[63]

De Voe, who wrote his book to provide consumers with a sweeping view of what was available at the markets of New York, included dozens of vegetables in his discussion. Luxury goods, such as asparagus, abounded in and out of season. According to De Voe, asparagus "is one of the best and choicest luxuries of the vegetable kind, being a wholesome, digestible, and a light food."[64] In contrast, Eliza Leslie's 1851 cookbook presented a more realistic appraisal of what most people ate. The vegetable section of her book mentioned artichokes, asparagus, beans (both dried and green), lima beans (which she esteemed highly), beets, broccoli, cabbage, carrots, cauliflower, corn, cucumbers, eggplant, lettuce, mushrooms, onions, parsnips, peas, green peppers, potatoes, salsify, sea kale, spinach, summer squash, sweet potatoes, tomatoes, turnips, and winter squash. Some of these, however, appeared in multiple recipes, which suggested that they were used more frequently than the rest. Cabbage, mushrooms, onions, potatoes, and tomatoes formed the basis for four recipes each, whereas the rest were used for only one or possibly two recipes.

De Voe would certainly have agreed with Leslie about potatoes and tomatoes. Of potatoes, he wrote, "This most excellent edible root is, without doubt, the most useful, wholesome, and nutritive of all the roots now in use. Scarcely a dinner is prepared without having this vegetable on the table. 'They furnish flour without a mill, and bread without an oven.'" He felt similarly inclined toward tomatoes, largely for their health benefits, and quoted a Dr. Bennett, who had argued that the tomato, "when used as an article of diet, it is almost sovereign for dyspepsia and indigestion—that it should be constantly used for daily food; either cooked, raw, or in the form of catsup, it is the most healthy article now in use."[65] Tomatoes, healthful or not, were one of the earliest canned foods to be widely accepted. A cannery in Philadelphia processed 10,000 baskets of tomatoes in 1855, and a New Jersey processing plant processed 150 bushels a day in 1864. By 1870, tomato canneries had sprung up in many places, including Mystic, Connecticut.[66]

FRUITS

As with vegetables, fruit options expanded during the Victorian era, and for most of the same reasons. In addition to apples, pears, peaches, cherries, raspberries, blueberries, cranberries, plums, and other fruits, improvements in communication and transportation brought pineapples, oranges, lemons, limes, bananas, and other tropical or warm-weather fruits to markets in the North and Midwest. De Voe noted the difference in the way that fruits were regarded in Europe versus the United States, asserting that in Europe, "even to the wealthy, fruits are a luxury, a dessert," because European countries lacked the open space required for growing fruits. In the United States, however, "happily, the people have an opportunity to seek and to obtain a portion of God's favors to man; and although fruits are not sufficiently plentiful to supply the wants of all, yet fruit, to a certain extent, may be obtained by the poorest of city populations."[67]

Fruit formed the basis of many desserts in Victorian America, whether pastries, puddings, pies, or served alone. Jane Croly, writing in 1871 as "Jennie June," stated, "Fruit alone makes a very good dessert; when in the season, and plentiful, a very cheap one. Apples, grapes, melons, pears, and peaches, are all fine for dessert and can be used singly, or combined, according to means and occasion."[68] Generally, though, the American sweet tooth preferred its fruit in combination with sugar, flour, and fat, as is suggested in cookery literature. Lydia Child proposed apple, cherry, cranberry, and whortleberry pudding for dessert, as well as apple, carrot, cherry, cranberry, custard, mince, pumpkin, rhubarb, squash, and whortleberry pie. Roughly twenty years later, Eliza Leslie's "Sweetmeat" offerings included items made from apples, apricots, barberries, cherries, citron, crab apples, currants, gooseberries, grapes, lemons, morello cherries, oranges, peaches, pears, pineapple, plums, pumpkin, quinces, raspberries, rhubarb, strawberries, and watermelon.

SWEETENERS

The title page of Eleanor Parkinson's *The Complete Confectioner* stated that the book would provide directions for "all sorts of preserves, sugar-boiling, comfit, lozenges, ornamental cakes, ices, liqueurs, water, gum-paste, ornaments, syrups, jellies, marmalades, compotes, ... fancy biscuits, cakes, rolls, muffins, tarts, pies, &c., &c."[69] All of these ices, puddings, pastries, pies, and other confections required some sort of sweetener and by the mid-nineteenth century, many choices of sweetener were readily available. Honey and maple syrup had been widely used in earlier times because of their availability, and continued to be so, especially in more remote parts of the United States. De Voe, in his description of the goods available in New York City

THE CULTURE OF FRUIT.

Downing says that "fine fruit is the most perfect union of the use-ful and beautiful, that earth knows." It is alike the luxury of prince and peasant—of the President and the pathmaster. If we include pumpkins and watermelons, it is the cheapest kind of food. Nothing is more wholesome than well ripened fruit, in moderate quantities. Many words, however, are not wanted, to convince any one of the excellence or deliciousness of fruit, if we can only pre-sent him a dish of apricots, or a quart of strawberries and cream.

For most of the nineteenth century, rural families grew their own fruit. Books and articles on fruit culture and its benefits abounded, including this one in *The Pictorial Cultivator Almanac for the United States for the Year 1851*, published in Albany, New York. The summer season offered a succession of fruit crops to be washed, peeled, pitted, and transformed into jellies, jams, and conserves.

markets, mentioned honey, maple sugar, maple syrup, and molasses.[70] Molasses, a by-product of sugar production, became an alternative syrup for sweetening foods in the eighteenth century, but was typi-cally used for cookies, puddings, cakes, and other made dishes, rather than as a table sweetener. Cane sugar became the primary sweetener for most people in the nineteenth century, as a result of improvements in sugar cultivation and sugar processing, as well as in transportation. These improvements resulted in a 500 percent increase in British sugar consumption during the nineteenth century, and doubtless a corresponding increase among Americans as well.[71] Gradually, as refining techniques improved, sugar became not only more available (cheaper) but also whiter, which added to its status and appeal. *Godey's* editor, Sarah Josepha Hale, surveyed the different grades of sugar available in 1853, in terms of both visual appearance and perceived sweetness. The lowest priced and coarsest (brown sugar) Hale deemed the least desirable; she thought it was dirty and of inferior sweetness. She felt that the most refined sugar was best because it was the sweetest; moreover "best has a bright and gravelly appearance." Her ultimate preference was for loaf sugar, which she chose for its fineness and closeness of texture. She considered this best for everything except preserving, where any coarse, strong sugar would do.[72] By 1871, loaf sugar was being replaced by granulated sugar. Loaf sugar, sold in cone-shaped blocks, had to be cut into lumps or pounded into a powder before use. Granulated sugar was loose and much more convenient to use. Maria Parloa wrote about it, "The fine granulated sugar is the best and cheapest for general family use. It is pure and dry; therefore, there is more in one pound of it than in a damp, brown sugar, besides its sweetening power being considerably greater." She recommended purchasing it by the barrel as an economy measure.[73]

WINE, BEER, WATER, AND OTHER BEVERAGES

Americans consumed a variety of beverages, depending on the meal, the occasion, religious and political convictions, climate, and social status. Some of these, beer and ale, for example, were made at home. Others depended on international trade networks (tea, coffee, chocolate, and wine), or a growing commercial production in the United States (lager beer). In 1833, Lydia Child assumed her cost-conscious readers would want the knowledge to make beer, chocolate, coffee, currant wine, ginger beer, hop beer, lemon brandy, medicinal drinks, raspberry shrub, and spruce beer at home, as well as to brew tea.

Water, readily available in the countryside but not always reliable or healthy in the city, became a political beverage with the advent of the temperance and health reform movements. Bottled springwaters and manufactured soda waters began to appear on fashionable tables during the 1830s. As Lydia Child noted, water was not always a reliable option in cold-weather climates. "In winter," she noted, "always set the handle of your pump as high as possible before you go to bed. Except in very rigid weather, this keeps the handle from freezing."[74]

Milk, always a favored beverage, especially for children, was transformed in the late 1850s by Gail Borden, who developed a process for canning, and thus preserving and purifying, milk. William Alcott, health reformer and physician, expressed the fears related to milk drinking in his household manual of the late 1830s. "All the cows of Paris have tubercles in their lungs, (the beginning of consumption)," he wrote, "and there is no doubt that many of the cows about our own cities and towns are in the same sad predicament."[75] By the end of the century, milk, which had been purchased originally directly from local farmers, was sold in glass bottles, the product of farmer's co-ops and enormous milk-processing plants.[76]

Beer, once brewed at home by housewives, became a consumer product in the nineteenth century. By 1873, there were 4,131 breweries in the United States, rolling out 9 million barrels of beer a year.[77] Popular novelist William Dean Howells documented the dominance of commercial breweries, as well as middle-class beer-drinking habits, through one of his characters in *A Modern Instance*. Bartley Hubbard, a young clerk, had his beer "sent in by the gross—it came cheaper that way; after trying both the Cincinnati and the Milwaukee lagers, and making a cursory test of the Boston brand, he had settled down upon the American Tivoli; it was cheap, and you could drink a couple of bottles without feeling it." Bartley customarily drank a bottle for lunch and two bottles for dinner.[78]

Cider, a staple drink of early American life, retained its importance throughout the nineteenth century, especially in rural parts of the country. Families that had large orchards may well have pressed their own fruit at home, using a portable cider press. Others, however, could easily have taken their fruit to a local cider mill to have it pressed, or merely purchased cider ready-made at the mill. *Buckeye Cookery*, written by Ohio women and published in Minnesota, advised that it was better to wait until late in the season to press cider; the cooler temperatures would help prevent fermentation. "Use only the best-flavored grafted fruit," they wrote, "rejecting all that are decayed or wormy." The juice was to be strained and put up in barrels for a short time (one to three days), and then bottled.[79] Cider could serve as the basis for a number of other drinks. It could be mulled, mixed with beaten egg, sugar, and spices. It could be fermented and transformed into a potent alcoholic beverage. Moreover, it could be turned into cider vinegar, an important component of the pickling process. Hard cider, however, lost much of its following with the rise of the temperance

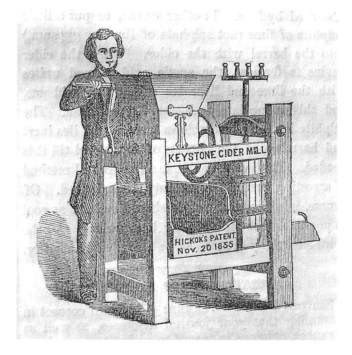

"This is the old-fashioned method of cider making," proclaimed the agricultural journal *Genesee Farmer* in October 1859. By that time, much cider was commercially produced in large, water-powered cider mills, although the process remained a rural-based occupation. (Collection of Harvey Green.)

movement. Temperance reformers, who urged sobriety in all areas of life, initially exempted beer, wine, and cider. By the 1870s, zealous reformers rampaged through the countryside destroying apple orchards by the acre.

In place of hard cider, many families turned to softer drink. Lemonade, always a refreshing summer drink, achieved a new status as a "Temperance Drink," along with root beer, shrub, and iced tea. Popular writer, agriculturist, and founder of the Lake County (Indiana) Temperance Society, Solon Robinson commented on his discovery of iced tea in 1860: "Last summer we got in the habit of taking the tea iced, and really thought it better than when hot."[80] *Buckeye Cookery* included a recipe for "Raspberry Shrub," a raspberry-flavored sweet vinegar that, when mixed with cold water, provided a refreshing cool drink on a hot summer day.

Raspberry Shrub

> Place red raspberries in a stone jar, cover them with good cider vinegar, let
> stand over night; next morning strain, and to one pint of juice add one pint of
> sugar, boil ten minutes, and bottle while hot.[81]

As wine became more and more fashionable among the middle classes during the Victorian era, cookbooks increased their number of recipes for making wine at home. Jane Croly included directions for making currant champagne, and wine from grapes, as well as from currants, blackberries, elder flowers, rhubarb, gooseberries, and ginger. She also described grape syrup, which she recommended as a non-alcoholic wine. In addition to wines, she provided recipes for other beverages, alcoholic and not, that would be useful for entertaining. These included blackberry and cherry brandies; hop, ginger, "quick," and spruce beers; mead, shrub, and claret punch; May Drink (a German favorite); Oxford Swig (a potent mix of beer, sherry, sugar, and lemon); Sack Posset; lemonade; milk punch; and Christmas eggnog.[82]

Coffee rivaled tea throughout the Victorian era as the hot beverage of choice in the United States. Coffee had risen in popularity during the American Revolution when British tea became too expensive (and unpatriotic) to drink, a trend that was solidified during the War of 1812. After that war, when the price of tea dropped again to an affordable level, it faced new competition from coffee grown in Brazil, as well as from the American fascination with things French.[83] The French connection with coffee stems from France's colonial holdings in the eighteenth century. While the British had access to tea through their colonial empire, the French did not, and they developed a national preference for coffee. As a result, French brewing techniques evolved to a high level during the nineteenth century, which further enhanced the national obsession with coffee: it tasted better because it was brewed better. Lydia Child bowed to the French mastery over coffee, stating, "French coffee is so celebrated, that it may be worth while to tell how it is made," although she added the caveat that "no prudent housekeeper will make it, unless she has boarders, who are willing to pay for expensive cooking."[84]

Chocolate had been favored by the European aristocracy as a less stimulating alternative to coffee and tea since the early sixteenth century. Typically consumed at breakfast (and ideally, in bed), chocolate conveyed associations of indolence and languor and was the antithesis of coffee, always a high-energy drink. By the nineteenth century, chocolate had been transformed by technology into a substance that was widely available for all, and especially children, to enjoy:

cocoa.[85] The traditional chocolate drink was made by dissolving solid chocolate, made from ground cocoa beans, in hot water or milk, often adding such other flavoring ingredients as sugar, vanilla, nutmeg, or even wine. *Buckeye Cookery* explained the differences between chocolate and cocoa:

> Cocoa is from the seed of the fruit of a small tropical tree. There are several forms in which it is sold, the most nutritious and convenient being chocolate, the next cocoa, then cocoa nibs, and last cocoa shells. The ground bean is simply cocoa; ground fine and mixed with sugar it is chocolate; the beans broken into bits are "nibs." The shells are the shells of the bean, usually removed before grinding. The beans are roasted like coffee, and ground between hot rollers.[86]

In 1828, a Dutch chocolate maker named Van Hooten developed a process for extracting cocoa butter from cocoa beans, 50 percent fat by weight. Van Hooten's process removed two-thirds of the cocoa butter, leaving behind a residue that he called cocoa. Because cocoa was less rich, it was more easily digested than full-fat chocolate; it was also easily soluble in water and made an ideal, nourishing drink for children, invalids, and anyone who wanted a hot beverage that was less stimulating than tea or coffee. The cocoa butter extracted during Van Hooten's process became the basis for molded chocolate bars and candies—an entirely new use for chocolate. The British firm Cadbury Brothers began to market chocolate bars in 1842; the Swiss chocolatier Henri Nestlé was manufacturing milk chocolate, the final piece of the modern chocolate calculus, after 1876.[87]

NOTES

1 Thomas Dublin examined the transformation of trading relationships between local consumers and their general store in "Women and Outwork in a Nineteenth-Century New England Town: Fitzwilliam, New Hampshire, 1830–1850," in *The Countryside in the Age of Capitalist Transformation: Essays in the Social History of Rural America*, ed. Steven Hahn and Jonathan Prude (Chapel Hill: University of North Carolina Press, 1985), 51–69.

2. Thomas Farrington De Voe, *The Market Assistant* (New York: Hurd and Houghton, 1867), 21; digital edition available at "Feeding America: The Historic American Cookbook Project," Michigan State University Library Web site, http://digital.lib.msu.edu/collections/ (accessed November 14, 2005).

3. Ibid., 9.

4. *Oxford Encyclopedia of Food and Drink in America*, s.v. "Canning and Bottling" (by Andrew F. Smith). See also, Andrew F. Smith, "The Well Preserved Tomato," chapter 3 in *Souper Tomatoes: The Story of America's Favorite*

Food (New Brunswick: Rutgers University Press, 2000), 45–62. Waverly Root and Richard De Rochemont, *Eating in America: A History* (New York: Ecco Press, 1976), 159, 187–91; Sandra L. Oliver, *Saltwater Foodways: New Englanders and Their Food at Sea and Ashore in the Nineteenth Century* (Mystic, CT: Mystic Seaport, Inc., 1995), 48.

5. Mary Randolph, *The Virginia House-Wife*, ed. Karen Hess (1824, 1825, 1828; reprint Columbia: University of South Carolina Press, 1984), iii–viii.

6. Prudence Smith's cookbook is described in Eleanor Lowenstein, *Bibliography of American Cookery Books, 1742–1860* (Worcester: American Antiquarian Society, 1972), 30.

7. Eliza Leslie, *Miss Leslie's Directions for Cookery: An Unabridged Reprint of the 1851 Classic* (1851; reprint New York: Dover Publications, Inc., 1999), 11.

8. Estelle Woods Wilcox, ed., *Buckeye Cookery and Practical Housekeeping: A Nineteenth Century Best Seller* (1880; reprint St. Paul, MN: Minnesota Historical Society Press, 1988), 7.

9. William Woys Weaver, ed., *A Quaker Woman's Cookbook: The Domestic Cookery of Elizabeth Ellicott Lea* (Philadelphia: University of Pennsylvania Press, 1982), xxii, 59–61.

10. Lydia Maria Child, *The American Frugal Housewife* (1832; reprint Worthington, OH: Worthington Historical Society, 1965), 76–80.

11. Leslie, *Directions for Cookery*, 379–82.

12. See Joan M. Jensen's comprehensive study of the women's butter economy in *Loosening the Bonds: Mid-Atlantic Farm Women, 1750–1850* (New Haven: Yale University Press, 1986), especially 102–113.

13. De Voe, 400–401.

14. Richard J. Hooker, *Food and Drink in America: A History* (Indianapolis and New York: Bobbs-Merrill Co., Inc., 1981), 227. The persistence of farm butter into the 1870s is suggested by Jane Cunningham Croly, *Jennie June's American Cookery Book* (New York: American News Co., 1870), 317–318.

15. Leslie, *Directions for Cookery*, 383–384; *Oxford Encyclopedia of Food and Drink in America*, s.v. "Cheese" (by Gerd Stern).

16. De Voe, 402–403.

17. Ibid., 402. Waverly Root claimed that brick cheese was invented in 1877, not 1871, by John Jossi, who was perhaps Swiss. Root and de Rochemont, 304.

18. Menu, Parker House, Boston, Massachusetts, August 17, 1874, Menu Collection, Library Company of Philadelphia (5763 F63c).

19. *Quaker Woman's Cookbook*, 31.

20. Child, 59.

21. Ibid., 48.

22. Ibid., 55.

23. See Andrew Smith's discussion of "Renaissance Soup" for fuller historical background on the history of soup, in *Souper Tomatoes*, 10–12.

24. Randolph, 28–38. For a discussion of the rising fashionability of soup on gentry tables, see Smith, *Souper Tomatoes*, 21.

25. Randolph, 29.

26. Leslie, *Directions for Cookery*, 13–41.

27. Boston grocer Fabens & Graham advertised that they carried Huckins's soups; see their advertisement in *The Boston Directory*, no. 70 (Boston: Sampson, Davenport & Co., 1882), 1552; see also Susan Williams, *Savory Suppers and Fashionable Feasts: Dining in Victorian America* (1985; reprint Knoxville: University of Tennessee Press, 1996), 98. For a history of Franco-American, see Smith, *Souper Tomatoes*, 81–84.

28. Child, 57–60.

29. *Fitchburg Almanac, Directory, and Advisor* (Fitchburg, MA: S & C Shepley, 1848), 53.

30. *The Fitchburg Directory* (Fitchburg, MA: Price, Lee & Co., 1876), 138.

31. *The Fitchburg Directory* (Fitchburg, MA: Price, Lee & Co., 1880), 145, 222–23.

32. *Fitchburg Almanac, Directory, and Business Advertiser for 1854* (Fitchburg, MA: Shepley & Wallace, 1854), 64

33. Root and de Rochemont, 155.

34. Eliza Leslie, *The Ladies' Guide to True Politeness and Perfect Manners* (Philadelphia, T. B. Peterson & Bros., 1864), 128–129. For an exploration of the changing social significance of the lobster, see George H. Lewis, "The Maine Lobster as Regional Icon: Competing Images over Time and Social Class," in *A Taste of American Place*, ed. Barbara G. and James R. Shortridge (Lanham, MD: Rowan & Littlefield Publishers, Inc., 1998), 65–83. See also Oliver, 380–382.

35. Maria Parloa, *Miss Parloa's New Cook Book, A Guide to Marketing and Cooking*, (Boston: Estes & Lauriat, 1888), 41–47.

36. *Fitchburg Directory* (1880), 155, 222–223.

37. *Buckeye Cookery*, 295, 303

38. "Fifty Years Success," *New England Grocer* (May 6, 1892), available from "Emergence of Advertising in America: Advertising Ephemera" Web site, Rare Book, Manuscript, and Special Collections Library, Duke University, http://scriptorium.lib.duke.edu:80/ (accessed January 2, 2006).

39. *Fitchburg Directory* (1854, 1868).

40. De Voe, 103–104.

41. Parloa, 9–29.

42. Ibid., 36–7.

43. Ibid., 35–36.

44. Ibid., 37–38

45. De Voe, 132.

46. Leslie, *Directions for Cookery*, 140–161.

47. Larry Zuckerman, *The Potato: How the Humble Spud Rescued the Western World* (New York: North Point Press, 1998), 48.

48. Fannie Merritt Farmer, *The Original Boston Cooking School Cookbook, 1896* (facsimile edition; New York: Weathervane Books, n.d.), 287.

49. Manuscript cookbook, 1390, cited in Constance B. Hiett and Sharon Butler, *Pleyn Delit: Medieval Cookery for Modern Cooks* (Toronto: University of Toronto Press, 1976), 44.

50. Robert Roberts, *The House Servant's Directory* (Boston, 1827; reprint Bedford, MA: Applewood Books, 1993), 67–68.

51. A Practical Housekeeper, *The American Practical Cookery Book* (Philadelphia: G. G. Evans, 1860), 218.

52. Robert Buist, *The Family Kitchen Gardener* (New York: C. M. Saxton & Co., 1855), 65.

53. Child, 36–37.

54. Amy Bess Miller and Persis Fuller, *The Best of Shaker Cooking* (New York: Macmillan & Co., 1985), 11–13.

55. Buist, 24, 33, 48, 59, 60, 62, 74, 97, 119, 138, 139, 140, 145, 146.

56. Parloa, 59.

57. J. M. Sanderson, *The Complete Cook* (Philadelphia: J. B. Lippincott & Co., 1864), 124–125; digital edition available at "Feeding America" Web site, http://digital.lib.msu.edu/collections/ (accessed January 13, 2006).

58. Child, 15–16.

59. H. J. Heinz Company, "Heinz Milestones" Web site, http://www. heinz.com/jsp/milestones.jsp (accessed October 16, 2005). See also Donna R. Gabaccia, "As American as Budweiser and Pickles?" in *Food Nations: Selling Taste in Consumer Societies*, ed. Warren Belasco and Philip Scranton (New York and London: Routledge, 2002), 175–193.

60. Marion [Mary Virginia Hawes Terhune] Harland, *Common Sense in the Household: A Manual of Practical Housewifery* (1871; reprint Birmingham, AL: Oxmoor House, Inc., 1985), 193.

61. Harland, *Common Sense in the Household*, 195.

62. For an extended social and cultural analysis of potato eating in America, see Zuckerman, "The Democratic Table," chapter 5 in *The Potato*.

63. De Voe, 321.

64. Ibid., 323.

65. Ibid., 342, 353.

66. Root and de Rochemont, 159, 187–191; Oliver, 48. See also Sue Shephard, *Pickled, Potted, and Canned: How the Art and Science of Food Preserving Changed the World* (New York: Simon & Schuster, 2000), 245-247.

67. De Voe, 367.

68. Croly, 142.

69. Eleanor Parkinson, *The Complete Confectioner* (Philadelphia: J. B. Lippincott & Co., 1864), title page; digital edition available at "Feeding America" Web site, http://digital.lib.msu.edu/collections/ (accessed January 13, 2006).

70. De Voe, 406–407.

71. Sidney W. Mintz, *Sweetness and Power: The Place of Sugar in Modern History* (New York: Viking Penguin Inc., 1985), 69, 73.

72. Sarah Josepha Hale, *The New Household Receipt Book* (New York: H. Long & Brother, 1853), 214.

73. Parloa, 58.

74. Child, 16.

75. William A. Alcott, *The Young Housekeeper, or Thoughts on Food and Cookery* (Boston: Waite, Peirce & Co., 1846), 271–272; digital edition available at "Feeding America" Web site, http://digital.lib.msu.edu/collections/ (accessed July 26, 2005).

76. For a general history of milk production in the nineteenth century, see *Oxford Encyclopedia of Food and Drink in America*, s.v. "Milk" (by Daniel Block).

77. Ibid., s.v. "Beer" (by Peter LaFrance).

78. William Dean Howells, *A Modern Instance* (1882; reprint New York: Library of America, 1982), 407.

79. *Buckeye Cookery*, 143.

80. Solon Robinson, *How to Live, or Domestic Economy Illustrated* (New York: 1860), 157, cited in Richard J. Hooker, *Food and Drink in America: A History* (New York: Bobbs-Merrill Co., 1981), 276.

81. *Buckeye Cookery*, 144.

82. Croly, 265–276.

83. Root and de Rochemont, *Eating in America*, 128–129.

84. Child, 83.

85. Wolfgang Schivelbusch, *Tastes of Paradise: A Social History of Spices, Stimulants, and Intoxicants* (New York: Vintage Books, 1993), 87–92.

86. *Buckeye Cookery*, 142.

87. Davidson, *Oxford Companion to Food*, 179.

CHAPTER 3
FOOD PREPARATION AND COOKERY

Women in the 1820s cooked meals for their families over open fires, using cranes, trammels, and trivets. The work was backbreaking because, for the most part, cooking occurred at floor level, on the hearth. By the 1870s, women were up off the hearth, cooking on commodious cast iron ranges and using a wide array of "modern" utensils. As cooking techniques became more scientific, recipes no longer called for "butter the size of an egg," or "a teacup of sugar." New, standardized tools for precisely weighing and measuring ingredients ensured that the final product could be widely replicable—without necessarily requiring previous training or experience. Other cooking tools became increasingly specialized. Kitchen cupboards by the 1880s stored multiple new options for baking, paring, beating, molding, grinding, straining, squeezing, chopping, frying, and freezing. These enhancements in cookery tools and techniques not only changed the variety of foods available from home kitchen but also raised expectations about what American families wanted to eat—potentially increasing a cook's workload at the same time as they streamlined it.

With the growth of an American-based publishing industry during the early 1800s, cookbooks, domestic advice manuals, and household management literature became widely available. These texts offered their readers a window into cooking cultures that far exceeded the traditional bounds of place and family. New issues of economy, nutrition, fashion, and taste entered the American kitchen, reshaping daily menus and family diets.

Finally, larger systems improved accessibility to more diverse foodstuffs for Victorian Americans, in particular the widespread availability

By 1876, in a "modern" kitchen, cooks had moved up from hearth level to stovetop and countertop work surfaces. The presence of cupboards, closets, and pantries implied more tools and ingredients, as well as fancier cookery. Ultimately, these modern improvements required that the cook be more educated and more ambitious in her cookery. Although modern cookery remained a somewhat intuitive process, the clock on the wall suggests some degree of science added to the mix. Mass-produced clocks began to appear by the 1820s; by the Civil War era, they were ubiquitous. (Courtesy of the Library of Congress, Prints & Photographs Division, Washington, D.C., LC-USZ62-478.)

of ice and hence, refrigeration. Railroads and steamships meant that seasonality and distance from the source no longer posed a problem for cooks who wanted to serve lobster in Buffalo or Des Moines or Denver. Other technologies related to canning and preserving food further contributed to a growing consumer culture of foodstuffs, transforming family menus all over the country.

FROM OPEN HEARTH TO STOVETOP COOKERY

Hearth cooking, as had been practiced in America since the beginning of European settlement, required a minimum of equipment. Cooks needed to be able to create and maintain a cooking fire, using axes, shovels, tongs, and pokers, along with andirons or fire dogs. To actually cook, they needed either a lug pole, which extended across the mouth of the chimney, or an iron crane, and a selection of pots and kettles that hung from the pole or crane on pothooks or trammels. On the hearth, which served as a cooking surface, griddles, toasting racks, spiders, and other smaller cooking vessels completed the kit. Baking occurred in a large brick oven, built into the chimney, or in the more

A transitional kitchen, from the era before cast iron ranges. Cooking was done on the hearth or over the fire, using hanging pots, kettles, trammels, skillets, and trivets; meat could be roasted in the "tin kitchen" in front of hearth. This image appeared as the frontispiece in Mrs. E. A. Howland's *The American Economical Housekeeper* in 1845. (Courtesy of Special Collections, Michigan State University Libraries.)

recently invented tin reflector oven or "tin kitchen"—which enabled open-hearth roasting.[1]

By the 1820s, cookstoves had begun to appear, and gradually made fireplace cooking a thing of the past. Although box stoves had been around since the eighteenth century, they had been used mainly for heating rather than cooking. At the outset, many women resisted cookstoves, in part, because they were skilled at hearth cookery and did not see any need to change. In her 1889 autobiography, Lucy Larcom (who was born in 1824) commented about this reluctance, referring nostalgically to the romance of the open hearth:

Cooking-stoves were coming into fashion, but they were clumsy affairs, and our elders thought that no cooking could be quite so nice as that which was done by an open fire. We younger ones reveled in the warm, beautiful glow, that we look back to as to a remembered sunset. There is no such home-splendor now.[2]

She preferred her family's fireplace, with its andirons (in the form of "two Continental soldiers in full uniform, marching one after the other") and its "swinging crane with its sooty pot-hooks and trammels." In the household of her childhood, all cooking was conducted in the fireplace and on the hearth. She noted that "the coffee-pot was set for breakfast over hot coals, on a three-legged bit of iron called a 'trivet,'" and that "potatoes were roasted in the ashes, and the Thanksgiving turkey in a 'tin-kitchen,' the business of turning the spit being usually delegated to some of us, small folk, who were only too willing to burn our faces in honor of the annual festival."[3]

William T. James patented his version of this new cooking device in 1815, the "Saddlebags" model—a stove that not only heated but also boiled water, baked, and cooked food. Essentially, the stove consisted of a cast-iron firebox, a baking oven above it, and a stovetop cooking surface. As James and his competitors advertised, these stoves could be further equipped with hot water boilers and other cooking equipment that fit into two round openings in the stovetop. The advantage of these new box stoves was twofold. By burning wood more efficiently, they could cut to half the amount of wood required for cooking—a significant savings in labor. They were also cheaper to install than a fireplace and chimney and could be moved if necessary. In terms of the comfort of the cook, they raised the cooking surface up off the hearth, thus eliminating heavy lifting and allowing women to stand while cooking rather than crouching, kneeling, or squatting in front of their vessels on the hearth.[4]

The stove industry expanded rapidly, testament to the growing popularity of this new style of cooking. By 1828, Mrs. William Parkes, author of *Domestic Duties; or, Instructions to Young Married Ladies on the Management of their Households*, commented that the kitchen range was "now in common use." She described the device as having an oven on one side of the fire and a hot water boiler on the other or behind—fed with water from a cistern with a ball cock.[5] The availability of hot water on demand must have been a compelling feature of these new ranges for many women. A Massachusetts farmwife, Lucy Watson Draper, wrote enthusiastically to her daughter about their new stove in 1839: "We have a stove like Mrs. W. Bemis's with the addition of an oven. . . . I am very much pleased with it. It is very warm and convenient. It cost three dollars more for the oven. I do almost all my cooking in it."[6] Many other women agreed with Lucy Draper's assessment and the stove industry boomed. More than five hundred stove-related patents were issued between 1820 and 1850; by midcentury, there were 230 stove manufacturers operating in the United States. Domestic advice writer Mary Cornelius commented to the readers of the 1859 edition of her cookbook that "stoves and cooking ranges have so generally taken the place of brick ovens, that the following directions [for constructing a brick oven], which were appropriate when this book was first published [in 1845] will seldom be of use now."[7]

The stoves themselves had evolved from a relatively small box, with a two- hole cooking surface, to massive ranges, with between four and eight potholes, multiple ovens, and large attached tanks for heating water.[8] In their design, these modern cookstoves reflected the prevailing taste for complex surface decoration. Their relief-molded side panels and doors and nickel-plated ornamentation frequently resembled finely carved furniture. "The Housekeeper," a high-end range produced by Philadelphia stove maker Charles Noble & Co.,

was intended by the manufacturers to be, in every respect, first-class. It has nickel-plated knobs and ornaments, front illumination, nickel-plated shifting guard-rail (in order that a tin kitchen can be used), shaking and dumping clinkerless grate, ash flue, hot-air arrangements to heat any number of room, and many other desirable characteristics.[9]

This grandiose range, for which its manufacturer won a medal at the Philadelphia Centennial Exhibition in 1876, had six burners, two ovens, and was embellished with cast-iron panels depicting standing stags, bunnies, and lion's heads; Renaissance ornaments crowned the top. In appearance, it would have been just as suitable in a bedroom or parlor as in a kitchen. As cookbook author Maria Parloa reminded her readers, "No single piece of furniture contributes so much to the comfort of a family as the range or stove, which, therefore, should be the best of its kind."[10] The range, and the domain that it inhabited, had become part of a highly civilized sphere, requiring both tools and ambiance to support genteel tastes.

One important outcome of the shift from fireplace cooking to stove cooking was that on a stove, a woman could more easily cook multiple items at once. As a result, ordinary family menus became more complex, involving more courses and more complicated recipes. Women had to acquire new skills to engage in range cookery. Opening and closing dampers and flues could modulate the temperatures, but it was only through experience that most women gained a close familiarity with the workings of their ranges. A summer family dinner, proposed by Maria Parloa in 1880, reflected the new assumptions brought about by the potential of range cookery. The menu began with asparagus soup, followed by boiled blue fish with *Maître d'Hôtel* butter, and then veal cutlets with white sauce, green peas, dressed cucumbers,

"THE HOUSEKEEPER" RANGE.

Charles Noble & Company's "Housekeeper" range won a medal at the Philadelphia Centennial Exhibition in 1876. The hot water heater beside the range offered cooks and housewives relief from the drudgery of hauling heavy kettles of water to the kitchen. (Courtesy of Dover Publications.)

mashed potatoes, and, for the conclusion, charlotte russe.[11] To produce such a meal required multiple cooking surfaces operating at once, as well as an oven (and cook) capable of baking the delicate sponge cake necessary for the charlotte russe.

Stoves, whether fueled by wood or coal, generated ash, dust, and soot, necessitating regular maintenance. While a fireplace and hearth also required some degree of cleaning—mainly, sweeping and shoveling out the ashes—a cookstove had a much larger surface area and multiple materials to keep tidy. Their cast-iron surfaces had to be kept rust-free and needed regular blacking. Likewise, their nickel trim had to be kept polished, and the ash bin emptied daily. Juliet Corson's cooking school textbook detailed for her students the process of cleaning stoves:

> FIRST.—Let down the grate and take up the cinders and ashes carefully to avoid all unnecessary dirt; put them at once into an ash sifter fitted into the top of a keg or pail with handles, and closed with a tight fitting cover; take the pail out of doors, sift the cinders, put the ashes into the ash-can, and bring the cinders back to the kitchen.
>
> SECOND.—Brush the soot and ashes out of all the flues and draught-holes of the stove, and then put the covers on, and brush all the dust off the outside. A careful cook will save all the wings of game and poultry to use for this purpose. If the stove is greasy, wash it off with a piece of flannel dipped in hot water containing a little soda.
>
> THIRD.—Mix a little black-lead or stove-polish with enough water to form a thin paste; apply this to the stove with a soft rag or brush; let it dry a little and then polish it with a stiff brush.
>
> FOURTH.—If there are any steel fittings about the stove, polish them with emery paper; if they have rusted from neglect, rub some oil on them at night, and polish them with emery paper in the morning. A "burnisher" composed of a net-work of fine steel rings, if used with strong hands, will make them look as if newly finished.
>
> FIFTH.—If the fittings are brass they should be cleaned with emery, or finely powdered and sifted bath brick dust rubbed on with a piece of damp flannel, and then polished with dry dust and chamois skin.
>
> SIXTH.—Brush up the hearthstone, wash it with a piece of flannel, dipped in hot water containing a little soda, rinse and wipe it dry with the flannel wrung out of clean hot water.[12]

Thus, while they may have saved women some forms of labor, especially heavy lifting of pots and kettles, the new stoves generated their own new forms of labor, which were in some ways equally onerous. As expensive objects of consumer consumption, cooking ranges served to express a family's taste and gentility to the public and, thus, held women accountable to different standards of cleanliness and presentation than had their more humble fireplace precedents.

STANDARDIZATION OF COOKERY

The 1833 edition of Lydia Maria Child's *The Frugal Housewife*, included the following recipe for pancakes:

Pancakes should be made of half a pint of milk, three great spoonfuls of sugar, one or two eggs, a tea-spoonful of dissolved pearlash, spiced with cinnamon, or cloves, a little salt, rose-water, or lemon-brandy, just as you happen to have it. Flour should be stirred in till the spoon moves round with difficulty. If they are thin, they are apt to soak fat. Have the fat in your skillet boiling hot, and drop them in with a spoon. Let them cook till thoroughly brown.[13]

The style of this recipe reflected a long tradition of cookery narrative, in which directions and quantities were often vaguely defined, and prior skills were assumed. A comparable recipe from the early seventeenth century advised, "To make the best pancake, take two or three eggs, and break them into a dish, and beat them well; then add unto them a pretty quantity of fair running water, and beat them all together." That recipe continued with directions for flavoring: "Then put in cloves, mace, cinnamon, and nutmeg, and season it with salt." Finally, "make it as thick as you think good with fine wheat flour."[14]

Child's recipe is somewhat more modern than Gervase Markham's "best pancake" recipe from 1615. She improved upon "a pretty quantity of fair running water" with "a pint measure of milk" and distinguished between "great spoonfuls" and "tea-spoonfuls," but the recipe as a whole retained the casual approach to measuring that had characterized its seventeenth-century predecessor. Neither recipe specified any quantities for the spices or flour—the amounts depended on the cook's experience or taste.

By 1851, Eliza Leslie noted in her best-selling *Directions for Cookery*, "Accuracy in proportioning the ingredients is indispensable; and therefore scales and weights, a set of tin measures (as least from a quart down to a jill) are of the utmost importance."[15] Her rationale stemmed from her belief that cooking, and especially baking cakes, was difficult, perhaps even doomed to failure, without proper tools. She could not imagine that any of her readers would wish to risk the disappointment and "needless expense" of a failed cake. The notion of risk (and the desire to minimize it) is an important aspect of Victorian cookery. As middle-class Americans became more educated, more cosmopolitan, and more able to participate in a growing consumer economy, they became increasingly reluctant to engage in behaviors or activities that might put their social position at risk. Risk could be minimized through standardization of techniques, measurements, and tools—in the kitchen as successfully as on the factory floor. To achieve more certain results, modern cooks preferred to follow recipes that were more explicit, and the plethora of newly available tools facilitated that objective.[16] Recipes for pancakes reflected this new desire for certainty and standardization of cookery. Leslie's "Plain Pancakes" called

The "Universal Family Scale," patented in 1865, suggests a trend toward more precise measurement and a standardization of recipes. Martha Skofield of Brunswick, Maine, purchased this scale for her kitchen, probably in the late 1880s. (Courtesy of the Pejepscot Historical Society, Brunswick, Maine.)

for "half a pound or a pint of flour," using two different measurements to avoid confusion. By 1876, *Buckeye Cookery* offered eleven different versions of pancake, gathered together under the general rubric of "Griddle Cakes." The author introduced these recipes with a general discussion of eggs (better if separated first), griddle types (soapstone versus iron), and greasing techniques (less is more). The beginning of the "French Pancakes" recipe reveals the extent to which measurements had become standardized and precise: "Beat together till smooth six eggs and a half a pound of flour, melt four ounces of butter and add to the batter, with one ounce of sugar and half a pint of milk, and beat until smooth."[17]

By 1875, when this recipe appeared in Marion Harland, *Breakfast, Luncheon and Tea*, the structure of recipes had evolved into a familiar formula, with the ingredients and amounts listed at the beginning, followed by cookery instructions and commentary.

Sour Milk Griddle Cakes

1 quart sour, or "loppered" milk.

About 4 cups sifted flour.

2 teaspoonsful soda, dissolved in boiling water.

3 table-spoonfuls molasses.

Salt to taste.

Mix the molasses with the milk. Put the flour into a deep bowl, mix the salt through it; make a hole in the middle, and pour in the milk, gradually stirring the flour down into it with a wooden spoon. The batter should not be too thick. When all the milk is in, beat until the mixture is free from lumps and very smooth. Add the soda water, stir up fast and well, and bake immediately.

These cakes are simple, economical, wholesome, and extremely nice. "Loppered" milk, or "clabber," is better than buttermilk. Try them![18]

To prepare this recipe according to the directions, the cook would have needed measuring spoons, a set of measuring cups (probably made of tin), and a kitchen scale. Maria Parloa illustrated a quart measure, with markings around the perimeter at half-pint intervals. "Being divided into half pints," she commented, "the one vessel answers for all quantities." Furthermore, "a kitchen should be furnished with two measures, one for dry material and the other for liquids."[19] These items, along with clocks, timers, and various types of cooking thermometers, represented the incursion of science into the American kitchen. By the end of the nineteenth century, cooking had come into its own as one of the "domestic sciences," and women learned to cook from a wide assortment of published cookbooks, as well as, in formal educational settings, from the newly established cooking schools that were opening up in cities all over the country.

COOKS, COOKBOOKS, AND COOKING SCHOOLS

The beginning of the Victorian era in America coincided with the publication of increasing numbers of American-authored cookbooks. Building on the momentum initiated in 1796 by Amelia Simmons's *American Cookery . . . Adapted to This Country and All Grades of Life*, American cooks began to write their own native cookbooks. Simmons had drawn many of her recipes from published English sources, although she also included many references to American customs and products. By 1824, when Mary Randolph published *The Virginia Housewife*, Americans were fully conscious of their own national identity, as well as the culture of their specific regions. *The Virginia Housewife* was followed by Eliza Leslie's *Seventy-Five Receipts, for Pastry, Cakes and Sweetmeats*, first published in Boston in 1828.[20]

Eliza Leslie, one of the most prominent figures in American cookery throughout the Victorian era, was born in Philadelphia in 1787. She spent much of her childhood in England, but returned to Philadelphia in 1798 or 1799. Because her family had suffered financial reverses (including the death of her father in 1803), Leslie and her mother had to devise strategies for maintaining their gentility while finding economic security. They did what many women in those circumstances did: took in boarders. Ultimately, Leslie became a pupil at Mrs. Goodfellow's Cooking School in Philadelphia and published a cookbook of recipes she had acquired there. Leslie stated in the preface to *Seventy-Five Receipts* that the recipes were, "in every sense of the word, American." She qualified that statement, however, confirming a lingering American deference to the cultural power of Europe. Her recipes may have been consciously constructed as American, "but the writer flatters herself that (if exactly followed) the articles produced from them will not be found inferior to any of a similar description made in the European manner." The book went through twenty editions by 1847.[21]

Emily Norcross Dickinson, mother of Emily Dickinson, received a copy of Lydia Maria Child's recently published cookbook, *The Frugal Housewife*, in 1832 as a gift from her husband, Edward.[22] *The Frugal Housewife*, dedicated by its author "To Those Who are Not Ashamed of Economy," cited no less eminent a social commentator than Benjamin Franklin on its cover. Readers were reminded of Franklin's adage "A fat kitchen maketh a lean will," advice that directly countered the potential problem of European aristocratic culinary decadence with American republican virtue.[23] Child's tone throughout the book was in keeping with her larger reformist ideology. She was an active antislavery advocate, as well as a tireless worker for social justice. The book was immensely popular, had already gone through seven editions by the time Mrs. Dickinson received her copy, and remained in print until 1850.

From the 1830s on, the American cookbook industry flourished. Increasing numbers of women wrote cookery books, representing increasingly diverse geographical constituencies. The earliest publishers were located in New York, Boston, and Philadelphia, but editions followed the westward movement of the country, first into the trans-Appalachian West (Ohio, Illinois, Indiana), and then up and

down the Mississippi Valley, over the mountains, and into the Far
West. Robert Roberts, the first African-American cookbook author,
published his *House Servant's Directory* in 1827. In 1839, another of
the female constellation of important cookbook authors, Sarah Josepha
Hale, released her first book, *The Good Housekeeper*. As the editor of
Godey's Lady's Book for forty years, Hale held a position of great influence with American women. The magazine included regular advice about cooking and other domestic pursuits, as well as numerous
recipes. In the 1840s, Catharine Beecher made her entrance with her
Treatise on Domestic Economy (1841)—essentially a guide for women
to fulfill their God-given destiny as homemakers by better organizing
and managing their households. Beecher's first cookbook, *Domestic
Receipt Book* (1846), combined recipes for traditional dishes with advice about the use of such modern innovations as cookstoves, cream
of tartar, and the ice cream freezer. In collaboration with her sister,
renowned author Harriet Beecher Stowe, she published her final work,
The American Woman's Home in 1869.[24] This book offered its readers much instructive information about scientific domesticity, ranging
from discussion of the science of ventilation to the functioning of
modern stoves and furnaces to issues of physiology, diet, health, and
of course, cookery. The pair drew heavily on their own experiences
as homemakers when offering advice to their readers, which doubtless
added to the book's appeal. In the chapter on cookstoves, for example,
they advocated a particular stove that they themselves had thoroughly
vetted. "With proper management of dampers," they wrote,

> one ordinary-sized coal-hod of anthracite coal will, for twenty-four hours, keep
> the stove running, keep seventeen gallons of water hot at all hours, bake pies
> and puddings in the warm closet, heat flat-irons under the back cover, boil
> tea-kettle and one pot under the front cover, bake bread in the oven, and cook
> a turkey in the tin roaster in front.[25]

Beecher and Stowe's book, written immediately after the end of the
American Civil War, reflected a new sense of female professionalism.
Women had become the primary cookbook writers by then, sharing
that stage with a much smaller number of males, generally chefs or
physicians. The legacy of the war, however, inspired a new kind of
cookbook, an offshoot of the kind of collaborative work many women
performed during the war itself – raising money to support their troops
and the war effort through Sanitary Fairs and charitable cookbooks.
Buckeye Cookery, written by the women of the First Congregational
Church of Marysville, Ohio, to raise money for a new parsonage, was

a very successful example of this type of cookbook. Written by "ordinary" women (most of the recipes were identified with specific contributors), the book was certain to resonate strongly with its readers. By 1900, sales of *Buckeye Cookery* had exceeded a million copies.[26]

In the years following the war, which had modernized the nation in so many ways, the food industry itself grew rapidly, consolidated, industrialized, and began to publish its own literature. Much of this literature was authored by newly educated professional cooks, graduates of college programs in home economics or of the newly established cooking schools that had begun to appear throughout the United States. The cooking school movement began in 1873 in England, at the National Training School for Cookery in South Kensington.[27] As the population of poor women and their families increased during the Victorian era, women reformers sought to ameliorate their situation by teaching them new vocational skills. In the United States, the Morrill Act of 1862 had begun the process of establishing schools to educate the "industrial" classes. Congress passed this act to set up colleges in each state,

> where the leading object shall be, without excluding other scientific and classical studies and including military tactics, to teach such branches of learning as are related to agriculture and the mechanic arts, in such manner as the legislatures of the States may respectively prescribe, in order to promote the liberal and practical education of the industrial classes in the several pursuits and professions in life.[28]

Passed during the Civil War, the Morrill Act reflected a growing awareness that the United States was changing, both socially and economically, and that new forms of education would be required to serve the needs of an increasingly diverse, industrial society. After the war, organizations dedicated to the same goals as the Morrill Act began to appear on the local level. Some of this work had been ongoing since the 1820s, through the efforts of women's moral reform societies. In New York City and elsewhere, however, urban reformers began to see vocational education as a strategy for improving society, and cookery became one of the skills emphasized by these new programs. The Women's Educational and Industrial Society of New York opened its Free Training School for Women in 1873 with classes in sewing, bookkeeping, and proofreading. A year later, they added cooking classes. These were team-taught by Juliet Corson, secretary of the Society, who lectured, and a professional chef, who demonstrated. Corson had no prior experience as a cook, but she educated herself

LADIES' CLASS.

The New York Cooking School held classes for ladies, servants, and even children, all under the guidance of Juliet Corson. Here, a professional chef demonstrates technique for the ladies' class. (Courtesy of Cornell University Library, Making of America Digital Collection, F. E. Fryatt, "The New York Cooking School," *Harper's New Monthly Magazine* 60:355 (December 1879): 22–30.)

by reading French and German cookery sources. The classes were a great success and Corson opened the New York Cooking School in 1876. The following year, she wrote her *Cooking Manual*. The emphasis of her school was training working-class women for careers as cooks in private homes. Corson also tried to uplift the working class generally, with publications that preached frugality, economy, and efficiency. When she could not find a publisher for *Fifteen Cent Dinners for Families of Six* (1877), she subsidized the expense herself, which only enhanced her public image. Corson lectured widely for the remainder of her career and continued to write both cookbooks and cooking school curricula.[29]

Boston followed a similar path into the cooking school movement. Mrs. Samuel Hooper, who chaired the committee on industrial education for the Women's Education Association, visited the National Training School for Cookery in London and was inspired to open a similar program at her home institution. The Boston Cooking School opened in March 1879. Volunteers largely staffed the program, working with two paid teachers, Joanna Sweeney and Maria Parloa. Parloa, already a well-known author and lecturer, demonstrated once every two weeks. Within seven months, however, Sweeney had resigned, and been replaced by Mary Lincoln. Mrs. Lincoln, a minister's daughter from South Attleboro, Massachusetts, had been educated to teach at Wheaton Female Seminary, although after her marriage she abandoned that career, at least temporarily. She spent a month working with Sweeney and Parloa and then took over the teaching responsibilities for the cooking school, where she taught until 1885. She was ultimately succeeded by one of her students, Fannie Merritt Farmer, whose name remains a household word today. *Mrs. Lincoln's Boston Cooking School Cook Book*, published in 1884, became a widespread best seller. The book included cooking school curriculum materials, as well as lecture outlines, examination questions, and sections on the science of cookery—chemistry, physiology, and hygiene.[30]

Both the New York and the Boston Cooking Schools had an impact that far exceeded their initial progressive agenda of educating poor women. Generations of middle-class women learned the new, scientific cookery philosophy espoused by these schools, and American cooking was transformed forever. Cooking became a scientifically organized system of procedures, measurements, techniques, and dietary requirements, but at the expense, as one food historian has argued, of taste itself. As cooking came to be dominated by middle-class professional standards, other notions of middle-class gentility, notably self-restraint and a distaste for gluttony, undermined the purely sensual experience of cooking and eating that had characterized traditional European and American foodways.[31]

ELABORATION OF COOKING UTENSILS AND EQUIPMENT

Stoves were only a first step in the overall elaboration of cookery in Victorian America. New cookery mandated new kinds of specialized utensils and tools to execute recipes efficiently and successfully. Mrs. Parkes had recommended an array of tools associated with stove cookery in 1829, including saucepans and kettles; stewing, preserving, and frying pans; gridirons, spits, basting ladles, egg-slices, and dredgers; coffee and pepper mills; Dutch ovens; and tins for baking bread, cakes, and pastry. She particularly recommended that saucepans and kettles be made of iron or tin, not copper (which she felt was dangerous).[32] This array changed somewhat over the next fifty years and would, of course, have varied according to economic means. Elizabeth Putnam, who wrote *Mrs. Putnam's Receipt Book* in 1858, assumed that her readers would have ranges in their kitchens, as well as the "usual quantity of utensils fitted into it." She offered an explicit list of other necessary items:

Copper saucepans, well lined, with covers, from three to six different sizes; a
flat-bottomed soup-pot; an upright gridiron; sheet-iron breadpans instead of
tin; a griddle; a tin kitchen; Hector's double boiler; a tin coffee-pot for boiling
coffee, or a filter—either being equally good; a tin canister to keep roasted and
ground coffee in; a canister for tea; a covered tin box for bread; one likewise
for cake, or a drawer in your store-closet, lined with zinc or tin; a bread-knife;
a board to cut bread upon; a covered jar for pieces of bread, and one for fine
crumbs; a knife-tray; a spoon-tray;—the yellow ware is much the strongest, or
tin pans of different sizes are economical;—a stout tin pan for mixing bread; a
large earthen bowl for beating cake; a stone jug for yeast; a stone jar for soup
stock; a meat-saw; a cleaver; iron and wooden spoons; a wire sieve for sifting
flour and meal; a small hair sieve; a bread-board; a meat-board; a lignum vitae
mortar, and rolling-pin, &c.[33]

In 1871, Marion Harland recommended that cooks obtain a raisin
seeder, a good eggbeater, a farina kettle, a syllabub churn, an apple-
corer, a potato peeler, and a slicer. She noted that these items were
mostly made of tin and were "therefore cheap and easily kept clean."[34]
Nine years later, Maria Parloa presented a two-page list of the essential
utensils for a well-furnished kitchen, ninety-three different items in all.
Her list began with pots and pans for stovetop cooking and baking,
and then addressed the items needed for beating, measuring, straining, molding, paring, storing, dredging, chopping and boning, mixing,
larding and trussing, roasting, grating, coring, scooping, squeezing,
rolling, mashing, scrubbing, and blacking. She assumed that her readers would need tools for making and serving coffee and tea, chocolate,
waffles, bread, muffins, squash, gravy, pudding, cake, vegetables, biscuits, toast, fish, apples, cold meats, lobster, brown bread, and baked
beans. Other foodstuffs on Parloa's list that required specialized utensils for their storage, use, and preparation included spices, meat, flour,
powdered sugar, ordinary sugar, salt, pepper, Graham flour, Indian
meal, rye meal, rice, tapioca, crackers, soda, cream of tartar, butter,
and pork.[35] In terms of materials of which these tools should be made,
Parloa assumed that her readers would choose either tin—the old-
fashioned medium—or the newer graniteware, a porcelain enameled
metal. She hoped that her readers would "have no more heavy, cast-
iron articles than are really needed, for they are not easily handled, and
are, therefore, less likely to be kept clean, inside and out, as the lighter
and smoother ware."[36]

Tinsmiths had been turning out a variety of wares since the late eighteenth century. Many of these transcended the transition from hearth
and bake oven to cookstove and range. As the United States industrialized during the nineteenth century, country tinsmiths were replaced
by larger firms, mass-producing tinwares for a national market. On

a local level, hardware merchants distributed these wares. Garfield & Bullock of Fitchburg, Massachusetts, advertised themselves in 1848 as "Dealers in Foreign and Domestic Hardware and Cutlery, Stoves, Britannia, Tin, Japan'd Ware." Ten years later, L. Patch & Co., also in Fitchburg, advertised themselves as purveyors of stoves, tin, brass, Japanned ware, glass, Britannia ware, wooden ware. They also noted that they could do "job work in tin, sheet iron, etc.," suggesting that they had retained the skills of tinsmithing, but that the economics of mass production had led them to turn to large-scale tinware producers for their consumer goods. [37]

Eliza Leslie specifically mentioned tinwares in several places in her cake baking instructions. She recommended "a set of tin measures" as being "of utmost importance." Other tin items on Eliza Leslie's list included spice boxes, graters for lemon, chocolate, coconut, and nutmeg, and block tin pans for baking both straight-sided and tube pans, as well as "little tins for queen cakes," and tin cutters for biscuits and cookies.[38] Maria Parloa also illustrated a number of tinware items, beginning with the ubiquitous, if old-fashioned, tin kitchen. Tin kitchens simplified the process of roasting meat on an open hearth. According to Parloa, "When possible, a tin kitchen should be used, as meat cooked before a bright fire has a flavor much nicer than when baked in an oven."[39] Another tinware item was advocated by Parloa, a bain-marie, which she described as being "a great convenience for keeping the various dishes hot when serving large dinners. It is simply a large tin pan," she explained, "which is partially filled with boiling water and placed where this will keep at a high temperature, but will not boil. The sauce pans containing the cooked food are placed in the water until the time for serving."[40] The use of a bain-marie, however, was probably limited to those who had servants in the kitchen to fetch and carry numerous courses to the table. The trade catalogs of hardware purveyors contained many other tinware items for cooking—especially, utensils that needed to be able to conduct heat and cold well, to convey a shape cleanly and crisply, or to be pierced for straining or draining. Simmons Hardware in St. Louis illustrated tin cake cutters, patty pans (in the shapes of hearts, horses, stars, and rosettes), and many different fancy food molds for cakes, jellies, and ice creams.[41]

Graniteware, a new material for kitchenwares in the Victorian era, gradually replaced tin and cast-iron wares by the late nineteenth century. Its popularity stemmed from the fact that it weighed much less than cast iron, and its enameled surface was far easier to clean than either tin or iron, as well as less susceptible to rust. For families of lesser means, however, cast-iron cookware remained available

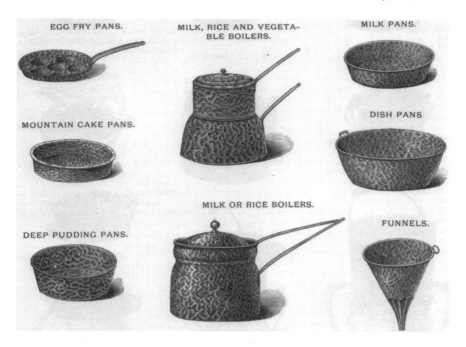

Graniteware, enameled iron cooking and table wares, became a popular alternative to tin wares during the second half of the nineteenth century. These new wares were colorful, easy to clean, durable, and did not rust. (Courtesy of Dover Publications.)

throughout the period, at the cheapest price. A price comparison for the same article in all three materials indicates the wide disparity of prices. The item, an "escaloped shell," for baking and serving creamed shellfish, cost $2 per dozen when made of tin and $4 per dozen in graniteware. The same article in silver plate cost ten times as much as graniteware.[42]

Paring, Coring, Grinding, and Chopping

Anyone who has ever made an apple pie knows that the first step is to peel, core, quarter, and slice the apples, the most time-consuming part of the process. Until the 1850s, most cooks performed this task the traditional way, with a small knife. Mechanical devices that would pare apples had existed at least since 1804, when Moses Coates of Chester County, Pennsylvania received the first patent for an apple parer. One reviewer who tested the device "found it to pare apples with great rapidity."[43] The appearance of mechanical apple parers coincided with two events: the expansion of the United States into the

trans-Appalachian West and beyond—prime apple-growing territory—
and the development of an American fascination with mechanized
production. As Americans spread out onto the frontier, as well as into
the rural countryside of older parts of the country, they often planted
apple orchards. Quakers Thomas and Elizabeth Lea, for example, converted part of their 200-acre farm at Walnut Hill, Maryland, into apple
orchards, producing apples and cider for the market. Elizabeth Lea's
cookbook included fourteen recipes for apples, as well as for cider and
apple butter.[44]

Tools that looked "mechanical"—generally because they used gearing mechanisms to perform their functions—were readily accepted if
the price was right, whether or not they actually saved any labor. Most
patent apple parers operated on a simple principle, as expressed in
Robert W. Mitchell's patent of 1838. Mitchell, who lived in Martin's
Mill, Ohio, patented "A Machine for Paring, Coring, and Dividing
Apples." To operate the parer, "the apple is to be placed on a fork at
the end of a shaft, or mandrel, turned by a crank, whilst the paring
knife, furnished with a guard, is held in the right hand, and passed from
end to end over the apple; this is then pushed towards the shaft which
is furnished with knives that cut it into quarters; a centre, tubular knife
removing the core."[45]

A flood of patented parers appeared after 1850, many of them from
Massachusetts makers. In Leominster, hometown of "Johnny Apple-
seed," Horatio Keyes patented a model that clamped to the edge of
the kitchen worktable. According to his patent papers, "As the promi-
nences and cavities of the apple pass ... the cutter will be moved in
a corresponding inverse manner ... and consequently the apple will
be pared in a perfect manner."[46] By 1881, the Simmons Hardware
Co. catalog included devices for paring apples, potatoes, and peaches,
as well as for stoning cherries. The specific types offered included
the Reading Apple Parer, patented in 1878, with "Covered Works,"
to protect the user from blade ($1.00); the White Mountain Potato
Parer ($1.25); and William Frankfurth Hardware Co.'s White Moun-
tain Apple Parer, Corer, and Slicer ($9.00 per dozen).[47] All were
cast-iron table-mounted food lathes, using gear-driven rotary crank-
turned paring mechanisms. The lathe device rotated the fruit while a
floating arm with a cutting blade rode over rotating fruit and pared
off skin. For apples, the lathe drove through the center of the fruit,
removing the core. The cutting edge could also slice fruit into long
spiral sections, for pies and applesauce.

Potatoes, another staple of the Victorian American diet, generated
their own mechanical processing devices, both for peeling off the skin

GOLD MEDAL APPLE PARER.

O. K. PARER AND SLICER.

Gold Medal Apple Parers,   -   -   -   -   -   -   -   -   -   per dozen, $8 00
O. K. Parer and Slicers,   -   -   -   -   -   -   -   -   -   "   1 25

WHITE MOUNTAIN APPLE PARER, CORER AND SLICER.

No. 40.

Mechanical apple parers greatly simplified the task of paring apples for pies, applesauce, and other apple desserts. The William Frankfurth Hardware Company in Milwaukee, Wisconsin, wholesaled many different mechanical peelers and parers in 1886. (Courtesy of Dover Publications.)

and for specialized cutting. "Saratoga chips" (potato chips), a newly fashionable menu item of the late nineteenth century, required that the potatoes be sliced paper-thin before frying. Two devices, Herring's Patent Ribbon Potato Slicer, which was specifically marketed for making Saratoga chips, and the Saratoga Potato Parer and Slicer, sold for seventy-five cents each in 1881.[48]

Besides paring, one of the other tedious tasks of fruit processing was removing the seeds, pits, or stones before the fruit could be dried or made into preserves. The same companies that were transforming the art of peeling fruit and vegetables also produced devices that mechanized the process of pitting and stoning. Cherry stoners and raisin seeders, which began to appear after the Civil War, were met with great approval. Marion Harland praised them to her readers in 1871, stating, "A raisin seeder costs a trifle in comparison with the time and patience required to stone the fruit in the old way."[49] That same year, an editor of the *American Agriculturist* remarked, "Every housekeeper knows that raisins are all the better for being stoned, and she also knows how tedious is the operation when performed in the ordinary manner. With this machine, the stoning is performed with comparative rapidity." He explained that the raisin stoner could be clamped to a worktable, then

the raisins are pushed one by one upon the grating. The crank being turned, the plate above comes down and holds it in place; then another place which contains numerous blunt needles which pass through the holes in the second plate is pressed down. These needles punch out the seeds of the raisins through the grating, and to make sure that they will be removed, there works underneath this grating a blunt knife, moved by a notch on the moving wheel as it is cranked. As the driving wheel revolves, an arm comes over and pushes the seeded raisin away to make room for another.[50]

How widely used these devices were remains a question. *Buckeye Cookery*, first published in 1876, described raisin seeding the old-fashioned way in their recipe for fruitcake. "Raisins should never be mashed," they began, "as it is difficult to dry out the moisture absorbed by them, and every particle of moisture retained tends to make the cake heavy." Instead, they advised their readers to remove the stems by rolling the raisins in a coarse towel until clean. After picking the raisins over carefully, "clip with the scissors, or cut with a sharp knife" to remove the seeds. Care should be taken not to chop the raisins too finely: "if for light fruit cake, seeding is all that is necessary."[51]

Home processing of meat enjoyed similar time-saving improvements with the invention of various devices for "mincing" or grinding meat, which could be then used to make mince pies, Salisbury steak, meat loaf, hash, force meat balls, sausages, and other similar menu items. Most of these grinders worked on one of two principles. The earlier versions were in the form of tubs with chopping blades that would be cranked up and down rapidly to automate the chopping. Leroy Starrett of the Athol Machine Company, Athol, Massachusetts, patented this type of chopper in 1865. A metal drum, which ranged between eight and twelve inches in diameter, rotated on a ratchet while the guillotine-type blade chopped the meat.[52] A testimonial in a Milwaukee hardware company's catalog in 1886 proclaimed that the Starrett, "for cutting Pie Meat, Hash, Sausage Meat, Fruit, Vegetables, &., &c.," was "one of the most useful and greatest labor-saving inventions of the day." It served for both family and butcher use. The testimonial continued, "Every housewife knows that it requires from 1 to 3 hours tedious labor with the common hand-knife and tray, to cut the meat and apple for an ordinary 'batch' of mince pies. With the American Chopper a *child 6 years of age* can do the same work in from *5 to 15 minutes* with the greatest ease."[53]

Mince pies, a traditional American staple of the Thanksgiving table, required extensive chopping, as the Starrett literature detailed in an accompanying recipe. First, the cook had to chop half a pound of beef kidney, suet, and then half a pound of cooked beef heart, as well as citron, candied orange peel, and two pounds of apples (in addition to seeding a pound and a half of raisins and currants). Once spices (cinnamon, nutmeg, allspice, ginger, and coriander) and brown sugar, cider, rum, brandy, and lemon peel had been added, the whole was set aside in a stoneware crock for fifteen days to ripen.[54] Only then was it ready to be put into pies.

Another food that today is an American staple became much more readily available after the advent of food choppers: the hamburger, as Starrett's recipe for "Salisbury Steak" suggests.

> Put two pounds of tenderloin of beef in the chopping machine; this machine is far superior to any other, for in chopping the meats the sinews and the other hard parts collect at the bottom of the machine, on the shelf; the meat arising to the surface is the best part; take this out, leaving the hard, fibrous pieces at the bottom. Mold the Salisbury steak in a ring three-quarters of an inch high by three inches in diameter or less in a small empty goose-liver terrine. These raw steaks are frequently served without any seasoning or else seasoned and broiled very rare.[55]

The hamburger, an import from northern Germany, came to the United States in the 1830s with the many German immigrants who arrived here during the middle years of the nineteenth century. Delmonico's restaurant put "Hamburg Steak" on their menu in 1834 as an ethnic offering. By midcentury, "Beefsteak a la Hamburg," as well as "Hamburg Steak" and "Salisbury Steak," appeared frequently in American cookbooks.[56]

Later meat grinders utilized the same lathe principle as the parers: the meat went into a hopper at the top and then was forced by a screw lathe through cutting blades. The extruded product could be as coarse or as fine as the cook required simply by changing the cutting blade. Sargent & Company's "Gem Chopper" included five grades of cutter, ranging from "Pulverizing," through "Fine," "Medium," "Coarse," and culminating in a final cutter for "Nut Butter."[57]

Sausages, long a staple of the traditional European diet, were doubtless the chief motivation and the chief beneficiary of this new chopping and grinding technology. Particularly in rural households, slaughtering and processing of pork and beef was a standard part of the agricultural year. Quaker farmwife and cookbook author Elizabeth Lea, who lived in rural Maryland, commented extensively on sausage meat. She advised her readers to prepare well for this event:

> It is a good plan to have plenty of bread and pies baked, and a quantity of apples stewed, vegetables washed and ready to cook, so that every member of the family, that is able, may devote herself to the work of putting away the meat which is of so much importance for the coming year; while some are cutting up the fat to render into lard, others may be employed in assorting the sausage meat, and cutting it into small pieces for the chopping machine, by trimming off every part that can be spared. You can have one hundred pounds of sausage from a twelve hundred weight of pork, and since the introduction of sausage choppers, a great deal more sausage is made, than formerly, by the old method.[58]

Lea's *Domestic Cookery* (1853) included instructions for pickling, salting, smoking, and storing sausages, as well as recipes for liver sausage, bologna sausage, hog's head cheese, souse, and scrapple.[59] Scrapple, a ubiquitous Pennsylvania "pot pudding," made from "scraps of pork that will not do for sausage," was boiled, chopped, seasoned with sage, summer savory, salt, and pepper, and then mixed with cornmeal and buckwheat flour and cooked until thick.[60]

Bologna sausage, despite its name, had culinary origins far more English rather than Italian. Based loosely on the Italian *mortadella* sausage (a product of Bologna), the American incarnation of this sausage typically referred to a spicy beef sausage, which was brined and then smoked. To make her version of bologna sausage, Lea chopped together ten pounds of beef and two and a half pounds of fresh pork fat, seasoned the whole with mace and cloves, and then stuffed it into large sausage skins. She brined her sausage first, and then hung it up to smoke for several days before eating.[61]

Fanny Lemira Gillette, whose *White House Cook Book* was published almost forty years later, also included a recipe for bologna sausage. Gillette's recipe differed considerably, however, calling for pork, veal, beef, salt pork, suet, sage, parsley, savory, marjoram, thyme, cayenne and black pepper, cloves, minced onion, and salt to taste. "Chop or grind the meat and suet," she instructed her readers, suggesting that by 1887, Gillette was aware of the mechanical options for meat processing. While "chopping" could have been done by hand or with a knife or a cleaver, "grinding" would have required a specialized tool. To finish, cooks were to stuff the sausage into beef skins, prick, and boil for one hour. When done, remove the sausage from the pot and lay out to dry in the sun "upon clean, sweet straw or hay." Finally, rub exterior with oil or butter, and store. Like Mrs. Lea's bologna, Gillette's finished product could be eaten without further cooking. "Cut in round slices and lay sliced lemon around the edge of the dish," the recipe concluded, "as many like to squeeze a few drops upon the sausage before eating."[62]

PICKLING AND CANNING

In a world where seasonality continued to define menu planning and cookery, the art of preserving fresh fruits and vegetables remained an important housewifery skill. During the growing months, American kitchens bustled with canning activities and the production of jams, jellies, preserves, marmalades, fruit butters, pickles, relishes, chutneys, catsups, vinegars, bottled sauces, and a wealth of other tasty comestibles.

Putting food by to counter the scarcity of the winter months was not a new phenomenon in the Victorian era. The first Europeans to arrive in America in the fifteenth century brought with them a culinary culture that emphasized preservation as well as production of foodstuffs. Grains and legumes were stored in barrels and sacks, or converted into beer. Meat, poultry, and fish were smoked, salted, dried, or pickled. Fruits and vegetables were generally dried and hung up on strings in the hall (or kitchen), pickled, or made into jams, jellies, and pastes that could be packed into ceramic crocks.[63]

Two factors transformed home canning and preserving in the nineteenth century. The first was the availability of comparatively inexpensive sugar. The second was the development of glass canning jars. The British had begun the process of transforming sugar from a scarce luxury into an ordinary commodity during the seventeenth century, with the establishment of their colony on the island of Barbados in 1627. The growth of slavery during the eighteenth century made sugar production on a massive scale possible, and by the 1820s, Americans were accustomed to sugar—although most people still considered it a luxury. During the nineteenth century, technological advances in sugar processing coupled with the development of beet sugar increased the supply and lowered the price correspondingly.[64]

Cookbooks reflected and documented the popularity of sweetness as a food value in nineteenth-century America, offering a profusion of jellies, preserves, jams and other "sweetmeats."[65] In terms of the specific tools required, cooks could choose either a traditional brass or bell-metal kettle, or the newer porcelain-lined iron kettle, along with a perforated skimmer. These kettles were preferably broader than deep, since, according to Eliza Leslie, "the fruit cannot be done equally if it is too much heaped." Sugar, the defining ingredient in sweetmeats, was to be the best quality obtainable and improper storage could also affect the outcome:

> In putting away sweetmeats, it is best to place them in small jars, as the more frequently they are exposed to the air by opening, the more danger there is of their spoiling. The best vessels for this purpose are white queen's-ware pots, or glass jars. For jellies, jams, and for small fruit, common glass tumblers are very convenient, and may be covered simply with double tissue-paper, cut exactly to fit the inside of the top of the glass, laid lightly on the sweetmeat, and pressed down all round with the finger. This covering, if closely and nicely fitted, will be found to keep them perfectly well, and as it adheres so closely as to form a complete coat over the top, it is better for jellies or jams than writing-paper dipped in brandy, which is always somewhat shriveled by the liquor with which it has been saturated.[66]

Sweetmeat recipes commonly began with a clarified sugar syrup, made by combining a large quantity of loaf sugar, broken up or powdered, with fresh springwater and beaten egg whites. Once cooked, this syrup could be used immediately, or bottled and used as needed.[67] Producing sweetmeats involved a considerable investment in time, labor, and materials. These were items for the tea and dessert table, for special occasions when sociability, rather than nutritional value, was the focus, or to end a modest family dinner with a bit of sweet frivolity and whimsy. For middle-class housewives like Sophia Wallace, of Fitchburg, Massachusetts, they were also an important indication of respectability. During the first year of her marriage to Rodney Wallace, she carefully recorded activities she deemed significant in her diary. She and Rodney were just setting up housekeeping in 1854 and she reported that in late August she went to Boston, where she "Purchased carpets, crockery, &c." A week later, she washed her newly acquired crockery and put down the carpets in her new house. On 16 September, she went to Rindge, New Hampshire and "moved furniture with Mother." On the 28th, she and Rodney "commenced housekeeping." Among the first cookery activities she recorded were "Made quince preserve" on 17 October, and "Made quince jelly" three days later. Shortly afterwards, "Rodney's father dined here," and within a month, Sophia and Rodney had borne a son—two weeks before their first wedding anniversary.[68]

By 1871, however, Marion Harland wrote, "Within a few years canned fruits have, in a great measure superseded preserves. They are cheaper, more wholesome, and far less difficult to prepare."[69] The task of preserving fruits and vegetables had been transformed by the invention in 1858 of a glass "fruit jar" by John L. Mason. Mason's jar, with its screw-on zinc lid, made canning easier and safer. A rubber gasket between the neck of the jar and the lid enabled the lid to exhaust any air inside the jar during the canning process and then seal out any external air once the jar cooled. The jar's popularity was enhanced by the fact that they were reusable. As Harland pointed out to her readers, "glass cans . . . are cheapest in the end, for you can use them year after year, getting new elastics when you need them."[70]

The other advantage of the new Mason jars was their material: because they were made of glass, the contents were visible from within. Home cooks doubtless derived great satisfaction from the shining rows of glass jars filled with richly colored fruits and vegetables that lined their pantry shelves. Cookbooks reinforced the popularity of home canning; by the 1870s, they included detailed instructions, sometimes even whole chapters on canning (as had Marion Harland in 1871).[71] Mary Lincoln's *Boston Cook Book*, first published in 1883, differentiated carefully between canning and preserving. In canning, she explained, "the fruit is kept, either with or without sugar, by sealing in air-tight jars or cans, and is not cooked long enough to destroy its natural flavor." Preserves, however, required a great deal more sugar, usually close to a one-to-one ratio with the fruit. "Although too rich for daily use," Lincoln commented, "there are many people who prefer them to the canned fruit, and there are some fruits which are better with the full weight of sugar."[72]

While much home canning focused on preserving fruit, cooks also processed vegetables, especially tomatoes, either whole or in pickles,

MASON'S PATENT.

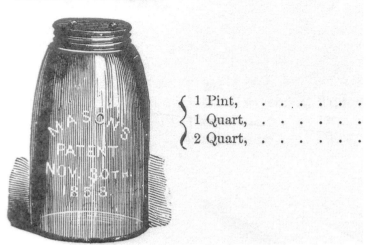

{ 1 Pint, ...

{ 1 Quart, ...

{ 2 Quart, ...

Glass canning jars, introduced in 1858 by John L. Mason, greatly improved the process of putting up fruit. The self-sealing jars were not only safer and more reliable but also were reusable. The transparency of the glass enhanced the visual appeal of the jar's contents. This jar appeared in the 1869 catalogue of the Dover Stamping Company of Boston. (Courtesy of Astragal Press.)

catsups, relishes, and chutneys.[73] Of the seventeen tomato recipes in Mary Randolph's *Virginia House-Wife*, two were for tomato marmalade and one was for tomato catsup. The catsup recipe, to be made in August, produced two bottles-full, which were to be corked tight. Lydia Maria Child also instructed the readers of her *American Frugal Housewife* about tomato catsup in 1833:

The best sort of catsup is made from tomatoes. The vegetables should be squeezed up in the hand, salt put to them, and set by for twenty-four hours. After being passed through a sieve, cloves, allspice, pepper, mace, garlic, and whole mustard-seed should be added. It should be boiled down one third, and bottled after it is cool. No liquid is necessary, as the tomatoes are very juicy. A good deal of salt and spice is necessary to keep the catsup well. It is delicious with roast meat; and a cupful adds much to the richness of soup and chowder. The garlic should be taken out before it is bottled.[74]

Catharine Beecher's recipe "A Hash of Cold Meat for Dinner" called for "six large tomatoes." She noted, however, "Dried tomatoes can be used," as well as catsup.[75] The availability of fresh tomatoes, even out of season, improved with the expansion of the railroad system—but they were expensive. "The fresh tomato comes to the market from the South in April and sometimes in March," noted Maria Parloa. "On account of the price it is then used only where the canned tomato will not answer."[76] With the advent of glass jars, home canning of whole tomatoes became much more common. Tomatoes required only to be skinned and packed into glass jars, then processed in a boiling water bath. Marion Harland made the task sound simple:

> Pour boiling water over the tomatoes, to loosen the skins. Remove these; drain off all the juice that will come away without pressing hard; put them into a kettle and heat slowly to a boil. Your tomatoes will look much nicer if you remove all the hard parts before putting them on the fire, and rub the pulp soft with your hands. Boil ten minutes, dip out the surplus liquid, pour the tomatoes, boiling hot, into the cans, and seal. Keep in a cool, dark place.[77]

By the 1870s, however, putting up one's own homegrown tomatoes was not the only option, nor was it necessarily the least expensive option. The tomato canning industry, which had begun in the 1840s, flourished during the Civil War, when canned tomatoes helped to feed the Union army. After the war, tomato consumption rose dramatically and by 1879, the industry was producing more than nineteen million cans of tomatoes per year.[78] Not surprisingly, canned tomatoes appeared with increasing regularity as a recipe enhancement. In 1877, Mary F. Henderson followed her bean soup recipe with one for "Bean and Tomato Soup," noting that "a pint of canned tomatoes, boiled and passed through a sieve, with a quart of bean soup, makes a very pleasant change." In a similar vein, Maria Parloa's 1888 recipe for "Tomato Sauce" began with "One quart of canned tomatoes."[79] While these both may have referred to home-canned tomatoes, put up in pint or quart glass canning jars, more commonly, women understood "canned tomatoes" to mean tin cans, purchased from a local grocer. The proliferation of patents for can openers, from 1858 on, confirms the growing popularity of canned foods for American consumers.[80]

MIXING AND BEATING

Two fundamental staples of the American diet, bread and butter, both required extended mixing in their production. To make bread, cooks had to combine flour with some liquid (including yeast) and then mix or knead until the dough had achieved the correct amount of elasticity and smoothness. For centuries, this process had begun in a bowl, made of either wood or crockery, and then moved out of the bowl and onto a table trough or board for kneading. Regardless, bread making was handwork. A spoon was the only utensil required, and not for too much of the preparation process. Dough machines, which used hand-cranked paddles to mix the dough, began to appear in the third quarter of the nineteenth century. Mary Lincoln mentioned them in 1883, noting that kneading dough "may be done by cutting or chopping, either with the hand or machinery." She concluded, however, that "there is nothing that gives the fine, even grain to bread so well as hand-kneading."[81] She went on to discuss the benefits of bowl versus board kneading (she preferred a board) and to celebrate the inherent beauty of kneading bread by hand. "There is no mechanical operation in cooking more fascinating than the deft, quick touches a natural kneader gives to a mass of dough," she concluded.[82]

Much Victorian cookery emphasized lightness and airiness, especially recipes for cakes, creams, syllabubs, and other dessert items. Eggs provided the critical component for achieving this goal, but required careful handling to avoid failure. According to *Buckeye Cookery*, "If it is warm weather, place the eggs in cold water, and let stand a few minutes, as they will then make finer froth; and be sure they are fresh, as they will not make a stiff froth from any amount of beating if old."[83]

Correct cake-making technique required the proper tools. "Unless you are provided with proper and convenient utensils and materials," wrote Eliza Leslie, "the difficulty of preparing cakes will be great, and in most instances a failure; involving disappointment, waste of time, and useless expense." For beating eggs, she recommended either hickory rods (to be purchased from a wood turner), or a wire whip. Beating eggs by hand was a lengthy and potentially tiring procedure. According to Leslie, first, the eggs were to be broken into a saucer, one at a time ("that, in case there should be a bad one among them, it may not spoil the others"). The eggs went into a "broad shallow pan," not tin, however, because the cold metal would prevent the eggs from becoming light. They were then to be beaten,

> not merely till they froth, but long afterwards, till the froth subsides, and they become thick and smooth like boiled custard. White of egg by itself may be beaten with small rods, or with a three-pronged fork, or a broad knife. It is a very easy process, and should be continued till the liquid is all converted into a stiff froth so firm that it will not drop from the rods when held up.[84]

Buckeye Cookery offered an entire chapter on the subject of cake making, including an extended discussion of eggs and the process of beating. The authors warned their readers about the pitfalls of "unskillful mixing":

> There is a great "knack" in beating cake; don't *stir*, but *beat* thoroughly, bringing the batter up from the bottom of the dish at every stroke; in this way the air is driven into the cells of the batter, instead of out of them—but the cells will be finer if beaten more slowly at the last, remembering that the motion should always be upward. In winter it is easier to beat with the hand, but in summer a wooden spoon is better.[85]

The task of beating eggs became far less strenuous with the development of the eggbeater. It is not clear who first came up with the notion of applying a rotary gearing mechanism to a wire whip, but in 1863, Timothy Earle of Smithfield, Rhode Island, registered a patent for such a device.[86] Other patents followed in rapid succession, with the Dover Stamping Company of Boston emerging by the early 1870s as the best-known manufacturer of the new kitchen tool. Dover's original eggbeater patent, issued on May 31, 1870, combined a handle at the top with a side-mounted gear wheel that could be turned by its handle to rotate intersecting wire "wings," which beat the eggs quickly and efficiently. The "Dover," as it was generally known, came in a range of sizes, suitable for individuals, families, large families, and hotels.[87] By the 1880s, there were a multitude of different types of eggbeaters available and literally millions in use. Milwaukee hardware distributor William Frankfurth, listed a wire spoon eggbeater, a wire whip or "French" eggbeater, a spiral eggbeater, and various rotary models. In addition to the Dover, his customers could have "The Acme," "The Easy," "Monroe's Mammoth," the "Peerless," and others—all suggesting that this tool would make eggbeating easier, and superb, light, smooth, high volume results.[88]

Cookbook writers capitalized on the new easy availability of well-beaten eggs. Cooking School leader, Juliet Corson, taught her students in the "Plain Cooks Course" how to make Sponge Cake in 1881. First, the students had to line a cake pan with buttered paper, grate the rind of half a lemon, and then "put the sugar and two eggs into a bowl, and beat them for two minutes; add another egg and beat two minutes; then add three yolks and beat three minutes." Then, "beat the whites of three eggs to a stiff froth." On the basis of the amount and length of time beating, eggbeaters were assumed, although not always. Corson's recipe for pound cake required the cook to use her bare hands to beat the eggs. "Put the butter, sugar, and one egg into a bowl and beat them with the hand to a cream," she wrote, "then

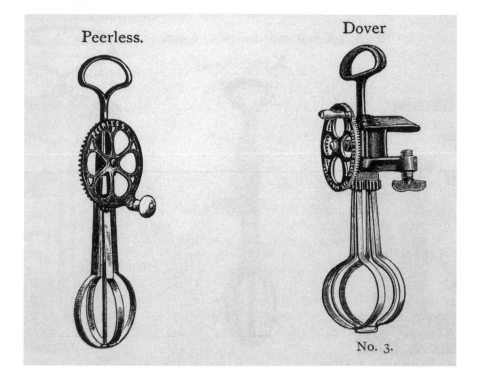

Peerless.

Dover

No. 3.

Mechanical eggbeaters greatly reduced the amount of time and energy required to whip up a cake. Beginning in 1863 with Timothy Earle's patent, they were produced by many different companies in a variety of beater configurations. (Courtesy of Dover Publications.)

add the rest of the eggs, one at a time, beating the cake with the hand two minutes after each egg is added." She verified that this unusual technique "of beating the cake with the hand is in vogue with many excellent pastry cooks." As a final comment, however, she noted "extreme cleanliness is indispensable when this method is employed."[89]

BREWING

Beer, tea, coffee, wine, cordials, shrub, bounce, brandy, lemonade, and punch formed yet another branch of the Victorian cook's repertoire. Beer, and its cousin, ale, were both made from fermented grains. At the beginning of the Victorian era, housewives still made their own beer and ale on occasion, but the roots of industrial production had already been well planted during the eighteenth century. That frugal housewife, Lydia Maria Child, noted, "Beer is a good family drink," and proceeded to tell her readers how to make it, in great variety. So did Sarah Josepha Hale in her first cookbook, *The Good Housekeeper*, published in 1839.[90] Both of these authors also mentioned Spruce Beer and Ginger Beer, two popular variants. To brew, however, "the rule is the same for all beer," wrote Child in *The American Frugal Housewife* in 1833.

> Boil the ingredients two or three hours, pour in a half-pint of molasses to a pailful, while the beer is scalding hot. Strain the beer, and when about lukewarm, put a pint of lively yeast to a barrel. Leave the bung loose till the beer is done working; you can ascertain this by observing when the froth subsides. If your family be large, and the beer will be drank rapidly, it may as well remain in the barrel; but if your family be small, fill what bottles you have with it; it keeps better bottled.[91]

By midcentury, however, the temperance movement, coupled with the arrival of massive numbers of German immigrants who introduced Americans to commercially produced lager beer, spelled the end for homemade beer. Although recipes for both spruce and ginger beers persisted in cookbooks, the American brewing industry quickly gathered momentum after the Civil War.

Tea continued to be consumed in large quantities by Americans of all walks of life throughout the nineteenth century. Eliza Leslie discussed the attributes of different teas, as well as the techniques for brewing them. "In buying tea," she wrote, "it is best to get it by the box, of an importer, that you may be sure of having it fresh … If green tea is good, it will look green in the cup when poured out." She continued, "Black tea should be dark colored and have a fragrant flowery smell."[92] She recommended pekoe and pouching as being the best black teas, and imperial, young hyson, and gunpowder the best green. American tea preferences were gradually reshaped, however, during the course of the century, away from the traditional preference for Chinese green and black teas toward newly available green tea from Japan after 1854, as well as oolong from Formosa, and teas from India, Ceylon, and Africa. Most tea was drunk with sugar and often milk or cream, as it had been since colonial times, but once the transcontinental railroad made citrus fruit readily available, many tea drinkers began to drink their tea with lemon instead.[93]

The process of making coffee involved several important steps. Once the beans had been acquired, they had to be roasted. "Every family should be provided with a coffee roaster," wrote Eliza Leslie, describing this device as "an iron cylinder to stand before the fire, and is either turned by a handle or wound up like a jack to go of itself."[94] By 1881, the Simmons Hardware Company catalog illustrated five varieties of coffee roaster, all of them metal vessels (cast iron or tin) in which the coffee beans could be roasted, with a crank-turned rotary spreader to prevent the beans from scorching. Most writers agreed that the roasted beans should be then ground and used as quickly as possible for the best cup of coffee, including Lydia Child, who wrote, "Those who pride themselves on first-rate coffee, burn it and grind it every morning."[95] Coffee mills varied in form—one hardware company presented fifteen different models to its customers in their 1886 catalog. Most of these were wooden boxes with a cast-iron crank grinding mechanism mounted on the top. The freshly ground beans dropped down into the box, where the cook could retrieve them from a small drawer. Eliza Leslie believed that "A coffee mill affixed to the wall is far more convenient than one that must be held on the lap."[96]

Once the grounds were prepared, the brewing process varied from household to household and place to place. The simplest method of brewing coffee was to use a tin or graniteware coffee pot, mix the coffee grounds with boiling water, allow the coffee to steep, and then clarify the substance with egg whites or isinglass. For more elegant serving, the coffee could be moved into to a silver or china coffee pot. According to Maria Parloa, in 1880, "the old method of boiling coffee is still practiced by at least one-half the housekeepers in this country."[97]

"French coffee," however, was made by a filtering process, and required more specialized brewing equipment, either a percolator or a biggin. The biggin had a perforated tin strainer that held the coffee grounds; when hot water was added, filtered coffee would result—without the necessity of boiling the coffee and grounds together. A related device, the percolator, which was developed in France in 1819, forced the hot water upwards through a tube, after which it dripped down through a filter or series of filters. In both cases, the resulting coffee was commonly decanted into a warmed china or silver coffee pot for serving at the table. Maria Parloa described use of the biggin in her *New Cook Book* of 1880:

Another—and really the most economical and the easiest—way of making coffee is by filtering. The French coffee biggin is valuable for this. It consists of two cylindrical tin vessels, one fitting into another, and the bottom of the upper being a fine strainer. Another coarser strainer, with a rod running from the centre, is placed upon this. Then the coffee, which must be finely-ground, is

Good Morning Coffee Makers,

FABRIC FILTER FOR GROUND COFFEE

Textile Fabric Filter, used in all "Good Morning" Coffee Makers.

No. 12, 3 Pints, Planished Tin Coffee Biggins, Tin Bottom,   -   -   -   per dozen, $13 00

A biggin brewed coffee by pouring boiling water through a series of filters, metal and cloth, onto the coffee grounds. This system of filtering coffee produced a far smoother brew than the customary tradition of boiling the grounds and water together in a metal coffee pot. These biggins, marketed as "Good Morning Coffee Makers," used a fabric filter and were sold by the William Frankfurth Hardware Company of Milwaukee in 1886. (Courtesy of Dover Publications.)

put in, and another strainer is placed at the top of the rod. The boiling water is poured on, and pot set where it will keep hot, but not boil, until the water has gone through. This will make a clear, strong coffee, with a rich, smooth flavor.[98]

French coffee, in addition to its taste, was widely thought to aid digestion when drunk after dinner, without milk or sugar.

CHILLING AND THE RISE OF REFRIGERATION

Ice, and the ability to keep foods cool, cold, or even frozen, became an important consumer commodity in the nineteenth century. Since ancient times, beverages had been chilled using ice or cold spring water, but its connections with food preservation began much later. Before the nineteenth-century discovery that coldness retarded the activity of microorganisms, food preservation had been accomplished through smoking, salting, spicing, picking, or drying. The new science led people to use their wells, spring houses, cellars, and by the early 1800s, ice houses to keep food cool and to avoid spoiling. In Mary Randolph's directions for making ice cream in 1824, she assumed her Virginia readers would have an icehouse: "Observations on Ice Cream. It is the practice of some indolent cooks, to set the freezer, containing the cream, in a tub with ice and salt, and put it in the ice-house; it will certainly freeze there, but not until the watery particles have subsided, and by the separation destroyed the cream." British traveler Frances Trollope mentioned how happy she was to move out of the city of Cincinnati during the summer of 1832 to a "pretty cottage" where "we had an ice-house that never failed."[99] An icehouse was built under a mound of earth or constructed as part of a house, barn, or separate building, where blocks of ice, packed in sawdust, would keep foods cold during the heat of the hottest summer.

Icehouses and their urban counterparts, iceboxes, were linked to the transportation revolution and the rise of an ice harvesting industry. Ice, harvested from the lakes and ponds of New England and other cold climate states, was used to transport fish from the East Coast to inland cities and towns via the Erie Canal and the burgeoning railroad system. In 1842, the Boston & Albany Railroad explored the notion of railroad cars filled with ice that could carry fish from Boston to the interior. That same year, oysters moved west from New York City to Buffalo on the Erie Canal, packed in ice.[100]

The idea of refrigerated transportation quickly led to the ice-cooled warehouses in depot cities, further stimulating the ice industry. In 1858, Moses Underwood, Jr., of Fitchburg—an important railroad town in Massachusetts—advertised ice, which "will be ordered from one of the best ponds in Massachusetts."[101] Ice and refrigeration helped to transform the availability of commercially produced food products, beer and meat, in particular. Refrigeration was required for the production of lager beer to keep the beer cool while it matured. The American meat industry was likewise transformed by the possibilities of refrigerated transportation. The first patent for refrigeration, issued to J. B. Sutherland in 1867, introduced the concept of regulating air circulation in railroad cars, using blocks of ice overhead, and evacuating the warm air. The first shipment of meat from Chicago to Boston followed within a year and experimentation continued. By 1882, meatpacker Gustavus Swift had discovered that when the ice was overhead, cold air sank—a discovery that greatly enhanced the trans-shipment of beef around the country, greatly reducing its price. These technological changes in refrigeration changed the diets of ordinary Americans, as well as their shopping and cooking habits.[102]

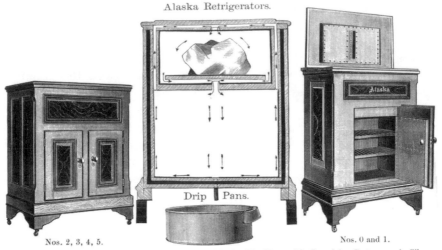

Alaska Retrigerators.

Drip | Pans.

Nos. 2, 3, 4, 5.   Nos. 0 and 1.

Beautifully grained in Oak and Black Walnut, Lined with Zinc, with Porcelain Castors and Silver Mounted Trimmings.

Home ice boxes or "refrigerators" became an important kitchen appliance by the 1880s. They worked on the same principle as Gustavus Swift's refrigerated railroad cars: cold air sinks. Stylistically, ice boxes were designed to look like furniture, with the doors closed. These Alaska Refrigerators, sold by the Simmons Hardware Company of St. Louis, might pass as elegant cupboards, made either of solid oak and walnut, or grain painted to appear that way. (Courtesy of Dover Publications.)

At home, urban Americans began to have iceboxes or "refrigerators" as they were widely known, in the late 1820s.[103] By the 1840s, commercially made refrigerators were available for those who could afford them, but women continued to use whatever resources they could muster to keep food cool. Ice and refrigeration was critical for the production of one of the most highly prized American deserts, ice cream. Made from expensive ingredients, cream and sugar, ice cream required skill, timing, and ice in order to avoid a runny mess. Ices, ice creams, and other frozen desserts abounded in Victorian cookbooks. Mary Randolph included recipes for fourteen different frozen creams and ices in *The Virginia House-Wife* in 1824. Many of these remain familiar today—vanilla, raspberry, chocolate, strawberry, coffee, lemon, and peach. Some however, seem more exotic. Randolph made creams out everything she could think of, including quince, citron (made from a melon syrup), almond, cocoa-nut, and most unusual, oysters ("Make a rich soup, . . . strain it from the oysters, and freeze it.").[104] Randolph, like other Victorian food writers, assumed that ice creams would either be molded into shapes or served in individual handled glasses, not unlike punch cups. Eliza Leslie described the molding process in 1828:

> If you wish to have it in moulds, put the cream into them as soon as it has frozen in the tin. Set the moulds in a tub of ice and salt. Just before you want to use the cream, take the moulds out of the tub, wipe or wash the salt, carefully from the outside, dip the moulds in lukewarm water, and turn out the cream.[105]

Twenty years later, Leslie described making lemon ice cream using an ice cream freezer. Once frozen, the ice cream was decanted and poured into a mold for an hour or so for further freezing, after which it was unmolded onto a glass plate or china dish. Leslie mentioned molds in the shape of doves, dolphins, lapdogs, fruit, and baskets, as possible forms. These hinged metal molds imparted a crisply sculpted surface to the ice cream, and made the process of unmolding relatively easy. "Serve it up immediately lest it begin to melt," she advised. "Send round sponge-cake with it, and wine or cordials immediately after."[106]

By the 1850s, the art of ice cream making had become standardized and simplified by the availability of commercially produced ice cream freezers. Patents for these devices had begun to appear during the previous decade, typically for a wooden tub that held a combination of ice and salt, into which a watertight metal canister could be inserted, and filled with the ice cream base. The top of the mixing canister had a gear mechanism through which an interior vertical paddle could be turned with a crank handle. Nancy M. Johnson of Philadelphia had received the first patent for an ice cream freezer of this type in 1843.[107] *The Young Housekeeper's Assistant*, however, was still describing how to make ice cream using more makeshift methods in 1859:

> Mix equal quantities of coarse salt and ice shopped small; set the freezer containing the cream into a firkin, and put in the ice and salt; let it come up well around the freezer. Turn and shake the freezer steadily at first, and nearly all the time until the cream is entirely frozen. Scrape the cream down often from the sides with a knife. When the ice and salt melt, do not pour off any of it, unless there is danger of its getting into the freezer; it takes half an hour to freeze a quart of cream; and sometimes longer. A tin pail which will hold twice the measure of the cream, answers a good purpose if you do not own a freezer. In winter, use snow instead of ice.[108]

By the 1880s, freezer models with names such as "Arctic" and "White Mountain" were cranking out many gallons of ice cream in American kitchens, in assorted flavors. *Mrs. Lincoln's Boston Cook Book*

Ice cream freezers could be operated by means of a crank or, as shown here, by an improved fly wheel, which apparently reduced the fatigue factor inherent in homemade ice cream production. (Courtesy of Dover Publications.)

offered recipes for a myriad of ice creams and ice cream desserts including almond, baked apple, banana, glazed bombe, brown bread, caramel, chestnut, chocolate, cocoanut, coffee, frappés, fruit mousse, biscuit glacé, lemon, macaroon, mouse, Neapolitan, Nesselrode, Philadelphia, pineapple, pistachio, plombière, Café Parfait, Café Pralines, banana sherbet, lemon ginger sherbet, white velvet sherbet, Roman punch, strawberry, sultana, tutti frutti, vanilla, and walnut.[109]

As this list suggests, the array of foods available, the quality, and the methods of producing those foods had changed dramatically over the course of sixty years. By the 1880s, American consumers had access to a wide variety of menu options, limited only by price. The distinct culinary cultures that had been so visible before the nineteenth century had been gradually eroded by mass transportation and technological innovation, new culinary literature that "Americanized" the nation's cookery, and a highly mobile population. Regional differences did persist, however, and were joined by new ethnic foodways, despite the forces of industrial conformity.

NOTES

1. Ruth Schwartz Cowan, *More Work for Mother: The Ironies of Household Technology from the Open Hearth to the Microwave* (New York: Basic Books, 1983), 34–37; Joyce W. Carlo, *Trammels, Trenchers, & Tartlets: A Definitive Tour of the Colonial Kitchen* (Old Saybrook, CT: Peregrine Press, 1982), 22–32; Jane C. Nylander, *Our Own Snug Fireside: Images of the New England Home, 1760–1860* (New York: Alfred A. Knopf, 1993), 185–187.

2. Lucy Larcom, *A New England Girlhood, Outlined from Memory (Beverly, MA)*, eBook (1889; 2004); available at http://www.gutenberg.org/ctext/22932004 (accessed January 7, 2005). I thank Sandra Oliver for pointing me toward this reference.

3. Ibid.

4. Nylander, 214–15, Cowan, 54–56, 61.

5. Mrs. William Parkes, *Domestic Duties; or, Instructions to Young Married Ladies on the Management of their Households*, 3rd American ed. (New York: T. & J. Harper, 1829), 171; digital edition available at "Feeding America: The Historic American Cookbook Project," Michigan State University Library, http://digital.lib.msu.edu/collections/ (accessed January 3, 2006).

6. Quoted in Priscilla J. Brewer, "Home Fires: Cookstoves in American Culture, 1815–1900," in *House and Home: The Dublin Seminar for New England Folklife Annual Proceedings 16–17 July 1988*, ed. Peter Benes (Boston: Boston University, 1990): 75.

7. Mary Hooker Cornelius, *The Young Housekeeper's Friend*, rev. ed. (Cambridge: Allen & Farnham, 1859), 21.

8. Brewer, 71–73; Cowan, 59–60.

9. "'The Housekeeper' Range," *The Metal Worker, A Weekly Journal of The Stove, Tin, Plumbing, and House Furnishing Trades* 8 (September 8, 1877), reprinted in Ronald S. Barlow, ed., *Victorian Houseware, Hardware, and Kitchenware* (Mineola, NY: Dover Publications, 1992), 64.

10. Maria Parloa, *Miss Parloa's New Cook Book: A Guide to Marketing and Cooking* (Boston: Estes and Lauriat, 1880), 65.

11. Parloa, 409.

12. This excerpt was published in the 1881 *House Furnishings Catalogue* of the Simmons Hardware Company, St. Louis, Missouri. Reprinted in Barlow, 75. See also Juliet Corson, *Cooking School Text Book and Housekeeper's Guide* (New York: Orange Judd Co., 1877), 21.

13. Lydia Maria Child, *The American Frugal Housewife* (1832; reprint Worthington, OH: Worthington Historical Society, 1965), 74.

14. Gervase Markham, *The English Housewife*, ed. Michael R. Best (London, 1615; reprint Montreal: McGill-Queen's University Press, 1994), 68–69.

15. Leslie, Eliza, *Miss Leslie's Directions for Cookery: An Unabridged Reprint of the 1851 Classic* (Mineola, NY: Dover Publications, 1999), 334.

16. For a discussion of a general cultural transition from workmanship of risk to workmanship of certainty, see David Pye, *The Nature and Art of Workmanship* (Cambridge: Cambridge University Press, 1968), 4–8.

17. Estelle Woods Wilcox, ed., *Buckeye Cookery and Practical Housekeeping*, with a preface by Virginia M. Westbrook (Buckeye Publishing Company, 1880; reprint edition, St. Paul: Minnesota Historical Society Press, 1988), 52.

18. Marion Harland, *Breakfast, Luncheon and Tea*, (New York: Scribner, Armstrong & Co., 1875), 191.

19. Parloa, 73.

20. See Alan Davidson's survey of the history of American cookbooks in *The Oxford Companion to Food* (New York: Oxford University Press, 1999), 15–16.

21. Janice Bluestone Longone, Introduction to *Directions for Cookery* viii–x.

22. Nancy Harvis Brose, Juliana McGovern Dupre, Wendy Tocher Kohler, and Jean McClure Mudge, *Emily Dickinson, Profile of the Poet as Cook* (1976; reprint Amherst, MA: Dickinson Homestead, 1981), 5.

23. Child, *American Frugal Housewife*, cover. The word "American" was added to the title of Child's book when it began to be sold in Germany and England. For biographical information about Child, see *Oxford Encyclopedia of Food and Drink in America*, s.v. "Child, Lydia Maria" (by Barbara Haber).

24. *Oxford Encyclopedia of Food and Drink in America*, s.v. "Beecher, Catharine" (by Alice Ross).

25. Catharine E. Beecher and Harriet Beecher Stowe, *The American Woman's Home* (New York: J. B. Ford and Co., 1869), 74.

26. Virginia M. Westbrook, Introduction to *Buckeye Cookery*, vii–xi.

27. For more information about the linkage between the South Kensington School and the American cooking school movement, see Mary Tolford Wilson's biography of Juliet Corson, in Edward T. James, ed., *Notable American Women, 1607–1950*, 3 vols. (Cambridge: Belknap Press of Harvard University Press, 1971), 387–388.

28. *Morrill Act, Statutes at Large* 12, 503 (1862).

29. *Notable American Women, 1607–1950*, s.v. "Corson, Juliet." Corson was so successful that she was even consulted by the government of France about procedures for setting up cooking schools.

30. Ibid., s.v. "Mary Johnson Bailey Lincoln" (by Mary Tolford Wilson).

31. See Laura Shapiro's extended discussion of the impact of cooking schools on American women and American foodways in *Perfection Salad: Women and Cooking at the Turn of the Century* (New York: Farrar, Straus and Giroux, 1986), especially chapters 3–4.

32. Parkes, 172.

33. Elizabeth H. Putnam, *Mrs. Putnam's Receipt Book, and Young Housekeeper's Assistant*, new and rev. ed. (1858; reprint New York: Sheldon & Co., 1867), 318.

34. Marion Harland [Mary Virginia Hawes Terhune], *Common Sense in the Household: A Manual of Practical Housewifery*, reprint (New York: Charles Scribner's Sons, 1871; Birmingham, AL: Oxmoor House, Inc., 1985), 21–22.

35. Parloa, 66–67.

36. Ibid., 68.

37. *Fitchburg Directory* (1848), 42. *Fitchburg Directory* (1858), 64.

38. Leslie, *Directions for Cookery*, 334–337.

39. Parloa is reflecting a long-held belief that "baked" beef was inferior than that roasted in front of a fire. This antimodern notion slowed down the movement toward cookstoves and ranges somewhat, and persisted in literature as a nostalgic critique of kitchen progress. Parloa, 68.

40. Parloa, 69–70.

41. Barlow, 106–114.

42. Parloa, 81.

43. Anthony Willich illustrated Coates's apple parer in his *Domestic Encyclopedia* in 1804; see Linda Campbell Franklin, *300 Years of Kitchen Collectibles*, 4th ed. (Iola, WI: Krause Publications, 1997), 7.

44. Weaver, ed., *Quaker Woman's Cookbook*, xxii.

45. Franklin, 7.

46. Ibid., 8.

47. Barlow, 77–80.

48. Barlow, 77–80.

49. Harland, *Common Sense in the Household*, 21.

50. Franklin, 64.

51. Wilcox, 61–62.

52. Franklin, 32.

53. From the catalog of the Wm. Frankfurth Hardware Co., Barlow, 223.

54. Ibid.

55. Barlow, 223.

56. *Oxford Encyclopedia of Food and Drink in America*, s.v. "Hamburger" (by David Gerard Hogan).

57. Barlow, 222.

58. Elizabeth Ellicott Lea, *Domestic Cookery, Useful Receipts, and Hints to Young Housekeepers* (Baltimore: Cushings and Bailey, 1853), 169; reprinted in *A Quaker Woman's Cookbook*, ed. William Woys Weaver (Philadelphia: University of Pennsylvania Press, 1982).

59. Lea, 170–171

60. Lea, 172. In his introduction to Lea's text, editor and food historian William Woys Weaver described scrapple as "a pot pudding made by thickening a butcher's broth (*Metzelsuppe*) with scraps of meat and buckwheat flour. After the pudding 'sets,' it is sliced and fried like sausage." Scrapple's origins were European; cornmeal appeared only in the American version. Blood was sometimes added to enhance both the consistency and color of scrapple. See Weaver's Glossary, lxxi–lxxii.

61. Lea, l–li, 170.

62. Fanny Lemira Gillette, *The White House Cook Book: A Selection of Choice Recipes Original and Selected, During a Period of Forty Years' Practical Housekeeping* (Chicago: R. S. Peale & Co., 1887), 135; digital edition available at "Feeding America" Web site. (accessed January 14, 2005).

63. Keith Stavely and Kathleen Fitzgerald, *America's Founding Food: The Story of New England Cooking* (Chapel Hill: University of North Carolina Press, 2004), 124–125.

64. Sidney W. Mintz, *Sweetness and Power: The Place of Sugar in Modern History* (London and New York: Viking Penguin, 1985), 37–51 and especially chapter 3, "Consumption."

65. A Lady of Philadelphia [Eliza Leslie], *Seventy-Five Receipts, for Pastry, Cakes, and Sweetmeats* (Boston: Munroe and Francis, 1828; reprint Cambridge: Applewood Books, 1988), 77–88.

66. Leslie, *Directions for Cookery*, 231,

67. Ibid., 232.

68. Sophia J. Wallace, Diary, 1854, recorded in *Fitchburg Almanac, Directory, and Business Advertiser for 1854* (Fitchburg, MA: Shepley & Wallace, 1854). Special Collections, Fitchburg State College, Fitchburg, MA.

69. Harland, *Common Sense in the Household*, 473.

70. Ibid., 474.

71. *Oxford Encyclopedia of Food and Drink in America*, s.v. "Canning and Bottling" (by Andrew F. Smith).

72. Mary J. Lincoln, *Mrs. Lincoln's Boston Cook Book*, rev. ed. (1883; reprint Boston: Little, Brown, and Co., 1909), 401, 398.

73. For a definitive look at the history of tomato canning, see Andrew F. Smith, "The Well Preserved Tomato," in *Souper Tomatoes: The Story of*

America's Favorite Food (Chapel Hill: University of North Carolina Press, 2000), 45–62.

74. *Oxford Encyclopedia of Food and Drink in Am*erica, s.v. "Tomatoes" (by Andrew F. Smith); Mary Randolph, *The Virginia House-Wife*, ed. Karen Hess (1824; reprint Columbia: University of South Carolina Press, 1984), 201; Child, 35.

75. Catharine Esther Beecher, *Miss Beecher's Domestic Receipt Book: Designed as a Supplement to Her Treatise on Domestic Economy* (1846; New York: Harper, 1850), 51–52; digital edition available at "Feeding America" Web site.

76. Parloa, 50.

77. Harland, *Common Sense in the Household*, 477.

78. *Oxford Encyclopedia of Food and Drink in America*, s.v. "Tomatoes" (by Andrew Smith).

79. Mary F. Henderson, *Practical Cooking and Dinner Giving* (New York: Harper & Brothers, 1877), 94; digital edition available at "Feeding America" Web site. Parloa, 229.

80. *Oxford Encyclopedia of Food and Drink in America*, s.v. "Can Openers" (by Linda Campbell Franklin).

81. Lincoln, 54.

82. Ibid., 55.

83. Wilcox, 61.

84. Leslie, *Directions for Cookery*, 336.

85. Wilcox, 59–61

86. Franklin, 91.

87. Ibid., 89; Barlow, 82–84.

88. Barlow, 82–84. An advertisement published in the March 1887 *Ladies Home Journal* claimed that there were four million in use; quoted in Franklin, 89

89. Corson, 135.

90. Child, 86; Sarah Josepha Hale, *The Good Housekeeper, or The Way to Live Well and To Be Well While We Live* (Boston: Weeks, Jordon and Co., 1839), 102–103.

91. Child, 86.

92. Leslie, *Directions for Cookery*, 388.

93. *Oxford Encyclopedia of Food and Drink in America*, s.v. "Tea" (by Jan Whitaker).

94. Leslie, *Directions for Cookery*, 389.

95. Child, 83.

96. "Farming Tools and House Furnishing Goods" Barlow, 42–47; Leslie, 389.

97. Parloa, 388.

98. Ibid., 389.

99. Oscar Edward Anderson, Jr., *Refrigeration in America: A History of a New Technology and Its Impact* (Princeton: Princeton University Press, 1953),

6–7; Randolph, 178–179; Frances Milton Trollope, *Domestic Manners of the Americans*, 4th ed. (New York: Whittaker, Treacher, & Co, 1832), 55.

100. Waverly Root and Richard de Rochemont, *Eating in America: A History* (1976; reprint New York: Ecco Press, 1981), 155.

101. *Fitchburg Directory* (1858), 83

102. Anderson, 15, 25, 31, 36; Siegfried Giedion, *Mechanization Takes Command* (1948; reprint New York: W. W. Norton Co., 1969), 220–222.

103. Strasser, Susan, *Never Done: A History of American Housework* (New York: Pantheon Books, 1982), 19–22. Linda Campbell Franklin notes that between 1790 and 1873, there was only one patent for an "ice box," but 190 patents (beginning in 1837) for "refrigerators." See Franklin, *300 Years of Kitchen Collectibles*, 5th ed., (Iola, WI: Krause Publications, 2003), 738.

104. Randolph, 174–178.

105. Leslie, *Seventy-Five Receipts*, 38.

106. Leslie, *Directions for Cookery*, 322–324.

107. For an extended discussion of the history of ice cream freezers, see Franklin, 5th ed., 740–744.

108. Henderson, 96–97.

109. Lincoln, 546–553.

CHAPTER 4

REGIONAL FOODWAYS IN VICTORIAN AMERICA

In 1876, the United States celebrated a century of independence, with a major international exhibition in Philadelphia. The country had a lot to celebrate: major improvements in communication, mass transportation, manufacturing technologies, and, most of all, sectional reunification after a bitter Civil War. Reunification, however, did not mean that nationalism had swept away all vestiges of regional differences. In fact, the national consensus had rarely meant a lack of difference in a country that had grown up from a handful of transplanted cultures. Regional identities, historically formed by a long process of blending, massaged into distinctive shapes by local contexts, seemed suddenly to be under siege from the twin forces of modernism and social mobility. The homogenizing power of industrial production threatened to eradicate local differences, whether in cheese, flour, apples, or any other part of a family's daily diet. At the same time, the glue that had held together community and regional custom had been breaking down since the beginning of the century. The inexorable movement of people westward or into the burgeoning cities all over the country threatened to splinter the continuity of culture through families and across familiar spaces. Simultaneously, many Americans were turning their cultural differences into marketable products for a growing nation of consumers.

In the middle of the eighteenth century, when Dr. Alexander Hamilton, an immigrant Scot living in colonial Maryland, toured the East Coast, he encountered a diverse array of people and foodways. After leaving Annapolis on March 30, 1744, Hamilton wandered as far north as Portsmouth, New Hampshire, before turning back toward home.

His *Itinerarium*, published upon his return to Annapolis in September, recorded a mélange of people, customs, fashions, and foodways. In Philadelphia, he noted that the local diet was based on bread and pork—probably not unfamiliar to Hamilton. When he reached New York, however, he "dined upon what I have never had to eat in my life before—a dish of fried clams, of which shellfish there is an abundance in these parts." Hamilton's Dutch landlady served the clams with rye bread and butter, but Hamilton noted that the clams required so much chewing that they cooled before dinner was over. The landlady then used a brass bed warmer as a chafing dish to reheat the clams.[1] Despite this unusual custom, Hamilton seemed to enjoy the fried clams and washed them down with quantities of beer.

One hundred years later, Americans traveled with much greater frequency than had Hamilton and with far greater ease. The trip from New York City to Buffalo, which had taken at least two weeks in 1800, was shortened to four days by the construction of the Erie Canal. A rapidly expanding railroad network, as well as steam-powered vessels on the major rivers of the Midwest, further facilitated trips into the interior. The completion of the transcontinental railroad after the Civil War made it possible to travel from coast to coast in a matter of days rather than weeks. These transportation improvements had a profound effect on regional American foodways. As they expanded the availability of foods and local cookery far beyond regional boundaries, American menus and diets became increasingly nationalized. At the same time, however, regional identities were perpetuated by a growing cookery literature that sought to preserve local food customs. Restaurants further expanded the reach of regional foodways, transplanting them far from home as exotic offerings—or as a taste of home for an increasingly migratory population. Finally, the demographic makeup of the United States changed dramatically during the nineteenth century, and newly arrived immigrants brought their own foodways along as baggage. For many of these immigrants, food customs functioned as an important link to home—and they engaged in food-related activities to preserve that link for their families and ethnic communities, as well as to offer it to their new American neighbors.[2]

By the conclusion of the U.S.-Mexican War in 1848, the United States had become a continental nation, with boundaries that ranged from Canada, south to Mexico, and from the Atlantic to the Pacific coasts. Within those boundaries, however, regional identities lingered, reminding inhabitants of their historical as well as geographical roots. The Northeast drew its regional identity from the Atlantic Ocean and its relative proximity to England, Scotland, Ireland, and Holland. Its

The abundance of the mid-Atlantic region is suggested by the cover of *The Philadelphia Companion*, published in 1844. The foods under preparation included a variety of game birds, hard, hams, sausage, fish, lobster, oysters, and a big terrapin in the foreground. The African American servant in the background is a reminder that slavery was widely practiced in Maryland and other mid-Atlantic states until the Civil War. (Courtesy of the Fitchburg Historical Society.)

regional foodways had been shaped from the beginning by its Puritan ancestry as much as by its coastal location. In the nineteenth century, an influx of Irish immigrants, fleeing from famine in their homeland, as well as French Canadians and Scandinavians, drawn to the burgeoning New England mills, helped transform local and regional culinary customs. Modern Puritans preserved the foodways of their English forbears but also adjusted to the modern metropolitan culture of Boston, as well as newly arrived ethnic food offerings.

In the Mid-Atlantic, long a region defined both by its agricultural bounty and by the rich aquatic culture of Chesapeake Bay, traditional Dutch, Swedish, English, and German culinary customs persisted throughout the Victorian era. New York City emerged as a major cosmopolitan fashion center, as well as an agent of new ethnic diversity for the region as well as for the nation. In Philadelphia, Quaker cookery customs coexisted with those imported from the most fashionable kitchens of Europe, commensurate with its continuing position as a major world city.

Southern American cookery had evolved as a hybrid of African and American cultures since the seventeenth century. As long as the institution of African slavery persisted, and undoubtedly well beyond its demise, many Southern kitchens reflected the blending of the Old World and the New. Moreover, Southern foodways also reflected the unique contributions of the Gulf culture, with strong French, Spanish, and Acadian influences shaping the resulting culinary customs and tastes.

The Victorian era in the United States marked the onset of a massive wave of westward migration and the peopling of the center of the country. Great new urban centers sprang up along the major rivers and around the shores of the Great Lakes—with Chicago, Cincinnati, and St. Louis as the greatest. These new cities generated their own regional offerings, shaped by their location at the heart of the country in a newly created agricultural breadbasket, as well as by the strong influences of recently arrived German and other northern European immigrants. "Buckeye" cookery—the title of a popular Ohio cookbook—came to signify "American" by the 1870s, as that part of the country filled up with ordinary farming folks whose lives were shaped by hard work, harsh winters, and economic uncertainty.

The Southwest, America's oldest area of European settlement, but its most recent regional acquisition as part of the United States, retained and spread its unique Hispanic culture during the nineteenth century. Most of this area had been part of the Spanish empire until 1821, when Mexico became an independent republic. Texas separated itself from Mexico in 1836, and the rest of Mexico's northern provinces were added to the United States by a treaty in 1848. This region contributed not only its indigenous foodways but also a culture that revolved around cooking beef in the open air, as well as methods of slow cooking and smoking beef.[3] The cultivation and use of chili peppers, long an important means of preserving and flavoring foods in the Southwest, gradually began to spread to mainstream American foodways as well.

The final piece of the regional map, the Northwest and California, although emerged late in the history of the United States, made a significant difference in American foodways. California, populated quickly after gold was discovered there in 1849, quickly became a "land of milk and honey." Its temperate climate and fertile valleys, coupled with a railroad system that could transport its produce in refrigerated cars, meant that American cooks in less compatible climate zones were no longer bound by seasonality. The railroad had also brought another sort of contribution to American foodways via California—the Chinese workforce that built the transcontinental railroad further diversified California cookery, giving it an Asian flavor. Finally, California, home to the High Sierra, became a tourist destination for hunters and sightseers alike. The trail foods, conveyed through the so-called "Mountain Men" and Native Americans to the larger population, enabled many urban and Eastern-bred visitors to experience the rigors of a less civilized life, including its cookery and diet.

In 1880, author Mark Twain, who had been on an extended European trip, reminisced about the American foods he missed most. He was tired of European food, and declared, "It has now been many months, at the present writing, since I have had a nourishing meal, but I shall soon have one—a modest, private affair, all to myself." Twain had written up a special menu, "which will go home in the steamer that precedes me, and be hot when I arrive." Twain's fantasy meal transcended American regional boundaries, selecting all the best that America had to offer:

Radishes. Baked apples, with cream.
Fried oysters; stewed oysters. Frogs.
American coffee, with real cream.
American butter.
Fried chicken, Southern style.
Porter-house steak.
Saratoga potatoes.
Broiled chicken, American style.
Hot biscuits, Southern style.
Hot wheat bread, Southern style.
Hot buckwheat cakes.
American toast. Clear maple syrup.
Virginia bacon, broiled.
Blue points, on the half shell.
Cherry-stone clams.
San Francisco mussels, steamed.
Oyster soup. Clam Soup.
Philadelphia Terapin soup.
Oysters roasted in shell—Northern style.
Soft-shell crabs. Connecticut shad.
Baltimore perch.
Brook trout, from Sierra Nevadas.

Lake trout, from Tahoe.
Sheep-head and croakers, from New Orleans.
Black bass from the Mississippi.
American roast beef.
Roast turkey, Thanksgiving style.
Cranberry sauce. Celery.
Roast wild turkey. Woodcock.
Canvas-back-duck, from Baltimore.
Prairie hens, from Illinois.
Missouri partridges, broiled.
'Possum. Coon.
Boston bacon and beans.
Bacon and greens, Southern style.
Hominy. Boiled onions. Turnips.
Pumpkin. Squash. Asparagus.
Butter beans. Sweet potatoes.
Lettuce. Succotash. String beans.
Mashed potatoes. Catsup.
Boiled potatoes, in their skins.
New potatoes, minus the skins.
Early rose potatoes, roasted in the ashes, Southern style, served hot.
Sliced tomatoes, with sugar or vinegar. Stewed tomatoes.
Green corn, cut from the ear and served with butter and pepper.
Green corn, on the ear.
Hot corn-pone, with chitlings, Southern style.
Hot hoe-cake, Southern style.
Hot egg-bread, Southern style.
Hot light-bread, Southern style.
Buttermilk. Iced sweet milk.
Apple dumplings, with real cream.
Apple pie. Apple fritters.
Apple puffs, Southern style.
Peach cobbler, Southern style
Peach pie. American mince pie.
Pumpkin pie. Squash pie.
All sorts of American pastry.

"Fresh American fruits of all sorts," Clemens concluded, "including strawberries, which are not to be doled out as if they were jewelry, but in a more liberal way. Ice-water—not prepared in the ineffectual goblet, but in the sincere and capable refrigerator."[4] As is evident from Clemens's list, certain foods had retained their regional identities, despite the modernizing effects of the nineteenth century. It seems just as evident, however, that by 1880, "American" had become a melting pot of regional and ethnic foodways, to be sampled, blended, and enjoyed, regardless of specific geographic origins.

NEW ENGLAND AND THE NORTHEAST

What Is "New England" Cookery?

New England foodways have long held special, almost iconic significance for Americans—especially during the nineteenth century. Because New England was one of the earliest points of European settlement, it served continuously as a cultural hearth. The descendents of those first arrivers took their foodways with them as they spread out across the continent. Thus, "New England" regional customs often seem familiar to a much wider spectrum of Americans, albeit transformed in many ways by local climate, soils, and topography, as well as by infusions from other cultures. As the country emerged from its colonial status into a modern nation, Americans, and particularly New Englanders, began to cling to the culture of the past as a means of staving off change. For any cultural group in transition, food is an important anchor, helping people retain their cultural identity. In the case of New England, the English yeoman diet that the original Puritan settlers had brought with them to the New World retained its potency well into the nineteenth century. That diet, based on wheat, barley, rye, peas, beef, mutton, pork, butter, cheese, and fruit, eventually flourished in the New World—although the grains were initially replaced by maize, native to America.[5] Pease porridge, brown bread, boiled dinner, dark beer, and fermented cider—the staples of seventeenth-century New Englanders—continued to grace tables in Boston, Salem, New Haven, Hartford, and elsewhere throughout the old colonies. By the Victorian era, however, Puritan notions of austerity and aversion to the temptations of the flesh ran up against new consumer offerings imported from afar or shipped in from other parts of the United States.

In attempting to describe New England regional foodways, one must distinguish between what nineteenth-century New Englanders actually ate and what they conceived of as "New England" about that diet. By the end of the Victorian era, New Englanders ate a diet that was modern, diverse, and the result of a wide range of influences. New England foodways combined locally produced fish, produce, and dairy products, with nationally distributed meat, grains and flours, canned foods, tropical fruits, and imported comestibles. But certain items, fish chowder, Indian pudding, or pumpkin pie, for example, conveyed deep connections to a specific New England past. When colonial revival historian Alice Morse Earle described the "Supplies of the Larder" of "Old New England" in 1893, she mentioned numerous foods that had remained on New England tables from Puritan times up to her present day. Her list included Indian pudding, succotash, hoecakes, popcorn, "Jonne-cake," pumpkin bread, pumpkin pie, cranberries, and turkey. According to Earle, early New Englanders had apple, pear, and quince pies, homemade preserves of all sorts ("They preserved everything that would bear preserving"), as well as excellent cheese, all washed down with prodigious quantities of beer and ale.[6]

Other sources confirm that New England–style cookery remained a popular genre throughout the nineteenth century (and indeed, up to the present). A search of cookery literature from that century revealed numerous recipes that were designated as being "New England," including codfish steak (New England style), boiled salt codfish (New England style), New England chowder, New England corn cake, New England doughnuts, New England fish chowder, New England hasty pudding or stir-about, New England raised loaf cake, New England sausages, New England squash, or pumpkin pie, and what has remained up to the present as a meal representative of this region, the New England boiled dinner.[7]

"Boston," another designation that associated recipes with New England cookery, appeared as a modifier even more frequently than did "New England" in nineteenth-century American cookbooks. Boston brown bread and Boston steamed brown bread, Boston baked beans (sometimes with pork), and Boston cream cake/pie/puffs were all common, but they were accompanied by other "Boston" recipes, including Boston (apple) pudding, Boston cake, Boston caramels, Boston cookies, Boston cooler, Boston corn bread, Boston favorite cake, Boston fish chowder, Boston (oyster) fry, and Boston pork and apple pie.[8] The same approach would yield even more New England–associated recipes by using the search terms "Indian" (as in "Indian Pudding" or anything made with Indian cornmeal), "Nantucket," "Cape Cod," "Plymouth," "Pilgrim," "Hartford," and, of course, "Yankee."

Ordinary New England Fare

These historic or "heritage" recipes offer one vision of New England foodways but do not reveal what New Englanders actually ate during the Victorian era. Mid-century grocers' advertisements offer a hint. A. F. Beaman of Fitchburg, Massachusetts, advertised "West India Goods and Country Produce," including "Superior Ningyong and Hyson Teas, Coffee, Sugars, Molasses, Foreign Fruit, . . . Salt, Beef, Pork Lard, Ham, Butter, and Cheese" in 1854. T. C. Caldwell offered much the same assortment, which he termed "best family groceries," as did R. M. Huntley, who offered his customers flour, salt, lard, pork, mackerel, fish, sugars, molasses, tea, coffee, rice, pearlash, and spices.[9] This list remained fairly constant until after the Civil War, when the range of goods available had expanded slightly to include more processed foods. By 1876, H. A. Hatch proclaimed, "Our aim is to keep the best teas, coffees, spices, flour, sugar, foreign and domestic fruits, in our line. Canned fruits, sauces, pickles, jellies, and everything pertaining to a first-class Grocery Store." Fitchburgers could also purchase hothouse produce grown under glass. Sylvanus Sawyer sold "Early Greenhouse Strawberries, Grapes, Cucumbers, Lettuces, etc."[10]

Butchers' advertisements demonstrated a similar proliferation of choice over the course of the Victorian era, as did those of fish dealers, bakeries and confectioners, and any other commercial food purveyor. In 1848, J. Bond & Co. advertised only beef, pork, and tripe. A competitor, C. B. Dupee, promised his customers, "So long as good meat is to be had at the Brighton Market, he will furnish them with a specimen of the same." Brighton was home to the largest slaughterhouses in the Boston area, although there were also some at Porter Square in Cambridge. Cattle, driven to market by farmers from the countryside, were slaughtered fresh daily. Butchers could then purchase the sides of beef and do the trimming themselves.[11] Dupee's reference to the Brighton Market—on the edge of Boston—confirms the movement of the market away from locally produced goods to regional and even national markets, distributed by carts, steamships, and railroads to urban centers, then outward, back to the hinterlands. Within a decade, his list of available meats had expanded to include mutton, veal, lamb, poultry, ham, tripe, sausages, and pig's feet—perhaps reflecting an influx of new immigrants from Germany, who brought their more developed tastes for pork products with them from their home country.[12]

New England's location on the coast made fish and shellfish an obvious dietary choice. If the cookery literature can be believed, the New England diet depended on such staples as "New England Codfish Steak," "New England Boiled Salt Codfish," and "New England Clam Chowder." Longstanding associations of fish with Roman Catholics, immigrants, and the poor, however, made fish a problematic choice for many New Englanders. As a food preference, meat and poultry far outweighed fish and shellfish throughout the Victorian era. When fish *was* served, it was typically sauced heavily or mixed with other foods to give it flavor and substance. Thus, fish cakes, chowders, and croquettes appeared with far greater frequency on the tables of ordinary people than did more upscale fish fillets, steaks, and other cuts. As the New England fishing industry, centered in Gloucester, Massachusetts, increased its yields during the nineteenth century (because of improved technologies for catching, transporting, and processing fish), fish and shellfish began to appear more frequently on Yankee breakfast and dinner tables, as well as on the tables of their more recently arrived neighbors.[13] Those who lived in or near fishing towns could easily purchase fresh cod, mackerel, salmon, clams, oysters, scallops, and lobster. Those who lived further inland had to depend on local fish dealers like William Atherton, who offered his customers "Fresh Fish, Lobsters, Oysters, Salt Fish, &c., &c."[14]

Clambakes

The clambake, perhaps the most beloved New England culinary tradition, seems to have been more of an "invented tradition" than a real one. The mythology surrounding the clambake placed it into a historical continuum, a Native American feasting custom readily adopted (perhaps even shared) by Puritan settlers and transmitted through their descendants to the present.[15] The ritual of the clambake came into its own during the nineteenth century, in concert with the growth of New England tourism and a widespread national interest in wilderness and historical romanticism.[16] By the end of the century, the clambake was a New England institution, enjoyed by the hoards of visitors who came during the summer months to partake of the region's scenery, fresh air, and quaint "old-time" ways. Visitors to Rocky Point, Rhode Island, could enjoy an authentic New England meal, as described in *Appleton's Illustrated Handbook of American Travel*:

> Hundreds come here early and feast upon delicious clams, just drawn from the water and roasted on the shore, in heated seaweed, upon true and orthodox "clam bake" principles. Let no visitor to Providence fail to eat clams and chowder at Rocky Point, even if he should never eat again.[17]

For those who wanted to do their own "impromptu" clambake, Mary Lincoln offered a prescription in her *Boston Cook Book*. She instructed her readers to wear "a short thick dress, shade hat, rubber boots—or, better still, no boots at all, if you can bring your mind to

Americans who lived far away from the coast of Maine could still enjoy Burnham & Morrill's Scarboro Beach Clam Chowder. The popularity of shore dinners and clambakes among summer vacationers to New England had, doubtless, spread the taste for clams across the country by 1878, when this product won a gold medal at the Paris Exposition. (Courtesy of the Maine State Archives, Augusta.)

the comfort of bare feet," and to bring along "a small garden trowel and fork, and a basket."[18] The tasks of preparing the clambake included gathering driftwood and seaweed and forming a circle of stones, with flat stones for a floor. A driftwood fire heated the stones, and once they were hot, clambakers were to line the pit with seaweed, then pile on the rinsed clams, and cover them with a thick layer of seaweed, topped by a canvas tarp. After the clams had steamed sufficiently to open their shells, the tarp and seaweed were removed and the feast began. According to Lincoln, "They are delicious eaten from the shell, with no other sauce than their own briny sweetness. Melted butter, pepper, and vinegar should be ready for those who wish them; then all may "fall to." Fingers must be used." As for the actual eating, Lincoln instructed readers to "pull off the thin skin, take them by the black end, dip them in the prepared butter, and bite off close to the end. If you swallow them whole," she added, "they will not hurt you."[19]

Squeamishness about eating clams dated back to early colonial times, when most of the English settlers believed that clams, which were enjoyed by Native Americans, were only fit food for hogs. By the Victorian period, however, clams, both fresh and canned, were consumed in a variety of forms—as fried clams, clam fritters, clam pie, and several different forms of clam soups. Chowder, however, was the clam concoction most closely associated with New England.[20] Its popularity stretched far beyond the boundaries of New England proper, as evidenced by its ubiquitous presence in cookbooks. Jane Cunningham Croly included two recipes in her *Jennie June's American Cookery Book*, published in New York in 1870. The first, "Cape Cod Chowder," began with the fat rendered from fried salt pork, layered with potatoes, onion, butter crackers, fish, and more fat. Her second recipe, simply called "Clam Chowder," called for "a great deal more pork," and most important, "be careful to get soft shell clams."[21]

Baked Beans

Baked beans, accompanied by brown bread, constituted Saturday night supper for many New Englanders throughout the nineteenth century, as it had for previous generations. The art of baking beans had been learned by early colonists from the Native Americans, who flavored their beans with maple syrup and baked them in a hole in the ground. Early English settlers had preferred to stew their beans, pottage style, as they had done at home. Daily diets typically included bean porridge: beans, boiled until soft, flavored by the addition of a piece of pork and perhaps a handful of cornmeal as thickener. By the nineteenth century, however, New Englanders baked their beans in bake ovens, flavored with salt pork and pepper. Families without an oven could carry their beans to the home of a neighbor or to a local baker, who would put the pots into his bake oven on Saturday night and return the finished products to their owners the following morning.[22] Lucy Larcom, who had been a Lowell mill operative in the 1840s, referred to "the Puritanic custom of saving Sunday-work by baking beans on Saturday evening, leaving them in the oven over night." Larcom explained that over time, families had abandoned their brick bake ovens, no doubt for cast iron ranges, in which case, "the bean-pots were taken by the village baker on Saturday afternoon, who returned them to each house early on Sunday morning, with the pan of brown bread that went with them."

Larcom reminisced further about this event:

> The Saturday's baking was a great event, the brick oven being heated to receive the flour bread, the flour-and-Indian, the rye-and-Indian bread, the traditional pot of beans, the Indian pudding, and the pies; for no further cooking was to be done until Monday.[23]

Molasses was added as a sweetener by the 1870s, although in much smaller quantity than today. Mary F. Henderson's recipe for "Boston Baked Beans" called for one and a half pints of navy beans and a quarter pound of pickled pork but only one tablespoonful of molasses. She baked her beans in a quart-sized bean pot for eight hours, adding water as necessary. To serve, she decanted the beans to a platter, arrayed around the piece of pork.[24] By the end of the century, Mary Lincoln had sweetened up the recipe somewhat, adding a quarter cup of molasses to a quart of beans. Her recipe also included a bit of onion and some mustard, which, she argued, "gives the beans a delicious flavor, and also renders them more wholesome."[25] By this time, however, women had a clear alternative to the laborious task of preparing Boston baked beans at home. Since the 1840s, the canning industry had been making steady inroads into the potential of processed foods, and canned beans were one of their earliest products. In 1867, Burnham & Morrill (B&M), a Portland canner began producing authentic "Brick Oven Baked Beans." All that was required for their preparation was a can opener and a saucepan or baking dish—although women could, and most certainly did, "doctor" them by adding onion, molasses or maple syrup, mustard, and perhaps more salt pork or bacon. With canned brown bread as an accompaniment, a meal of B&M baked beans could thus be made to taste almost homemade.

Potatoes in the New England Diet

The poorest New Englanders, those at the very bottom of the economic scale, often had little more to eat than some form of starch, washed down with coffee, tea, or cider. If that starch were bread, it would most likely have to have been purchased, since the poorest families could have afforded neither a stove nor fuel for extended baking. More likely, however, the family relied on potatoes for their sustenance, as had the poor since the seventeenth century. Potatoes had been on the North American continent since 1621, when the first potatoes arrived via Bermuda. They gradually gained favor with Americans throughout the eighteenth century because they were relatively easy to grow, cook, and eat, especially in the poor, rocky soils of New England. George Washington had planted them at Mount Vernon in 1767, as had Thomas Jefferson at Monticello. When a potato famine in Ireland caused the migration of hundreds of thousands of Irish families to the United States, many of them to New England, the potato, long a staple of Irish diets, came along with them. By the time the famine Irish arrived in Boston, they found potatoes waiting for them in abundance.[26] In 1863, a farmer in central Massachusetts noted in his pocket diary that he began to dig his early potatoes on September 9. He then continued digging potatoes on September 18, September 19, and on and on, several times a week, until he finally "finished digging potatoes" more than a month later, on October 27. On two occasions after that date, he took some of his potatoes into town, presumably to sell or trade. The bulk of them, however, seemed to have been for his own consumption and must have been a dietary staple for his family for the duration of the winter.[27] Like many other families who were struggling to get by, this farmer and his family could have roasted the potatoes and eaten them whole with their fingers or perhaps followed the directions in Lydia Child's bestselling *American Frugal Housewife*. Child instructed her readers to eat their potatoes either boiled or mashed and commented additionally that mashed potatoes "are good to use in making short cakes and puddings; they save flour, and less shortening is necessary."[28]

For New England mill workers, living in factory-owned boarding houses in Lowell, Lawrence, Manchester, New Hampshire, and numerous other mill towns that dotted New England's rivers and streams, potatoes were a daily occurrence. While the famine Irish did not technically bring potatoes to the United States, they certainly enhanced the consumption and variety of preparation of the tuber in New England. By 1850, Eliza Leslie discussed colcannon as a new way of preparing potatoes. She considered colcannon, a mixture of potatoes, stewed with turnips or cabbage and then mashed together, to be a delicious accompaniment for corned beef, salt pork, or bacon.[29]

Potatoes, once scorned by the elites as food fit only for animals or those of the lower classes, had become generally accepted as ordinary fare for all Americans by the Victorian era. Maria Parloa's guide for food shopping, aimed at the middle class, offered her readers information about buying potatoes. "Bermuda sends new potatoes into Northern markets about the last of March or first of April," she wrote in 1880. "Florida soon follows, and one Southern State after another continues to supply until June, when Northern and Eastern districts begin." But new potatoes were not for everyone. According to Parloa, "It is only the rich, however, who can afford new potatoes before July." She knew that among her more rural readers, growing and keeping potatoes was still relatively common practice, and she reassured those readers that "the old are good up to that time, if they have been well kept and are properly cooked."[30]

Foodways of "The Age of Homespun"

At the Philadelphia Centennial Exhibition in 1876, held in Fairmont Park in Philadelphia, visitors could experience the foodways of the past in the New England Log House and Kitchen exhibit. There, hostesses clad in linsey-woolsey gowns served dinners of boiled meat, beans, and gingerbread—items widely perceived to be, in the words of Miss Emma Southwick, the exhibit organizer, "food the old Puritans grew and waxed strong on."[31] In the background, a turkey—that most American of all foods—spit-roasted on the hearth. The exhibit was so popular that it continued after the fair closed in 1877, serving "Ye Old Tyme Meals" under the rubric of the "Log Cabin Restaurant." First on the menu were "Ye Baked Beans, prepared as in ye fafhion of ye Olden Tyme in ye Ancient City of Bofton, Brown Bread, Coffee or Tea," followed by cold ham, cold tongue, roast beef, corned beef, boiled potatoes, boiled or fried eggs, sandwiches, "Oat-Meal and Milk," bread and milk, pie, doughnuts, gingerbread, ice cream, soups, and iced coffee or tea.[32] In the New England Log House and Kitchen, regional character, history, and food had been blended into an appealing consumer event.

Traditional New England foods, many of which had consciously historical associations with the past, persisted into the modern era. Indian pudding, pumpkin pie, and gingerbread were presumed to have fed generations of New Englanders.[33] Indian pudding could either be baked in the oven in a pudding dish or boiled in a cloth pudding bag until cooked. Typical recipes called for "Indian" or cornmeal as a prime ingredient—hence its name—mixed with milk, molasses, ground ginger, and fat. Lydia Maria Child included recipes for both baked and boiled versions in her 1832 edition of *The American Frugal Housewife*, as did most cookery writers who followed her. Later authors modified the basic recipe, adding eggs to lighten the pudding and additional flavors, including apples, grated lemon peel, and more spices.

Mary Cornelius's 1859 version gave explicit directions about both ingredients and the cooking utensils required to uphold the historical integrity of the recipe. She listed her recipe for "Baked Indian" under the "Puddings without Eggs" category of her pudding chapter. "Boil a pint of milk, and set of off from the fire," she began. "Then stir in a large teacup of Indian meal, a cup of finely chopped suet, half a cup of white flour, the same of molasses, and a teaspoonful each of salt, ginger, and cinnamon." The batter was to be put into a "deep, fire-proof patty pan, or a brown earthen one with a small top, such as are made for baking beans," thus associating this dish with another traditional New England food relic. After adding a cup of cold milk, the pudding was to be baked at moderate heat for two hours. "The modern ovens do not bake this kind of pudding as well as a brick oven," Cornelius remarked, reflecting the ambivalence many women felt about encroaching modernity into their kitchens. Finally, if desired, housewives could serve a sour cream sauce, sweetened with a little sugar and flavored with nutmeg.[34]

Indian pudding persisted on New England tables well beyond "the age of homespun." Almost fifty years after Child, Maria Parloa published two new versions of the recipe, one for "Delicate Indian Pudding" the other for "Indian and Apple Pudding."[35] Indian and apple pudding was not really new—although this recipe called for a double boiler for thickening the cornmeal-and-milk mixture prior to baking. "Delicate" Indian pudding would have appealed to the more rarified sensibilities and tastes of later Victorians. It was made with sugar instead of molasses and called for butter (not suet or lard) and eggs—all of which would have enhanced its lightness and digestibility.[36]

The women organizers of the New England Log House and Kitchen exhibit at the Philadelphia Centennial Exhibition in 1876 identified gingerbread as one of the three basic elements of a recreated New England menu. Gingerbread, originally made from a mixture of breadcrumbs and honey, spiced with ginger, cinnamon, and pepper, gained its deep brown color from the addition of saffron or "sanders"— powdered sandalwood. English and Scottish bakers rolled out the mixture into thin sheets that could be cut into individual cakes and baked at a low temperature until crisp. Sometimes the gingerbread was pressed into wooden molds to create a relief-decorated surface. Other bakers formed the batch into a square cake, which was then embellished with box leaves pinned down with gilded cloves.[37] During the seventeenth century, flour replaced the breadcrumbs and gingerbread achieved the cake-like form that is familiar today. The sweetener also changed, from honey to sugar or treacle/molasses, or both, and some recipes called for the addition of dried fruits. By the nineteenth century, gingerbread persisted in a variety of forms—some traditional, some adapted to modern tastes. A perusal of nineteenth-century cookery sources reveals many different gingerbread recipes. Maria Parloa had three: soft, Canada, and fairy gingerbread.[38] Overall, the words "soft, hard, molasses, and sugar" prefixed the most common recipes, suggesting the basic forms. Other modifiers included "Cambridge" and "Flemington"—a reference to the British custom of towns having their own special gingerbread types; "cheap," "common," "eggless," "hot water," "sea voyage," and "hard times," implying more practical or economical forms; "sponge," which would been a yeasted gingerbread, as opposed to the more common use of pearlash, saleratus, or baking power as leavening; and "caraway," "orange," "superior," "sour milk," "spiced," "gossamer," and "white"—all of which suggested improved flavor, lightness, or color.[39] By the end of the

Victorian era, gingerbread recipes, whether for cake, cookies, or other forms, most commonly affirmed their New England heritage and the implied Puritan values of thrift, modesty, and simplicity through the use of molasses (instead of sugar). As New Englanders spread out across America during the nineteenth century, they carried a taste for gingerbread with them as part of their cultural heritage. As a result, gingerbread appeared as a ubiquitous presence in cookbooks, whether published in the Old South, the Midwest, or the Far West. For transplanted Yankees, gingerbread was a taste of their past and the primacy of their heritage.[40]

Thanksgiving

Thanksgiving, the greatest New England food heritage event of all, became a formal national holiday during the Victorian age. Although days of thanksgiving had been celebrated intermittently throughout the year from Puritan times, there had been no one specific calendar day designated for its celebration, until 1863, when President Abraham Lincoln issued his Thanksgiving Day Proclamation. Lincoln's proclamation, however, came about only after many years of work by New England author, editor, and social activist, Sarah Josepha Hale (1788–1879). Hale, born in Newport, New Hampshire, ultimately became the editor of *Godey's Ladies' Book*, perhaps the most influential women's magazine of the nineteenth century. Through her editorial activities at *Godey's*, Hale was continually in a position to influence American attitudes about domestic matters, art, politics, and, especially, food. Her crusade to make Thanksgiving a national holiday began in 1827, when she expressed the idea through the voice of Squire Romilly, a character in her book, *Northwood*. "We have too few holidays," the Squire explained to an English visitor who had joined the family for Thanksgiving dinner. "Thanksgiving Day, like the Fourth of July, should be considered a national festival and observed by all our people." The value of such a holiday was that the collective observance of Thanksgiving by all Americans "will be a grand spectacle of moral power and human happiness, such as the world has never witnessed."[41]

The menu for Romilly's Thanksgiving dinner centered on roast turkey "sending forth the rich odor of its savory stuffing and finely covered with the froth of basting." Other dishes on the table included chicken pie, several meats, a goose, and a pair of ducklings, surrounded by gravies, pickles, preserves, vegetables, and wine. The dessert course waited on a nearby side table: "There was a huge plum pudding, custards and pies of every name and description ever known in Yankee land; yet the pumpkin occupied the most distinguished niche. There were also several kinds of rich cakes, and a variety of sweetmeats and fruits."[42] This description offered a bounteous formula for generations of succeeding Thanksgiving dinners, all building on the basic components of turkey, stuffing, and pumpkin pie, and lots of it. Within a decade after the publication of this novel, Hale had begun an all-out campaign to make Thanksgiving a national holiday, using *Godey's* as her platform. In her November editorial in 1847, she wrote, "From this year, 1847, henceforth and forever, as long as the Union endured, the *last Thursday of November be the Day* set apart by every State for its annual Thanksgiving." From then on, she wrote two editorials a year, urging acceptance of her plan, but it was not until the turbulent years of the Civil War that she finally achieved her goal. Lincoln, sensing the potential for unification in such a holiday, proclaimed it so in 1863.[43] The institutionalization of Thanksgiving further inscribed historical New England foodways onto the national palate.

THE MID-ATLANTIC REGION

The foodways of the Mid-Atlantic region—New York, Pennsylvania, New Jersey, Maryland, and Delaware—have always been defined by two important factors: diversity of population and urban cultures. Since the early settlement period, these colonies lacked the homogeneity of New England, attracting instead a rich variety of immigrants. The Dutch dominated New York culture and foodways at the beginning, and that influence persisted through the nineteenth century but heavily intermixed with numerous newer influences. In Pennsylvania, William Penn's Quakers coexisted with Germans, Swedes, English, Irish, Scots, and many other European emigrants—and the resulting foodways reflected that diversity. Delaware, settled by Swedes in the seventeenth century, quickly became a pathway for many other cultures, as did New Jersey. This region, located "in the middle" of the coastal settlements, filled quickly with people in transition from one world to another, whether from Europe to America, from urban seaport to inland farm communities, or from settled agriculture to western frontier areas. By 1820, New York and Pennsylvania were the largest states in the Union, with 1.3 and 1.5 million residents, respectively, a rank that they held throughout the century. By 1880, New York had surpassed Pennsylvania in the census, and their populations had each roughly tripled to between 4 and 5 million. Part of the appeal of this region has been its rich agricultural lands and, in contrast with New England, its milder climate. But the physical size of New York and Pennsylvania meant that many appealing options existed for settlement and development.

Geographically, the region has been dominated by its coastal location, its estuaries and its inland rivers, and, in the nineteenth century, its canals and railroad depots. New York City and Philadelphia, the largest cities in the United States, were joined by newer urban places—such canal boom towns as Rochester and Buffalo (New York) and Pittsburgh (Pennsylvania). A flood of people moving into the hinterlands fed these new cities, and they quickly emerged as important commercial centers, both for the region and for the nation.

During the Victorian era, the influx of immigrants into the cities of the Mid-Atlantic brought the foodways of Ireland, Germany, Italy, Poland, and other world cultures to this region. New York led the country in the number of foreign-born white persons enumerated in the 1860 census—with almost all of them residing in New York City and King's County, home to Brooklyn. Their legacy, both to New York and to the newer cities to which they moved throughout the United States, included local groceries that grew up to cater to their ethnic preferences, as well as the food carts, saloons, and ethnic restaurants that served the population in general as well as ethnic insiders.[44] This urban immigrant population existed in counterpoint to the metropolitan elites, who enabled the transfer of high-style European fashions in food and drink to American society in general. When English traveler Frances Trollope arrived in New York City in 1828, she exclaimed, "I must still declare that I think New York one of the finest cities I ever saw, and as much superior to every other in the Union, (Philadelphia not excepted,) as London to Liverpool, as Paris to Rouen." Trollope compared New York to Venice and speculated that New York, "like that fairest of cities in the days of her glory, receives into its lap tribute of all the riches of the earth."[45]

Restaurants

By the 1850s, New York's restaurant culture rivaled Europe in its elegance and diversity, led by Delmonico's, the grandest restaurant in Victorian Manhattan. Delmonico's "raised dining out to the status of an event" for New Yorkers and visitors alike, according to culinary historians.[46] Delmonico's, which had begun as a wine shop, hired its first French chef in 1831. From the beginning, the restaurant was novel in many ways, from its presentation to its menu choices, as well

The scale and elegance of Delmonico's presentation and service are clearly evident
in this illustration of the twelfth annual dinner of the Dartmouth College Alumni
Association, held at the restaurant on January 19, 1876. (Courtesy of the New
York Public Library Digital Library [Digital ID=809549].)

as its practice of printing its menu both in French and English. Diners
at Delmonico's, typically unaccustomed to eating vegetables, were introduced to such delicacies as eggplant, artichokes, salads, endive, and
watercress. When the Delmonico family could not find the European
vegetable and salad items that they wanted to see on their dinner
menus, they grew them themselves. Dinner at Delmonico's always
included a fine selection of imported European wines—champagne,
Madeira, sherries, sauterne, and clarets, another sign of the increasingly lavish lifestyles of their rich and famous patrons. The restaurant
attracted New York's old and new rich, as well as such celebrities as
Jenny Lind, Boss Tweed, Louis Kossuth, Horace Greeley, and a host
of others, who only added to the cachet of Delmonico's.[47]

As New York society moved uptown, the restaurant did too, to
Broadway and Chambers Street in 1853 and then again in 1876 to
Madison Square. Where Delmonico's had been one of the only restau-
rants in New York when it began serving customers, by 1876, there

almost six thousand. Delmonico's had set a high standard, hosting dinners, balls, and parties and catering many more off-site. One of the most memorable, the so-called "Swan Banquet" of 1873, featured a fully landscaped banquet table, complete with mountains, trees, park-like grounds, and a lake with *real* swans, at which breakfast was served for seventy-two guests, a cost of $10,000.[48] The excessive grandeur and occasionally outlandish modes of entertaining among New York's elites was fed by the imagination of the Delmonico family, aided and abetted by newspaper accounts of their antics. These published reports fed the imaginations of more ordinary New Yorkers, creating a new metropolitan culture of "dining out."

Not all New Yorkers, however, could afford Delmonico's-style dining. For them, there were a host of alternatives, including the 850 oyster houses in New York by 1874. Oyster houses were not a new phenomenon in the 1870s. They had existed throughout the nineteenth century in New York, Philadelphia, and other urban centers, catering particularly to men, who went there to drink, smoke, engage in male comradeship, and eat oysters. One Philadelphia restaurateur advertised that he had "made arrangements to be supplied daily, in large quantities, direct from the boats, with the finest oysters brought to this market." He sold raw, stewed, panned, fancy roast, fried, broiled, roasted, and "escalloped" oysters to his restaurant patrons. He also offered oysters as takeout items, either as "Stewed Oysters put up in cans to order" or "Fried Oysters in Boxes, also, for Gents to take home, on eight minutes notice."[49] The city of Philadelphia imported four thousand tons of oysters from Chesapeake Bay in 1840. In 1859, according to one source, New Yorkers "spend more on oysters than on butcher's meat."[50] By the 1880, the oyster beds in Chesapeake Bay had already begun to experience depletion, overburdened by the demand not only from East Coast cities but also from every city with any proximity to a railroad line, all the way across the country.

In addition to oysters, shore birds from this region, canvasback ducks in particular, graced the menus of those who could afford to serve them, either in restaurants or at home. Franklin House, a Philadelphia "Gentlemen's Ordinary," included "Wild Duck" as one of its "Roast" offerings in early December 1855. Another Philadelphia establishment, the St. Louis Hotel, offered both canvasback ducks and "Red Head Ducks" to its patrons, under the general heading of "Game." Even Leach's Restaurant, which advertised itself as "The Cheapest Place in the City," included duck, both wild and tame, on its menu.[51]

Locker's, in Philadelphia, specialized in oysters, especially oyster stew. Patrons could have a bowl of stew for $.20, or a roast dinner for $.30. (Courtesy Print and Picture Collection, Free Library of Philadelphia [pdcl100107].)

In her discussion of ducks in the "Marketing" section of her popular cookbook, Maria Parloa noted, "Besides the tame bird, there are at least twenty different kinds that come under the head of game. The canvas-back is the finest in the list." She went on to discuss the seasonality of these ducks, adding that while domestic ducks were available throughout the year, "the wild ones only through the fall and winter." A pair of canvasbacks, in season, might have cost $1.50, but out of season, that price more than tripled to $5.00. According to Parloa, the ducks were to be roasted, stuffed only with an onion or two, until rare, and served with currant jelly and gravy.[52] The Philadelphian Eliza Leslie had previously included three different methods for preparing canvasback ducks in her 1847 cookbook: roasted, plain, and stewed.[53] Four years later, in yet another cookbook, Leslie commented that canvasback ducks should be roasted in the same manner as regular ducks but that "they will generally be done enough in three quarters of an hour. Send currant jelly to the table with them, and have heaters to place under the plates. Add to the gravy a little cayenne, and a large wine-glass of port."[54]

Everyday Cookery in the Mid-Atlantic

The food culture of Philadelphia had been shaped both by its Quaker heritage and by its influx of German immigrants during the nineteenth century. The Quakers, Philadelphia's ruling class since the eighteenth century, viewed luxury as a sign of God's grace and set a tone of abundance and quality in Pennsylvania foodways. According to one food historian, "Quaker shipping in Wilmington and Philadelphia kept tables within the Quaker network well stocked with things unobtainable in many parts of the country, such as fresh pineapples from the Caribbean, Seville oranges, and winter grapes from the Canary Islands, even when Philadelphia grocers went without."[55]

Quaker farmwife Elizabeth Ellicott Lea's cookbook, published in 1845, offered a glimpse into the everyday cookery of this region in the 1840s, as shaped by the cultural mix of Native Americans, African Americans, Anglo-Americans, and Pennsylvania Germans. Lea assumed that her readers would be rural women like herself, with easy access to fresh meat, fish, poultry, vegetables, fruits, and dairy products. She showed how to cook shad, a local specialty fish, as well as rockfish, salmon, mackerel, and herring. Lea prepared terrapins—small edible turtles found in the coastal marshes of Delaware and Chesapeake Bays—by boiling them "till the shells crack," then dismembering them, removing the eggs, and stewing the meat with salt, cayenne and black pepper, mace, and a lump of butter "the size of an egg." The resulting dish, when thickened with flour and flavored with two glasses of wine, was a regional delicacy, commonly known as "the bird."[56] According to politician and writer Colonel John W. Forney, "Terrapin is essentially a Philadelphia dish. Baltimore delights in it, Washington eats it, New York knows it; but in Philadelphia it approaches a crime not to be passionately fond of it."[57]

Oysters, another local menu item, appeared thirteen times in Lea's cookbook. She offered two recipes for oyster soup—both essentially oysters, water, seasonings, butter, and cream—as well as "Scolloped Oysters," fried oysters, oyster fritters, stewed oysters, "A Rich Oyster Pie," "A Baltimore Oyster Pie," "Plain Oyster Pie," oyster sauce, pickled oysters (two ways), and a final recipe for frying oysters in an egg yolk batter, "To Brown Oysters in their own Juice."[58]

Elizabeth Lea's Rich Oyster Pie

Strain off the liquor from the oysters, and put it on to boil, with some butter, mace, nutmeg, pepper and salt; just as it boils, stir in a thickening of milk and flour; put in the oysters, and stir them till they are sufficiently stewed; take them off, and put in the yelks of two eggs, well beaten; do not put this in while it is boiling, or it will curdle. Line a dish, not very deep, with puff paste; fill it with white paper, or a clean napkin, to keep the top crust from falling in; put on a lid of paste, and bake it. When done, take off the lid carefully; take out the paper or napkin, and pour in the oysters. Send it hot to the table.[59]

Lea's cookbook, as well as the cookbooks of other women from the Mid-Atlantic, reflected the agricultural abundance of the region. She discussed a wide variety of vegetables, including corn, hominy, potatoes, tomatoes, eggplant, salsify, mushrooms, cucumbers, lettuce, cauliflower, cabbage, greens, string beans, peas, asparagus, squash, pumpkins, parsnips, carrots, turnips, onions, and beets. Philadelphian Eliza Leslie added sweet potatoes, broccoli, spinach, artichokes, lima beans, celery, radishes, okra, and chestnuts to that list. Another Philadelphian, Robert Buist, advocated surrounding the vegetable crops with fruits. *The Family Kitchen Gardener*, published in 1855, laid out an ideal kitchen garden that integrated a grape arbor and pear, plum, quince, peach, or apricot trees, as well as current and raspberry bushes, into the plan. Buist offered a list of "Garden Seeds for Half an Acre," including asparagus, assorted beans, assorted beets, broccoli, cauliflower, assorted cabbage, celery, cress, cucumber, carrot, early corn, eggplant, endive, leek, lima beans, assorted lettuces, mustard, melons, okra, assorted onions, parsley, parsnips, peppers, pumpkin, peas, radish, salsify, squash, spinach, tomatoes, turnips, and "pot and sweet herbs."[60]

Catharine Beecher, although a New Englander by birth and by choice, included a recipe for "Pennsylvania Flannel Cakes" in her *Domestic Receipt Book* in 1846, suggesting a regional dimension to this basic griddlecake. Beecher's recipe used beaten egg whites to lighten the batter, in contrast to the more typical yeasted recipes found elsewhere.[61]

Pennsylvania Flannel Cakes

One quart of milk, and half a teaspoonful of salt.

Three eggs, the whites beaten separately to a stiff froth.

Mix the milk, salt, and yolks, stir in flour till a batter is made, suitable for griddle cakes. Then, when ready to bake, stir in the whites.

Rye flour is very fine, used in this way, instead of wheat, but the cakes adhere so much that it is difficult to bake them. Many love them much better than the wheat.

Surveys of nineteenth-century cookery literature yielded other recipes with specific associations to Mid-Atlantic places, including Pennsylvania cream cheese, Quaker oats, Quaker omelet, Philadelphia ice cream, Philadelphia pepper pot, and Philadelphia clam soup. Ice cream, with strong Philadelphia associations since the late eighteenth century, became a standard culinary treat after the invention of the ice cream freezer in 1846 and the rise of wholesale ice cream manufacturers. During the 1840s and 1850s, Philadelphia newspaper advertisements documented vanilla, lemon, strawberry, and pineapple as the favorite flavors.[62] Jacob Fussell has been credited with initiating the mass production of ice cream, in Seven Valleys, Pennsylvania, a small town in York County, west of Philadelphia. Although Fussell moved his business to Baltimore within two years of its founding, ice-cream production persisted in Seven Valleys for the remainder of the century.[63] "Philadelphia" style ice cream referred to a means of manufacture that predated commercial production, whereby sweetened whipped cream was flavored, frozen, beaten again, and refrozen.[64] Juliet Corson described Philadelphia ice cream as "pure cream, over-sweetened, over-flavored, and then frozen."[65] Catharine Beecher, however, offered a slightly less decadent version, using milk ("cream when you have it"), thickened with arrowroot and egg whites and flavored with half a vanilla bean, before freezing.[66]

Food on the Mid-Atlantic Frontier

During the nineteenth century, the Mid-Atlantic states increasingly divided into two distinctly different regions: the old coastal settlements and the frontier. The opening of the Erie Canal in 1825 connected New York City with the Great Lakes, giving rise to new areas of settlement and such boom towns as Rochester and Buffalo. The development of a rail system and the ensuing demand for iron, coal, and steel pushed the development of the interior of Pennsylvania and the growth of Pittsburgh as a new industrial hub. The Chesapeake Canal spurred the development of Baltimore as a new commercial city and rapid migration into western Maryland, Kentucky, and south into the mountains of Virginia. All of this development carried with it the foodways of the migrants, foodways that were then reshaped by the new environments on the frontier. In turn, the frontier itself, much of it rich agricultural lands, began to reshape the traditional foodways of the coast.

Rochester, New York, located at the fall of Genesee River, transformed itself from a sleepy settlement of 1,500 in 1820 into a thriving flour-milling center that fed much of the rest of the population of the East. Such growth created opportunities for the thousands of immigrants arriving through the port of New York City, Germans in particular. Hardworking and eager to imprint their own food customs on their new home, German settlers in Rochester began to produce sausages and beer—which were then transported both east and west through the new transportation network. Buffalo, another major beneficiary of the Erie Canal, capitalized on its situation at the gateway to the Great Lakes system, as well as becoming an important rail hub. Buffalo's population surged as Italians, Poles, Germans, and other European immigrants arrived daily in search of land, work, and a future. For the existing residents of both of these cities, many of them migrants themselves from New England and lower New York, the newer arrivals brought food options that enriched their diets and their tastes. The resulting food culture of these developing frontier areas was a heterogeneous blend of established Anglo-American foodways and those of the recent arrivals. Early in the century, the food and dining habits of those living on the frontier were decried as being primitive, rancid, coarse, and generally unappetizing. Over the course of the Victorian era, however, these early frontier places quickly became new cosmopolitan centers, populated by middle-class Americans who demanded and received the sophisticated culinary customs of New York, Philadelphia, Boston, and even Paris.

THE SOUTH

Mark Twain, in his nostalgic reminiscence about American regional cookery written from Europe in 1880, mentioned many Southern dishes. Fried chicken, hot biscuits, broiled Virginia bacon, New Orleans sheep-head and croakers, bacon and greens, hominy, "early rose potatoes, roasted in the ashes," hot corn pone with chitterlings, hot hoecake, hot egg-bread, hot light-bread, apple puff, and peach cobbler, all lovingly designated by Twain as "Southern style."[67] Twain's list captured much of the essence of nineteenth-century Southern foodways, which centered around pork, chicken, greens, corn, oysters, freshwater fish, outdoor cooking, airy baked goods, and rich fruit desserts.

Any discussion of regional "Southern" cookery, however, must take into account that the South consisted of multiple regions, shaped by topography, climate, economy, politics, and culture. In the Tidewater zone, comprising parts of coastal Maryland, Virginia, North and South Carolina, and Georgia, foodways of the nineteenth century reflected a complex mix of English, African, and Native American cultures. On the Gulf Coast, French and Cajun cookery combined with persistent Creole foodways. New Orleans became a powerful cultural force, blending French, Spanish, West Indian, and Mexican influences with an *haute* restaurant culture imported from Paris. In the upland South, encompassing parts of western Virginia, North and South Carolina, Georgia, Kentucky, Tennessee, Alabama, and Arkansas, successions of migrants from Scotland, Ireland, Germany, and central Europe laid their imprint on Southern foodways as they trekked through the mountains of Appalachia. Despite its multiple geographies, however, a predominantly agricultural economy, the institution of slavery, and a common purpose during Civil War bound the nineteenth-century South together, politically and economically. Some Southern foods, barbecues, collards, or grits, for example, have become iconic—products of the nostalgic affirmation of this region after the war; others are more closely linked to specific subregions and divergent ethnicities of the South.

Tidewater Cookery

Virginian Mary Randolph captured the flavors of the antebellum South in *The Virginia House-Wife*, which was first published in 1824. The book offered an impressive array of recipes that reflected the cultures of Randolph's Anglo-Virginia context in concert with other Southern foodways imported from Africa, India, and the Creole South. In Randolph's kitchen, the food traditions of Jacobean England were reshaped by the agricultural bounty of the Tidewater and cosmopolitan nineteenth-century tastes. Whereas Gervase Markham's seventeenth-century work, *The English Housewife*, had contained recipes only for varieties of "sallet" and no individual vegetable recipes, Randolph discussed a multitude of vegetables, including potatoes, Jerusalem and globe artichokes, cabbage, sprouts, asparagus, kale, cauliflower, beets, parsnips, carrots, turnips, French beans, broccoli, peas, beans of various sorts, eggplant, sweet potato, spinach, sorrel, squashes, salsify, mushrooms, and tomatoes.[68] Native American cookery appeared in Randolph's work in the form of maize, squash, beans, and sweet potatoes, albeit prepared using English cooking methods. Randolph offered a recipe for barbecuing shoat in *The Virginia House-Wife* (1824), although the sauce was flavored with red wine and mushroom catsup rather than the more spicy ingredients of the Lower South.

To Barbecue Shoat

This is the name given in the southern states to a fat young hog, which, when the head and feet are taken off, and it is cut into four quarters, will weigh six pounds per quarter. Take a fore quarter, make several incisions between the ribs, and stuff it with rich forcemeat; put it in a pan with a pint of water, two cloves garlic, pepper, salt, two gills of red wine, and two of mushroom catsup, bake it and thicken the gravy with butter and brown flour; it must be jointed and the ribs cut across before it is cooked, or it cannot be carved well; lay it in the dish with the ribs uppermost; if it be not sufficiently brown, add a little sugar to the gravy; garnish with balls.[69]

Slavery existed in Virginia until the end of the Civil War in 1865. Since many of the cooks in Virginia kitchens during that era were slaves, they had an obvious influence on the foodways, not only in Virginia but all over the South. Randolph offered many African-influenced recipes for gumbo, eggplant, field peas, benne, yams, sorghum, watermelon, and bananas. As one historian of Southern foodways has pointed out, African tastes were modified by exposure to West Indian cookery, which added more spicy dishes, seasoned with capsicum peppers and tomatoes, to Randolph's repertoire. Gumbo, pepper pot, and *à la daube* all clearly reflected this Creole heritage.[70] Other ethnic influences, both Spanish and Italian, in keeping with the cultural diversity and cosmopolitanism of nineteenth-century Virginia, appeared in the form of gazpacho, "pipitoria," "Olla—a Spanish Dish," and "Polenta," as well as recipes using vermicelli and macaroni.[71]

Perhaps because of Virginia's temperate climate, or maybe just because it was fashionable, Randolph offered twenty-two different ice cream recipes to her readers, including vanilla, raspberry, strawberry, coconut, chocolate, oyster, iced jelly, peach, coffee, quince, citron, almond, black walnut, lemon, and lemon ice. The hot climate of the South also generated a preference for quick breads, using saleratus or baking powder as leavening instead of yeast, as well as for a variety of sweetened cold drinks.

Gulf Coast Cookery

A very different culinary culture prevailed on the Gulf Coast of Louisiana, one which blended French, Spanish, Cajun, and Creole traditions. Termed the "tepid melting pot" by food historians, New Orleans foodways varied considerably from those of the Tidewater—although both are considered "Southern."[72] In New Orleans, jambalaya, a legacy of the Spanish, stood side by side with *bouillabaisse* and gumbo—two fish stews that characterize this region, unique in their use of *filé* (made from pounded sassafras leaves) or young okra pods as thickener. Lafcadio Hearn summarized the character of "La Cuisine Creole," or Creole cookery, in the introduction to his cookbook of the same title. Creole cookery, he wrote, "partakes of the nature of its birthplace—New Orleans—which is cosmopolitan in tis nature, blending the characteristics of the American, French, Spanish, Italian, West Indian, and Mexican." He specifically mentioned gumbo *filé, bouillabaisse, court bouillon*, jambalaya, *salade á la russe*, bisque of crayfish *á la Creole, pusse café, café brulée*, and *café brulot* as important New Orleans contributions to Southern cookery. His cookbook, *La Cuisine Creole: A Collection of Culinary Recipes, From Leading Chefs and Noted Creole Housewives, Who Have Made New Orleans Famous for its Cuisine* (1885) included a recipe for "Bouille-abaisse," as well as for nine varieties of "Gombo."

Bouille-Abaisse

Chop some onions and garlic very fine, fry them in olive oil, and when slightly colored add some fish cut up in slices; also a few tomatoes scalded, peeled and sliced, some salt, black and red pepper, thyme, sweet-bay, parsley, and half a bottle of white wine, and enough water to cover the fish. Put it over a brisk fire and boil a quarter of an hour. Put slices of toasted bread in a deep dish, place the fish on a shallow dish with some broth, and pour the balance on the bread and serve hot.[73]

Hearn's gumbos were made using either *filé* or okra and included chicken with oysters, oysters alone, crab, or shrimp.[74] "This is a most excellent form of soup," he commented, "and is an economical way of using up the remains of any cold roasted chicken, turkey, game, or other meats." He advised cutting up and seasoning the meat, then browning it in lard or drippings, adding water, and boiling for about two hours. Remove the bones and add either okra or "a preparation of dried and pounded sassafras leaves, called filee. This makes the difference in gombo." Either of these two ingredients "gives the smoothness so desirable in this soup." When in season, oysters, shrimp, or crabs may be added, as well as tomatoes and green corn, and the whole should be served over white rice.[75] Most of Hearn's gumbo recipes were further seasoned with onion, leeks, parsley, and frequently, a pod of red pepper.

The use of hot peppers and pepper sauces, another characteristic of Southern cookery, was a necessity of the hot climate, which required multiple ways of spicing and preserving foods. Pickles, chutneys, curries, barbecue sauces, flavored vinegars, and ketchups all helped to pique the appetite, as well as preserve foods. Taken in quantity, pepper and other "hot" spices also helped cool the body—an important attribute in the warm Gulf climate.[76] The McIlhenny Company began producing its hot pepper sauce on Avery Island in Louisiana in 1868. Within two years, Edmund McIlhenny had patented his fiery hot "Tabasco" sauce, made from capsicum peppers, salt, and vinegar. By 1872, the demand was so great that McIlhenny opened an office in London to manage the European market.[77]

African Heritage Cookery

African-American cooks exerted a strong and lasting influence on Southern cookery. Slave diets were strictly controlled by the generosity, or lack thereof, of the masters, as well as by traditional African culinary customs. Typically, small amounts of meat or fish had to be stretched into a larger one-pot dish such as Hoppin' John, jambalaya, burgoo, gumbo, pilau (pilaf), pepper pot, some other sort of soup or stew, through the addition of rice, beans, cornmeal, okra, yams, tomatoes, eggplant, and anything else that was readily available.[78] Hoppin' John, a classic Southern dish with African ancestry, combined ham hocks, black-eyed peas or other forms of local beans, and rice. In South Carolina, rice was especially important as a dietary staple, and rice soups, pilaus, and casseroles abounded in Southern cookbooks. Most of these rice dishes were traditional meat, fish, and vegetable combinations, but the common addition of okra as an ingredient put a Southern, and specifically African-American, spin on the recipes.[79] *The Carolina Rice Book*, a collection of traditional rice recipes collected and published in 1901, preserves the rice kitchen cookery that dominated the Lowland South during the nineteenth century. Many of the recipes came from the African-American cooks of the Carolina ladies from whom Louisa Cheeves Smythe Stoney sought contributions, cooks whose influence had been paramount but who were declining in numbers by the late nineteenth century. Stoney had used several important nineteenth-century sources for her compilation, including *The Carolina Housewife*, published in 1842, *Fifty Years in a Maryland Kitchen*, which appeared in 1873, and *Mrs. Hill's New Cook Book*, written by a Georgia widow in 1871. Her reliance on these, and other older recipe sources, makes her work an important source for Southern cookery of the Victorian era.[80] Stoney proclaimed the importance and value of rice in her prefatory remarks, stating, "Rice is more generally and widely used as a food material than any other cereal. A combination of rice and legume is a much cheaper, complete food ration than wheat and meat, and can be produced on a much smaller area."[81] Stoney's work demonstrated clearly the pervasiveness of rice in Southern cookery, with recipes for rice breads, cakes, soups, pilaus, pies, curries, casseroles, croquettes, puddings—both sweet and savory—dumplings, blancmange, and custards. Pilau, described as "the most characteristic dish of the Carolina rice kitchen," drew its origins from Persia, India, and France, but in Carolina became essentially a combination of chicken, bacon, and rice.[82] Stoney reprinted an 1842 recipe for "Carolina Pilau" (as well as eleven other varieties of pilau). The recipe began with bacon, boiled with washed rice and fowl and seasoned simply with salt and pepper. "In serving up, which should be done as soon as possible after the fowls are cooked through, put the rice in a dish, and the bacon and fowl on it."[83]

Other Southern food writers, including former slave Abby Fisher, also frequently mentioned rice dishes, including "Jumberlie—A Creole Dish." To make this dish, Fisher began with a chicken, which she cut up and then stewed with rice, six tomatoes, and sweet ham, well seasoned with pepper and salt. "It will cook in twenty-five minutes," she advised, "Do not put any water on it."[84]

Fried chicken, another African legacy, appeared routinely in nineteenth-century Southern cookbooks, from Mary Randolph on. Generally, the recipes called for dredging a cut-up chicken with flour and seasonings and then pan-frying in lard and bacon drippings. Gravy, made from fat, flour, and milk, completed the dish. These two recipes, although spread out over more than a half century, captured the essence of Southern fried chicken: hot, crisp, well seasoned, and swimming in a rich, creamy gravy. The first is from Mary Randolph, *The Virginia House-Wife* (1828), and the second from Lofcadio Hearn, *La Cuisine Creole* (1885).

Fried Chickens

Cut them up as for fricassee, dredge them well with flour, sprinkle them with salt, put them into a good quantity of boiling lard, and fry them a light brown, fry small pieces of mush and a quantity of parsley nicely picked to be served in

the dish with the chickens, take half a pint of rich milk, add to it a small bit of
butter with pepper, salt, and chopped parsley, stew it a little, and pour it over
the chickens, and then garnish with the fried parsley.[85]

Country Fried Chicken

Take a young, fat chicken, cut it up, pepper and salt it, dredge it over with
flour, and set it by while you mix a cup of lard, and some slices of fat bacon in a
frying pan. Let the lard get very hot, then drop in a few pieces of the chicken,
always allowing room in the pan for each piece to be turned without crowding.
As fast as you fry the pieces, put them on a dish over hot water to keep the heat
in them while you make the gravy. Pour off some of the grease the chicken was
fried in, and then dredge into the fryingpan some flour, let this brown nicely
and then pour into it a cup of sweet milk, little at a time; let it froth up, and
then place your chicken back into the gravy for three minutes. If you like the
chicken brown and dry, pour the gravy under it on the dish for serving.[86]

The Upland South

The upland South, which encompassed mountainous areas more
remote from the coast and urban influences, had its own food culture. Much of western Maryland, Virginia, North and South Carolina,
Georgia, and Alabama, as well as Kentucky, Tennessee, Arkansas, and
Missouri, were in the process of settlement during the nineteenth century or were always sparsely settled because of topography, and the
foodways reflected that isolation. Homesteaders relied on game and
foraged produce to a greater extent than their cousins on the coast.
Hogs, which were able to run wild in the wooded landscape, provided a
central menu item—in great variety. Slaughtered hogs presented their
owners with ham, bacon, sausage, salt pork, chops, steaks, and ribs.
The meat was typically smoked, salted, or brined to preserve it. Bits
of smoked ham could greatly enhance stews, soups, pilaus, casseroles,
and other one-pot meals. Pork steaks and chops were broiled or fried
in lard, and pork roasts were dressed with a side of applesauce. On
special occasions, a whole pig might be roasted, perhaps according
to the directions offered by former slave from Alabama, Mrs. Abby
Fisher. At the time that Fisher wrote this recipe (1881), she was living
in San Francisco, which explains her reliance on a butcher for her pig
instead of one that had been slaughtered in the farmyard.

Roast Pig

Examine when it comes from the butcher and see that it is completely cleaned.
The pig should be roasted the same way you would a turkey well done. For the
stuffing take a loaf and one-half of baker's bread cut thin, fry the bread in butter

or lard and mash it well; season it with salt and pepper according to taste, using a little red pepper. Then stuff the pig putting an apple in its mouth. Put it in the pan and baste with lard, then put it to roast, and while it is cooking keep basting it every five or ten minutes until it is cooked; you can tell when it is perfectly done by a fork passing through it easily. To make the gravy for the pig—After it is cooked, take about a tablespoonful of flour and put it in the pan where you cooked your roast and brown well on the stove, then add a little water; stir till it commences to get thick. A little onion in your stuffing is good.[87]

No part of the pig was wasted. Whatever was left over after butchering went into sausages of various kinds, including souse. Souse, a jellied sausage, was made by boiling down all the head, feet, ears, and other bits and bones into a tender mass, which was seasoned with salt, pepper, cayenne, green onion, and parsley. Finally, the picked-over cooked meat was pressed into bowls until it solidified. Souse was sliced onto plates and served cold.[88]

In addition to pig, Southern cooks and particularly those living in upland areas relied on small game and wild birds to supplement their diets. Squirrels were stewed, made into soups, pies, and dumplings. Southern food writer Martha McCulloch Williams reminded her readers, "Furred game, as rabbits, squirrels, possums, ought to be drawn before it is cold, if you would have the finest flavor. This is especially necessary with possums—which should be bought alive, and fattened for several weeks in a clean cage, feeding them on bread, milk, apples, potatoes, cabbage leaves, and grass. This makes them tender and much more delicate in flavor."[89] Quail, squab, woodcock, pigeon, pheasant, grouse, and other game birds were hunted, plucked, skinned, and roasted to perfection. "Of game birds the woodcock outranks all in delicate tenderness and sweet flavor," wrote *Buckeye Cookery* author Estelle Woods Wilcox in 1876, the year of America's Centennial. Despite the progress that had been made since the signing of the Declaration of Independence, those Americans living on the developing frontiers, especially in the upland South, utilized a hybrid cuisine of modern consumables and traditional foods that could be hunted and gathered locally.

Corn in Southern Cookery

Once the forests were cleared, frontier settlers planted corn and, to a lesser extent, wheat—which quickly became such Southern staples as hush puppies, corn pone, corn fritters, spoon bread, cornbread, mush, the ubiquitous hominy, and its equally ubiquitous kin, grits. Hominy, made by removing the hulls from the grains of corn, either by threshing or, more commonly, by prolonged soaking in a bath of lye and water, had been a staple on Southern tables since the earliest settlements. The word "hominy" actually refers to the dried, hulled, white grains of corn, which could then be ground into a fine meal called grits. Grits appeared commonly on breakfast tables, either as a cereal with milk and sugar or in some fried form. Mary Henderson included a breakfast recipe for "Baked Hominy Grits" in 1877 that involved boiling grits in milk for twenty minutes, then cooling and stirring in beaten eggs, and baking for half an hour.[90] Grits were also mixed with meats or fish and sometimes other vegetables to produce such dishes as hog and hominy, *grillades* and grits, grits and liver pudding, or batter-fried shrimp and hominy.[91]

Southern cooks prepared other forms of corn, whether green, ripe, on-the-cob, canned, parched, or pickled. Mark Twain had reminisced about "Green corn, cut from the ear and served with butter and pepper," as well as green corn on the ear, Southern-style hot corn pone with chitterlings, and Southern-style hot hoecake.[92] New Orleans writer Lofcadio Hearn discussed numerous corn-based recipes in *La Cuisine Creole*, including green corn on the cob, stewed green corn, green corn fritters, succotash, corn oysters, roasting corn pudding, okra and corn fricassee, corn batter bread, Mississippi corn bread, and three recipes using "Indian" or cornmeal.[93] Green corn fritters seemed to be a particular favorite of Hearn (as well as many other Victorian food writers), made by beating together eggs and milk and then adding a pint of boiled and grated green corn. The ensuing batter was seasoned with salt and pepper and thickened with flour until it could be mounded onto a spoon and then dropped into boiling lard. According to Hearn, "This is a great luxury and a good substitute for oysters during the hot season."[94]

Corn pone had such strong Southern associations that author Angelina Maria Collins prefaced her recipe for it with the phrase "Carry Me Back to Old Virginny." Corn pone was made from a cornmeal and boiling water batter. According to Collins, "This bread cannot be baked in anything but an oven, (Dutch oven,) or deep skillet; if baked any other way," she added, "it would not, could not, be CORN PONE."[95] Along similar lines, "Kentucky Corn Dodgers" were also made from cornmeal but formed into long, thin tea cakes, "the size of a hand, and an inch thick." Like corn pone, dodgers could be baked in Dutch ovens, a practice that persisted until the advent of cast iron ranges and baking pans that molded the corn stick into cakes that looked like corncobs.[96]

Southern Sweets

Regardless of where they lived, Southerners had a fondness for sweet desserts. Mark Twain had reminisced about Southern apple puff and peach cobbler, two of many dishes that combined locally grown fruit, some sort of sweetener—sorghum, molasses, cane syrup, or sugar—and a flour-based pastry. Southerners expressed their tradition of hospitality in elaborate creations that graced their tea or dessert tables. Local ingredients in concert with highly skilled cooks, both black and white, and a legacy of French cookery produced such sweet specialties as jam cake, red velvet cake, sweet-potato pie, pralines, and pecan-bourbon cake, to name only a few. This recipe is from former slave Abby Fisher's cookbook, *What Mrs. Fisher Knows About Old Southern Cooking* (1881).

Sweet Potato Pie

Two pounds of potatoes will make two pies. Boil the potatoes soft; peel and mash fine through a cullender while hot; one tablespoonful of butter to be mashed in with the potato. Take five eggs and beat the yelks and whites separate and add one gill of milk; sweeten to taste; squeeze the juice of one orange, and grate one-half of the peel into the liquid. One half teaspoonful of salt in the potatoes. Have only one crust and that at the bottom of the plate. Bake quickly.[97]

THE MIDWEST

During the nineteenth century, the land that today constitutes the Midwest was a series of constantly shifting frontiers as successive waves of immigrants, from New England and the South, as well as from Europe, settled in this region. Initially, the "Old Northwest" included the territories of Ohio, Indiana, Illinois, Michigan, and Wisconsin. By the 1820s, Ohio, Indiana, and Illinois had achieved statehood and the edge of settlement had crossed the Mississippi River into Missouri. Within two decades, Michigan, Iowa, and Wisconsin had enough citizens to apply for statehood, with Minnesota not far behind. The Kansas–Nebraska Act of 1854 opened up the remaining lands of the Louisiana Purchase territory for settlement, albeit amidst much bloodshed over the issue of slavery. By the end of the Civil War, with the admission of Nebraska in 1867, the prairie lands in the center of the nation had become states in the Union, a process completed with Congressional acceptance of the Dakotas as two more new states in 1889.

The foodways of this region too, then, must be defined as much by cultural transmission via migration as by local conditions and geography. Each new group that settled Midwestern places brought along its own food culture and cookery customs. Over time, these separate strands began to interweave, producing new, culturally blended food traditions. Moreover, because the Midwest as a region was in a constant state of transition throughout the Victorian era, its culture and foodways reflected a broad continuum, from rugged and basic frontier conditions, to the cosmopolitanism of such modern urban centers as Chicago, Cincinnati, and St. Louis. Finally, because the Midwest was "in the middle," people living there were constantly exposed to the cultures of those passing through, en route to Oregon, Texas, California, and other places further west. This factor gave the Midwest and its foodways openness to new ideas and new tastes that was not always apparent in the older regions of the country.

The impact of Native Americans on the foodways of Americans settling the Midwest cannot be underestimated. By the nineteenth century, they had been living on the plains and prairies for centuries and had developed skills in hunting and gathering, as well as agriculture. The new arrivals had to rely on the local knowledge that Native peoples could provide, albeit frequently with reluctance on both sides. When settlers reached the Illinois country, they found well an established sugar bush at Sugar Creek, where the Kickapoo had been producing maple syrup for generations.[98] Midwestern settlers learned to use buffalo chips (dung) instead of wood for their cooking fires and to hunt local game, especially buffalo—but also bear, moose, venison, and other smaller species. Women learned about maize from their Native American neighbors, as well as about how to grind acorns into a flour to make acorn mush or cakes or where to find edible roots and mushrooms, honey, or local grapes and berries. In exchange, pioneer women traded their own culinary products, especially bread—when they had enough of a surplus—with local Indians, whose lifestyle and access to food had been seriously disrupted by the incursion of white settlement.[99]

The lakes and rivers of the Midwest contributed greatly to Midwestern foodways. Lakes Erie, Huron, Michigan, and Superior formed the northern boundary of Ohio, Indiana, Illinois, Michigan, Wisconsin, and Minnesota. Fish caught in those waters appeared regularly in regional cookbooks, including *Jenny June's American Cookery Book* in 1870. Author Jane Cunningham Croly included two recipes for whitefish "Lake Superior Style," both boiled and broiled. Whitefish, she commented, "is the most delicious of lake fish."[100] In addition to the Great Lakes (and many smaller ones throughout the Upper Midwest), several great rivers bisected the region, beginning with the Mississippi. These rivers tied the region together geographically, economically, and culturally. They enabled Americans from Pittsburgh, for example, to ship their goods and produce down the Ohio River, to the Mississippi, and ultimately north to Minnesota, west via the Missouri River to Montana, or south to New Orleans and the Gulf of Mexico. An abundance of freshwater fish made their way from these waters onto Midwestern American breakfast and dinner tables, as well as into urban markets, including trout, pike, pickerel, perch, bass, catfish, and eels. These were typically dredged with flour and fried, creamed, stewed, or made into chowder.[101] New York butcher Thomas De Voe commented on the fish market in 1867, noting, "It is only a few years since a regular business has been established by which the many excellent varieties from the large Western lakes, rivers, etc., have—in their proper season—been found on the tables of the citizens of either New York, Boston, Philadelphia, or Brooklyn."[102] De Voe also discussed the new practice of "growing fish" for the market to meet the growing demand and diminishing stocks. By mid-century, the combination of environmental degradation of the streams, lakes, and rivers from lumbering and industrial pollution, coupled with a surge of sport and commercial fishing, necessitated the passage of laws to protect freshwater game fish. New York State passed the first of these on April 6, 1860, prohibiting the sale of "speckled brook-trout, or spotted trout, or lake trout, between the first day of September and the first day of March." Lake trout and muskellunge were also protected.

Perhaps more than any other feature, prairie lands best define the Midwest. The prairie, a vast sea of open grassland that stretched from parts of Texas north into Canada, was unlike anything most Eastern settlers had ever seen. Because the land was relatively flat, as well as treeless, there were few landmarks on the horizon and it was easy to get lost. Those who planned to farm the prairie quickly found that their wooden plows could not cut through the dense sod. John Deere solved that problem in 1837, when he patented his self-scouring metal plow. The steel cutting edge broke through the surface easily, and the cast iron moldboard enabled this plow to shed any soil that might have collected on its surface and slowed things down. This improvement, coupled with further advances in harvesting and threshing, as well as transportation, quickly made the Midwest a major wheat-producing region for the nation. By the eve of the Civil War, fifty percent of all wheat grown in the United States came from Ohio, Indiana, Illinois,

Wisconsin, and Iowa.[103] After the war, improvements in milling, us-ing steel rollers instead of flat mill stones, elevated Minneapolis to a position of prominence in the production of wheat flour. Washburn, Crosby Company's Gold Medal Flour and John Pillsbury's XXXX Flour competed for a national market by 1880.[104]

The transcontinental railroad, completed with the driving of the golden stake at Promontory Summit, Utah, in 1869, facilitated the rise of the Midwest as a center for commercial agriculture. The rail-road catapulted Chicago to the center of that universe, both for the transshipment of grain and for the processing and shipping of meat products. The Union Stock Yard, built in 1865 and continuously ex-panded thereafter, initially covered sixty acres and housed pigs and cattle in 500 pens. Within three years, the yard could handle 21,000 head of cattle, 75,000 hogs, 22,000 sheep, and 200 horses, all at once.[105] According to one scholarly study of the rise of Chicago, the ultimate purpose of "this vast network of rails and fences," was "to assemble the animal products of the Great West, transmute them into their most marketable form, and speed them on their way to dinner tables around the world." Hogs were slaughtered on the "disassembly line" and converted to ham, bacon, chops, roasts, lard, and sausage products.[106]

Beef, however, had traditionally been grown close to its market, and slaughtered by butchers at the location where it would be sold. Chicago greatly enhanced the movement of live animals from grower to market. By the end of the century, beef too had been transformed into a product that was regularly processed far from its end destina-tion. The development of the beef industry was linked to the story of settlement of the prairie. As migrants pushed across the prairie onto the high plains, they found it easier to grow cattle than grain crops. In order to do so, however, they had to eliminate the competition for the prairie grasses posed by the native bison. During the post–Civil War era, the railroads accomplished that within a generation. Sport hunters, shooting from train windows, felled buffalo by the thou-sands. Professional hunters slaughtered the remaining herds, sending the hides back East to be converted to leather goods. By 1883, the buffalo had disappeared from the Great Plains, and cattle, en route from Texas to the Union Stockyard in Chicago, had replaced them. Cowboys drove hundreds of Texas Longhorns overland, to Abilene, Kansas, where the trail met the railroad.

Meanwhile, cattle growers in Ohio, Illinois, and Iowa engaged in mixed agriculture, growing corn and using it to fatten up their herds for the market. With the development of refrigerated transportation, using ice harvested from northern lakes and ponds,

HOG-SLAUGHTERING—THE "CUTTING" ROOM.

Hog slaughtering by means of a "disassembly line" in Cincinnati, Ohio. This woodcut, published in *Harper's Weekly* on January 11, 1868, shows the cutting room in action. (Illustration from *Harper's Weekly* [Jan 11 1868]: 28. Courtesy of Library of Congress Prints and Photographs Division, Washington, D.C. [LC-USZ62-84433])

cattle, whether from Texas or elsewhere, could be shipped to Chicago, slaughtered, and dressed for consumption prior to shipment. American consumers, by the end of the nineteenth century, gradually—if reluctantly—accepted the notion that "dressed beef" was an acceptable alternative to that freshly butchered locally.[107]

German Beer and Other Ethnic Contributions

The ethnic diversity of the Midwest nurtured a strongly hybridized food culture, reflecting, in particular, the influence of immigrants from Germany and the countries of Scandinavia. Germans had been settling in this region since it opened up for settlement after the Revolution. By the late nineteenth century, Chicago, Cincinnati, Milwaukee, St. Louis, and other new Midwestern cities had major German enclaves. Wisconsin led the way, with a population in 1880 that was fourteen percent German-born—the highest concentration in the country.[108] German immigrants brought with them a skill that transformed American drinking habits, the ability to make lager beer. Johann Wagner, a Bavarian brewer, introduced bottom-fermenting yeast in Philadelphia in 1840, a brewing practice that produced a clear, light beer that appealed to American (and most European) tastes. These newer "Bavarian," "Bohemian," and "Pilsner" beers supplanted the darker top-fermented ales, porters, and stouts that had characterized British and earlier American brews. In Milwaukee, Wisconsin, Jacob Best's Empire Brewery, founded in 1844, evolved into the Pabst Brewing Company by 1889, with an annual output of 585,300 barrels. Pabst's competitors included Joseph Schlitz, who had taken over August Krug's brewery in 1849 and transformed it into the Joseph Schlitz Brewery in 1858, and Frederic Miller, who had purchased yet another German-run Milwaukee brewery in the mid-1850s.[109] The fame of Milwaukee's brewers was surpassed only by Anheuser-Busch in St. Louis, Missouri. Anheuser-Busch had begun as one of the many small German breweries that appeared in cities throughout the United States. Georg Schneider's Bavarian Brewery changed hands twice before Eberhard Anheuser acquired it. Anheuser, in partnership with his son-in-law, Adolphus Busch—a marketing specialist—transformed the Anheuser-Busch Brewing Association into the most successful brewery in the country by expanding their market from regional to national. They used refrigerated transportation to move their beer from St. Louis to depots around the nation. "Budweis," named after a popular Bohemian Pilsner, became the first mass-produced beer in America.[110]

In addition to beer, German Americans introduced many other food traditions to their new neighbors, including cheesecake, cream cheese, hot dogs, sauerkraut, meatloaf, pretzels, and numerous other forms of baked goods. American diners who visited German restaurants learned about Rhine wines, German sausages, potato pancakes, pumpernickel bread, potato salad, *Rouladen*, sauerbraten, and numerous other German specialties.[111] American cookbook authors quickly embraced German cookery, including recipes for many "German" items, including German puffs, German Lebkuchen, German pancake soup, German sauce (a rich custard sauce flavored with Madeira or brandy), German soup (veal stock with turnips, carrots, onions, and celery, flavored with lemon and thyme and thickened with egg yolks and cream), German steamer baked ice cream (a precursor to baked Alaska), German waffles, German toast (not unlike French toast), German cabbage, German coffee cake, German cookies, and more. The following recipe is from Mary Henderson's *Practical Cooking and Dinner Giving* (1877).

German Steamer Baked Ice-Cream

This dish was at least a curiosity, served at the table of one of the German steamers. A flat, round sponge-cake served as a base. A circular mold of very hard frozen ice-cream was placed on this, and then covered with a *meringue*, or whipped white of egg, sweetened and flavored. The surface was quickly colored with a red-hot salamander, which gave the dish the appearance of being baked.

The gentleman who told me about this dish insisted that it was put into the oven and quickly colored, as the egg surrounding the cream was a sufficiently good non-conductor of heat to protect the ice for one or two minutes. However, there is less risk with a salamander.[112]

Swedish, Norwegian, and Danish immigrants also settled largely in the Midwest. Minnesota had the largest population of Scandinavians in the country in both the 1870 and 1880 census, followed by Wisconsin, Illinois, and Iowa. Norwegian immigrants Ulrik Vilhelm and Elizabeth Koren settled in Iowa in 1853. Elizabeth recorded her impressions of American food in her diary in January 1854. "The dishes here vary from boiled pork to fried pork, rare to well done, with coffee in addition (milk when we can get it), good bread and butter. To this are added now and then potatoes ... fried onions once in a while, and above all, the glass jar of pickles. That is our meal, morning, noon and evening ... Oh that I had some new potatoes and mackerel from home!"[113] Koren and countless emigrants like her brought with them the tastes and cooking rituals of their native lands, hoping to replicate them whenever possible. Mainstream Americans encountered these new foodways only rarely, transmitted through neighbors and local community activities—most of the Scandinavians were economic immigrants fleeing rural poverty and did most of their cooking at home rather than establishing a public food culture through restaurants. Swedes, in particular, clung to their native food customs well into the twentieth century. Gradually, Swedish meatballs, potato sausage, *knäckebröd* (hardtack), *Jansson's Temptation* (a julienned potato gratin with anchovies), and *sil och potatis* (herring and potatoes) infiltrated the church suppers and Grange potlucks of the upper Midwest.[114]

THE WEST

The western half of the United States developed as a richly heterogeneous food region during the second half of the nineteenth century. Much of it had been part of the empire of Spain, and after 1821, Mexico, with corresponding food preferences. The movement west

began in earnest in 1841, when the Western Emigration Society organized the first wagon train across the Rockies. Half of the migrants
went to the Oregon country, the other half to California. En route,
women cooked according to custom and the necessities of the trail.
Removed from their kitchens, women had to prepare meals outdoors,
over a campfire, hanging pots and kettles from a makeshift tripod, or
frying everything in a large skillet.[115] Minnie Miller described her family's traveling kitchen in 1883: "At the extreme back end of the wagon
was the lunch box and camping equipment. Another box contained
home cured meats and a goodly supply of beans. There was a Dutch
oven frying pan and a coffee pot. The water bucket hung on behind
and dangled all day long."[116] Women and children gathered water and
fuel—firewood, when possible, and weeds and buffalo chips when not.
Esther Hanna's diary reflected the discomfort many women felt with
outdoor cooking: "Had to haul our water and wood for night ... I
have also had to bake tonight. It is very trying on the patience to cook
and bake on a little green wood fire with the smoke blowing in your
eyes so as to blind you, and shivering with cold so as to make the teeth
chatter." Baking was made possible by using either a Dutch oven or a
covered skillet. Women also tried to bake on hot rocks, underground.
Rain made things even worse because the wet fuel would not burn.
One woman recalled, "There is nothing to eat but crackers and raw
bacon."[117]

Although meals were makeshift, the cooks demonstrated their cookery skills and ingenuity. Out of a limited array of ingredients, they con-
cocted meals that reminded their families of home. Catherine Haun,
a young bride from Iowa who crossed the plains in 1849, bound for
California, described her cookery prospects:

> The third wagon contained our household effects and provisions. The former
> consisted of cooking utensils, two boards nailed together, which was to serve
> as our dining table, some bedding and a small tent. We had a very generous
> supply of provisions. All meats were either dried or salted, and vegetables and
> fruit were dried ... For luxuries we carried a gallon each of wild plum and
> crabapple preserves and blackberry jam. Our groceries were wrapped in India
> rubber covers and we did not lose any of them—in fact still had some when we
> reached Sacramento.[118]

Provisions for another traveling family included only "hard sea biscuit,
crackers, bacon, beans, rice, dried fruit, teas, coffee, and sugar." For
most families, flour, cornmeal, baking powder, yeast, and salt would
have fleshed out the menu options. Women typically cooked pancakes

Clovernook, Alice Cary's 1852 novel about her family's early settlement of Ohio, depicted the romance of the trail in its frontispiece.
The wagon served as a mobile bedroom, living room, and kitchen.
(*Clovernook; or, Recollections of Our Neighborhood in the West*, Taylor
1852 C37 C4, Early American Fiction Collection, Special Collections, University of Virginia Library.)

for breakfast and accompanied it with fried meat, beans, and tea or coffee. If not pancakes, bread completed the meal. They also baked pies, stewed fruits and berries, and made "Dutch cheese." Supper on the trail for the family of Charlotte Stearns Pengra included griddlecakes, stewed berries, and tea. After preparing supper, Charlotte baked two loaves of bread, stewed some apples, and prepared meat and potatoes for breakfast before retiring.[119]

Emigrant guides advised taking adequate provisions for the three-month journey, but miscalculations, bad luck, or accidents, which forced families to lighten their loads, frequently made it necessary to forage. Men hunted for rabbits, prairie chickens, sage hens, quail, doves, turkeys, goose, ground squirrels, deer, buffalo, or any other source of meat they could find, including frogs. Women gathered greens, wild onion, nuts, berries, mushrooms, and whatever else they thought might be edible.[120] Although there were trading posts at the military forts along the way, where the migrants might have been able to replenish their supplies, families without money or goods to barter with often went hungry. Buffalo, in particular, offered a great source of assistance to the migrants, both as food and as fuel. Catherine Haun described her first experience with buffaloes—a stampede during which two wagons in her group were demolished. The men managed to shoot two buffaloes, however, and "the humps and tongues furnished us with fine, fresh meat. They happened to be buffalo cows and, in consequence, the meat was particularly good flavor and tender." Moreover, "one family 'jerked' some of the hump. After being cut in strips about an inch wide it was strung on ropes on the outside of the wagon cover and in two or three days was thoroughly cured. It was then packed in a bag," she continued, "and in the Humboldt Sink, when rations were low it came in very handy." Haun also commented on buffalo chips, which, "when dry, were very useful to us as fuel. On the barren plains when we were without wood we carried empty bags and each pedestrian 'picked up chips' as he, or she, walked along."[121] Not all women regarded this task as objectively as Haun. Many found buffalo dung offensive, and some were so squeamish about touching the dung that they wore gloves to collect it. According to one observer, however, "most of them . . . discarded their gloves" once they became resigned to the necessity of buffalo chips as fuel.[122]

Upon reaching their destinations, migrants on the Overland Trail began the process of farming, finding the soils and farming conditions in the Willamette Valley and California to be far superior to the rocky New England farms they had left behind. The first winter,

however, fully tested many families, as Lucy Henderson Deady recalled in 1846:

> After a great hardship ... we finally made our way through ... to Oregon. It was late in the year and the winter rains had started. We had been eight months on the road instead of five, we were out of food, and our cattle were nearly worn out. ... We lived on boiled wheat and boiled peas that winter.[123]

Once spring arrived, however, farming began in earnest, and gradually, frontier families were able to recreate some the foodways of the homes they had left behind. Cooks found local substitutes for ingredients that were unavailable on the frontier—oatmeal for wheat flour, molasses for sugar, chicory for coffee, and "mock" apple pie, mincemeat, and oysters.[124]

The discovery of gold in California in 1848 launched a massive migration to the Pacific coast. Eighty-five thousand men (and a few women) rushed west to prospect for gold the following year. San Francisco, which had been established as a Spanish mission in the sixteenth century, quickly blossomed from a ramshackle cluster of tents and impermanent buildings into an urban center full of hotels and boarding houses.[125] Mining camps dotted the area, offering enterprising women an opportunity to make money, feeding the hungry prospectors. Supplies, however, were hard to come by: meat, flour, eggs, fruit, and vegetables typically had to travel "around the Horn" by ship; when they arrived, they were often putrefied, rancid, or inedible. According to Luzena Stanley Wilson, an early settler in Vacaville, California, "The flour we used was often soured and from a single sieve-full I have sifted out at one time a handful of long black worms. The butter was brown from age and had spent a year on the way to California."[126]

During that long sea voyage around Cape Horn to San Francisco, travelers ate according to their means. Elizabeth LeBreton Gunn, sailing on the ship *Bengal,* fared well despite her bouts of seasickness. She was offered a variety of meats and vegetables, interspersed with baked goods, relishes, and sweets during her journey. "I don't like the bread," she complained on February 12. "It is light and sweet but so salty." Moreover, she continued,

> I don't feel a bit of appetite for meat three times a day, and we always have two or three kinds, and always soup. Or stew, pork and cabbage, beans, potatoes, and beets. We have bread and butter, apples and cranberries for tea. Last night the Captain's wife made doughnuts. They were sweet, but not "short" like ours. She makes all the puddings, and often the bread. I am glad of it, for she is much cleaner than the cook and steward.

"I feel quite well today," she wrote on February 29. "We had boiled salt beef and ham—very nice indeed—beets, turnips, parsnips, baked beans, bean soup, potatoes, cranberry sauce, pickles, bread, boiled rice, and apple pudding with sauce, and raw tomatoes too—all that for dinner! For tea we have chocolate, water, hot and cold bread, butter, cheese, cranberry, cold meats, crackers, and sometimes tarts, cake, or pie!"[127]

Once they arrived in California, many migrants, especially the miners, survived on beans, bacon, and cornmeal mush, washed down with whiskey. The more fortunate found women who could cook for them. Mary Ballou, in a letter to her son in 1852 from Negrobar, California, detailed the primitive conditions under which she had to cook. "All the kitchen that I have is four posts stuck down into the ground and covered over the top with factory cloth no floor but the ground. This is a Boarding House kitchen." Nonetheless, Ballou made do with her situation, preparing mince pie, apple pie, squash pie, mince turnovers, doughnuts, "Indian jonny cake," minute pudding "filled with rasons," Indian pudding, plum pudding, blueberry pudding, soups, cranberry tarts, boiled cabbage and turnips, potatoes, ham, pork, broiled steak, baked chicken, oysters, codfish, salmon trout, rabbit, quail, squirrel, gruel for the sick, and very strong coffee for the French. "Three times a day I set my Table which is about thirty feet in length and do all the little fixings about it such as filling pepper boxes and vinegar cruits and mustard pots and Butter cups," she added.[128]

With the growth of the West, a vibrant restaurant culture developed in the cities. San Francisco, Sacramento, Seattle, Denver, and other western boomtowns benefited in a culinary sense from the excessive amount of gold floating around as enterprising emigrants opened up eateries of all kinds—some very luxurious. French restaurants had great appeal in San Francisco, beginning with the Poulet d'Or, which opened its doors in 1849. The following year, the Tadisch Grill, a seafood restaurant, commenced serving, and by 1875, The Palace, a grand hotel, opened with chef Jules Harder, imported from Delmonico's in New York.[129] Most residents of San Francisco, however, ate whatever they were served in the numerous small hotels and boarding houses that dotted the city. There, the fare offered combined traditional Anglo-Saxon tastes with Spanish-Mexican and Chinese influences.

In 1851, Elizabeth LeBreton Gunn wrote a letter to her mother and sisters in Philadelphia, describing her journey from San Francisco to Sonora. In Stockton, where her party stopped for the night at a private boarding house, the landlady served a dinner of "roast beef and veal

San Francisco offered restaurant diners a wide range of options, re-flecting the heterogeneous population of gold seekers. The Chinese, who came to California to build the transcontinental railroad, found that they could serve their own cultural food needs, as well as those of a hungry public. This Chinese restaurant, photographed sometime after 1873, was elaborately furnished with carved wooden screens, gas and kerosene light fixtures dripping with crystals, and framed panels. It must have seemed quite exotic to westerners. (Courtesy of the New York Public Library Digital Library [g89f406_025f].)

pie, mashed potatoes, bread and butter, tea and a very nice dried apple pudding." She went on to reassure her family back home that she was eating well, stating, "At tea and breakfast we had dried apple pie. The mother did the cooking. They had good water, with a pump close at the door."[130] Dried apple pie appeared with great frequency on the menus of Western travelers—both on and off the trail—no doubt because the ingredients were durable and easily portable. Jane Cunningham Croly provided a recipe in *Jennie June's American Cookery Book* (1870).

Dried Apple Pies

Wash the apples in two or three waters, and put them to soak in rather more water than will cover them, as they absorb a great deal. After soaking an hour or two, put them into a preserving kettle with the same water, and with the thin peel of one or two lemons chopped fine. Boil tender; when they rise, press them down, but do not stir them. When tender, add sugar, and boil fifteen or twenty minutes longer. Dried apples, soaked over night, are made tasteless, and are mashed up by being stirred. When cooked, stir in a little melted butter, some cinnamon, and powdered cloves. It is important that the apples be of a tart kind.[131]

Other travelers in the West dined on less desirable fare. Alice Cunningham Fletcher, an early anthropologist conducting fieldwork among the Sioux in 1881, discussed her eating experiences in her journal. "We breakfasted at the daughter's who is married to a half-breed and lives white fashion," she wrote in October 1881. "Buffalo meat, coffee, bread and molasses. I ate the latter." Although she was working and living among the Sioux, Fletcher apparently could not bring herself to eat buffalo meat. Later that same month, the quality of the food had deteriorated even further. "Our fire was made in a hole, the wind blowing, and I ate bread and apricots, sour and horrid—and drank wretched coffee. The management of food is being poor in many ways. Things are getting so disagreeable that I hardly know how to get on at all."[132]

Disagreeable or not, the foodways of the West were marked by extremes of abundance and paucity, refined taste, and rustic make-do. In the emerging urban centers, cosmopolitan culinary offerings abounded in direct relation to the availability of gold and silver. On the trail, cowboys, homesteaders, tourists, and others had to settle for whatever was available among the provisions they had carried with them, augmented by whatever local ingredients they could hunt, fish, or harvest from the land alongside the trail.

NOTES

1. Alexander Hamilton, *Itinerarium*, in *Colonial American Travel Narratives*, ed. Wendy Martin (1744; New York: Penguin Books, 1994), 205.

2. For an extended discussion of immigrant food-related customs and strategies during the nineteenth century, see Donna R. Gabaccia, "Immigration, Isolation, and Industry," chapter 2 in *We Are What We Eat: Ethnic Food and the Making of Americans* (Cambridge: Harvard University Press, 1998).

3. Terry G. Jordan, *North American Cattle-Ranching Frontiers: Origins, Diffusion, and Differentiation* (Albuquerque: University of New Mexico

Press, 1993), 187; *Oxford Encyclopedia of Food and Drink in America*, s.v. "Barbecue" (by Sylvia Lovegren).

4. Mark Twain, *A Tramp Abroad*, 1880. A facsimile of the first American edition with introduction by Russell Banks and afterword by James S. Leonard, ed. Shelley Fisher Fishkin (New York: Oxford University Press, 1996), 574–575 .

5. *Oxford Encyclopedia of Food and Drink in America*, s.v. "New England Regional Cookery" (by Sandra Oliver). See also Oliver's excellent book-length study of New England regional foodways, *Saltwater Foodways: New Englanders and Their Food, at Sea and Ashore, in the Nineteenth Century* (Mystic, CT: Mystic Seaport Museum, 1995).

6. Alice Morse Earle, *Customs and Fashions in Old New England* (New York: Charles Scribner's Sons, 1893), 146–162.

7. Search for "New England" as recipe title in "Feeding America: The Historic American Cookbook Project," Michigan State University Library Web site, http://digital.lib.msu.edu/projects/cookbooks/index.html (accessed April 1, 2005).

8. Search for "Boston" in "Feeding America" Digital Archive, http://digital.lib.msu.edu/projects/cookbooks/index.html (accessed April 1, 2005).

9. *Fitchburg Almanac, Directory, and Business Advertiser for 1854* (Fitchburg, MA: Shepley & Wallace, 1854), 64.

10. *Fitchburg Directory* (Fitchburg, MA: Price, Lee & Co., 1876), 157.

11. Clay McShane, e-mail message to author, April 16, 2005.

12. *Fitchburg Directory* (1848), 43, 46; ibid. (1858), 57.

13. For fresh insights into the realities of fish eating in New England, as well as the technological and marketing changes that occurred during the nineteenth century with regard to fish and shellfish, see Oliver, *Saltwater Foodways*, 331–352; 363–369.

14. *Fitchburg Directory* (1848), 53

15. Folklorist Kathy Neustadt has argued that clams did not appear as a symbolic New England dish until 1720, when they were consumed to commemorate the centennial of the landing of the Pilgrims. See Neustadt, *Clambake: A History and Celebration of an American Tradition* (Amherst: University of Massachusetts Press, 1992), 29–32, and Oliver, *Saltwater Foodways*, 282–289.

16. Neustadt, 41, 46.

17. *Appleton's Illustrated Handbook of American Travel*, ed. T. Addison Richards (New York: D. Appleton and Co., 1860), quoted in Neustadt, *Clambake*, 55, n. 25.

18. Mary J. Lincoln, *Mrs. Lincoln's Boston Cook Book* (Boston: Little, Brown and Co., 1883, 1900), 180.

19. Ibid., 180–181.

20. For a history of chowder in America, see Andrew F. Smith, *Souper Tomatoes: The Story of America's Favorite Food* (New Brunswick: Rutgers University Press, 2000), 71–73.

21. Jane Cunningham Croly, *Jennie June's American Cookery Book* (New York: American News Company, 1870), 72; digital edition available at "Feeding America" Web site, http://digital.lib.msu.edu/projects/cookbooks/index.html (accessed May 23, 2005).

22. Sarah McMahon has documented the transformation of rural New England diet from the seventeenth to the nineteenth century, describing in detail the meat stews or pottages, accompanied by bread, pudding, or cake that characterized early American meals. Sarah McMahon, "A Comfortable Subsistence: the Changing Composition of Diet in Rural New England, 1620–1840," *William and Mary Quarterly* 42, no.1 (January 1985): 31–32. See also Oliver, *Saltwater Foodways*, 79. For an extended discussion of New Englanders and their baked beans, see Kevin Stavely and Kathleen Fitzgerald, *America's Founding Food: The Story of New England Cooking* (Chapel Hill: University of North Carolina Press, 2004), 55–65.

23. Quoted in Stavely and Fitzgerald, *America's Founding Food*, 56.

24. Mary F. Henderson, *Practical Cooking and Dinner Giving* (New York: Harper & Brothers, 1877), 162–163.

25. Lincoln, 249–250.

26. Larry Zuckerman, *The Potato: How the Humble Spud Rescued the Western World* (New York: North Point Press, 1998), 88–90.

27. Manuscript diary, written in *The Fitchburg Almanac, Directory, and Business Advertiser for 1863* (Fitchburg, MA: R. Wallace & Co., 1863), Special Collections, Fitchburg State College Library, Fitchburg, MA.

28. Lydia Maria Child, *The American Frugal Housewife* (1832; reprint Worthington, OH: Worthington Historical Society, 1965), 34.

29. Zuckerman, 32.

30. Maria Parloa, *Miss Parloa's New Cook Book, A Guide to Marketing and Cooking* (Boston: Estes and Lauriat, 1888), 49.

31. Karal Ann Marling, *George Washington Slept Here: Colonial Revivals and American Culture, 1876–1986* (Cambridge: Harvard University Press, 1988), 42.

32. Rodris Roth, "New England Kitchen Exhibits," in *Colonial Revival in America*, ed. Alex Axelrod (New York: W. W. Norton & Co., 1985): 179.

33. Keith Stavely and Kathleen Fitzgerald have discussed the history of Indian pudding in *America's Founding Food: The Story of New England Cooking* (Chapel Hill: University of North Carolina Press, 2004), 15–19.

34. Mary Hooker Cornelius, *The Young Housekeeper's Friend* (Boston: Brown, Taggard and Chase, 1859), 84. Traditionally, Indian pudding was served as a side dish with roasted meat, or for breakfast. The inclusion of a sweet sauce suggests dessert, a change of use.

35. Child, 61; Parloa, 267–268.

36. Parloa, 267–268.

37. For histories of gingerbread, see Alan Davidson, *The Oxford Companion to Food* (New York: Oxford University Press, 1999), 338–339; Stavely and Fitgerald, *America's Founding Food*, 244–252.

38. Parloa, 328–329.

39. Search for "Gingerbread" in "Feeding America" Digital Archive, http://digital.lib.msu.edu/projects/cookbooks/index.html (accessed June 2, 2005).

40. Stavely and Fitzgerald, 252–252.

41. Sherbrooke Rogers, *Sarah Josepha Hale: A New England Pioneer, 1788–1879* (Grantham, NH: Tompson & Rutter, 1985), 96–97.

42. Ibid., 97.

43. Although Lincoln's proclamation established the custom of celebrating Thanksgiving as a national holiday, it was not until the presidency of Franklin Roosevelt that the *third* Thursday of November was established in law as a Thanksgiving holiday. His change of date was a concession to business interests, who wanted a longer pre-Christmas shopping season; see Rogers, 101–102.

44. Donna R. Gabaccia, "Ethnic Entrepreneurs," chapter in *We Are What We Eat: Ethnic Food and the Making of Americans* (Cambridge: Harvard University Press, 1998), 64–92.

45. Frances Milton Trollope, *Domestic Manners of the Americans*, 4th ed. (London; New York: Whittaker, Treacher, & Co, 1832), 173.

46. See Waverley Root and Richard de Rochemont's extended history of the Delmonico family and their restaurants in *Eating in America: A History* (1976; New York: Ecco Press, 1981), 321–334.

47. Ibid., 327.

48. Ibid., 333.

49. Menu, G. Byron Morse, Philadelphia, ca. 1875, Menu Collection, Library Company of Philadelphia (5763 43a).

50. *Oxford Encyclopedia of Food and Drink in America*, s.v. "Oyster Bars" (by Joan Reardon).

51. Franklin House Menu, 4 December 1855, Philadelphia (5763 F9); St. Louis Hotel Menu, November 16, 1863, Philadelphia (5763 F23); Leach's Restaurant Menu (5763 F55), Philadelphia, all from Menu Collection, Library Company of Philadelphia.

52. Parloa, *New Cook Book*, 39–40, 148–49.

53. Eliza Leslie, *The Lady's Receipt-Book; A Useful Companion For Large Or Small Families* (Philadelphia: Carey And Hart, 1847), 94–96, digital edition available on "Feeding America" Web site, http://digital.lib.msu.edu/projects/cookbooks/index.html (accessed June 22, 2005).

54. Eliza Leslie, *Miss Leslie's Directions for Cookery: An Unabridged Reprint of the 1851 Classic*. A facsimile of the 1851 edition with an introduction by Jan Longone (Mineola, NY: Dover Publications, 1999), 149.

55. William Woys Weaver, ed., *A Quaker Woman's Cookbook: The Domestic Cookery of Elizabeth Ellicott Lea* (Philadelphia: University of Pennsylvania Press, 1982), xix.

56. Elizabeth Ellicott Lea, *Domestic Cookery, Useful Receipts, and Hints to Young Housekeepers* (Baltimore: Cushings and Bailey, 1853; reprinted in

Weaver, *A Quaker Woman's Cookbook*), 38. For a more extended discussion of terrapin, see Mary Anne Hines, Gordon Marshall, and William Woys Weaver, *The Larder Invaded: Reflections on Three Centuries of Philadelphia Food and Drink* (Philadelphia: The Library Company of Philadelphia and The Historical Society of Pennsylvania, 1987), 50. See also William Woys Weaver, *35 Receipts from "The Larder Invaded"* (Philadelphia: The Library Company of Philadelphia and The Historical Society of Pennsylvania, 1987), 35–37.

57. Colonel John W. Forney, "Terrapin," *The Epicure* (New York: H. K & F. B. Thurber Co., 1879), 32, quoted in Weaver, *35 Receipts*, 37.

58. Lea, 38–42.

59. Ibid., 40.

60. Ibid., 44–57; Leslie, 183–205; Robert Buist, *The Family Kitchen Gardener* (New York: C. M. Saxton & Co., 1855), 16–18.

61. Catharine Esther Beecher, *Miss Beecher's Domestic Receipt Book: Designed as a Supplement to Her Treatise on Domestic Economy* (1846; reprint New York: Harper, 1850), 102.

62. Weaver, *35 Receipts*, 43.

63. Anne Cooper Funderburg, *Chocolate, Strawberry, and Vanilla: A History of American Ice Cream* (Bowling Green, OH: Bowling Green State University Popular Press, 1995), 51–53. See also *Oxford Encyclopedia of Food and Drink in America*, s.v. "Ice Creams and Ices" (by Jeri Quinzio).

64. Weaver, *35 Receipts*, 43.

65. Juliet Corson, *Miss Corson's Practical American Cookery and Household Management*, 4th ed. (New York: Dodd, Mead & Co., 1886), 527, digital edition available on "Feeding America" Web site, http://digital.lib.msu.edu/projects/cookbooks/index.html (accessed June 27, 2005).

66. Beecher, 167.

67. Twain, 574–575.

68. Gervase Markham, *The English Housewife*, ed. Michael R. Best (1615; reprint Montreal: McGill-Queens University Press, 1986), 60–124; Mary Randolph, *The Virginia House-Wife*, ed. Karen Hess (1824; reprint Columbia: University of South Carolina Press, 1984), v–vi.

69. Randolph, 63.

70. Karen Hess, "Historical Notes and Commentaries on Mary Randolph's *The Virginia House-Wife*," in *The Virginia House-Wife*, xxix–xxx.

71. Hess, "Historical Notes," xxxii–xxxiii.

72. Root and de Rochemont, 282.

73. Lafcadio Hearn, *La Cuisine Creole* (New Orleans: F. F. Hansell & Bro., Ltd., 1885), 252; digital edition available at "Feeding America" Web site, http://digital.lib.msu.edu/projects/cookbooks/index.html (accessed July 26, 2005).

74. Hearn, 252, 261.

75. Hearn, 18–19.

76. Davidson, *Oxford Companion to Food*, s.v. "Pepper."

77. Linda Stradley, "Tabasco Pepper Sauce," "What's Cooking in America" Web site, http://whatscookingamerica.net/History/Tabasco.htm (accessed June 20, 2005).

78. *Oxford Encyclopedia of Food and Drink in America,* s.v. "Southern Regional Cookery" (by John Martin Taylor).

79. Karen Hess, *The Carolina Rice Kitchen: The African Connection* (Columbia: University of South Carolina Press, 1992), 111–113. Hess has discussed the importance of okra as an agent of cultural transmission from Africa to the New World via slavery. Her analysis of African gumbo stews, whether in Louisiana or Carolina, points out the frequent relationship between okra and rice in Southern rice soups. See also Hess's discussion of the ethnohistory of Hoppin' John in chapter 5, "Hoppin' John and Other Bean Pilaus of the African Diaspora": 92–110.

80. Hess, *Carolina Rice Kitchen,* 152–155.

81. Mrs. Samuel G. Stoney, *Carolina Rice Cook Book* (Charleston, SC: Carolina Rice Kitchen Association, 1901; reprinted in Hess, *The Carolina Rice Kitchen*), 5.

82. Hess has carefully tracked the culinary ethnography of pilau in "Pilau and Its Kind," in *The Carolina Rice Kitchen*: 36–83.

83. Stoney, 51.

84. Abby Fisher, *What Mrs. Fisher Knows about Old Southern Cooking* (San Francisco: Co-op Printing Office, 1881), 57; digital edition available at "Feeding America" Web site, http://digital.lib.msu.edu/projects/cookbooks/index.html (accessed July 26, 2005).

85. Randolph, 253.

86. Hearn, 66–67.

87. Fisher, 19.

88. For a modern souse recipe, see John T. Edge, *A Gracious Plenty: Recipes and Recollections from the American South* (New York: G. P. Putnam's Sons, 1999), 19.

89. Martha McCulloch Williams, *Dishes & Beverages of The Old South* (New York: McBride, Nast & Co., 1913), 166.

90. See Betty Fussell's discussion of hominy and grits in *The Story of Corn* (New York: Alfred A. Knopf, 1992), 195–200; Mary F. Henderson, *Practical Cooking and Dinner Giving* (New York: Harper & Brothers, 1877), 71.

91. Fussell, 199.

92. Twain, n. 4.

93. Hearn, 84–86, 127–128, 135.

94. Ibid., 85.

95. Angelina Maria Collins, *The Great Western Cook Book* (New York: A. S. Barnes & Co., 1857), 62; digital edition available at "Feeding America" Web site, http://digital.lib.msu.edu/projects/cookbooks/index.html (accessed July 30, 2005).

96. Beecher, 102–203; Fussell, 223.

97. Fisher, 26.

98. John Mack Faragher, "Hunters and Sugar Makers," in *Sugar Creek: Life on the Illinois Prairie* (New Haven: Yale University Press, 1986), 10–17.

99. Julie Roy Jeffrey, *Frontier Women*, rev. ed. (New York: Hill and Wang, 1979), 53–59, 71–73; Cathy Luchetti, *Home on the Range: A Culinary History of the American West* (New York: Villard Books, 1993), xxviii–xxix.

100. Croly, 65.

101. See, for example, Marion Harland, *Common Sense in the Household: A Manual of Practical Housewifery* (1871; reprint Birmingham, AL: Oxmoor House, 1985), 65–68. Harland listed recipes for fried trout, fried pickerel, cream pickerel, fried perch and other pan-fish, stewed catfish, fried catfish, catfish chowder, fried eels, and stewed eels.

102. Thomas F. De Voe, *The Market Assistant* (New York: Hurd and Houghton, 1867), 180–189.

103. Brooke Hindle and Steven Lubar, *Engines of Change: The American Industrial Revolution, 1790–1860* (Washington, DC: Smithsonian Institution Press, 1986), 97–99.

104. *Oxford Encyclopedia of Food and Drink in America*, s.v. "Wheat" (by Andrew F. Smith).

105. William Cronon, *Nature's Metropolis: Chicago and the Great West* (New York: W. W. Norton & Co., 1991), 210.

106. Ibid., 211, 228–229.

107. Ibid., 233–247.

108. Minnesota (8.58%), Indiana (7.66%), New York (7%), and Nebraska (6.86%) followed Wisconsin in percentage of German-born versus total population in 1880, "United States in 1880 Persons Born in the German Empire/Total Population (Percent)." Retrieved from the University of Virginia Library Historical Census Browser, Geospatial and Statistical Data Center, http://fisher.lib.virginia.edu/collections/stats/histcensus/index.html (accessed August 17, 2005).

109. Bill Yenne, *Beers of North America* (New York: Gallery Books, 1986), 17–26.

110. Yenne, 31–35.

111. *Oxford Encyclopedia of Food and Drink in America*, s.v. "German American Food" (by Mark Zanger).

112. Search for "German" as recipe title in "Feeding America" Digital Archive, http://digital.lib.msu.edu/projects/cookbooks/index.html (accessed January 23, 2006); recipe from Henderson, *Practical Cooking and Dinner Giving*, 310.

113. Luchetti, 137–138.

114. Anne R. Kaplan, Marjorie A. Hoover, and Willard A. Moore, *The Minnesota Ethnic Food Book* (St. Paul: Minnesota Historical Society Press, 1986), 131–139.

115. Jeffrey, 52–53.

116. Luchetti, 46.

117. Lillian Schlissel, *Women's Diaries of the Westward Journey* (New York: Schocken Books, 1982), 80.

118. Catherine Haun, "A Woman's Trip Across the Plains, 1849," Manuscript Diary reprinted in Schlissel, 167.

119. Schlissel, 80–81. There are two possible interpretations for the term "Dutch Cheese." According to Aunt Babette's cookbook, this was a sort of cheese streudel. Mary Lincoln, however, included a recipe for sour milk cheese and noted that it was also known as "Dutch, Curd, or Cottage Cheese." See Bertha F. Kramer, *"Aunt Babette's" Cook Book* (Cincinnati: Block Publishing and Printing Co., 1889), 252 and *Mrs. Lincoln's Boston Cook Book* (Boston: Roberts Brothers, 1884), 283 [both accessed on "Feeding America" Web site, http://digital.lib.msu.edu/projects/cookbooks/index.html (accessed July 22, 2005)].

120. Luchetti, 111.

121. Schlissel, 176–177.

122. Jeffrey, 54.

123. Lucy Henderson Deady, "Crossing the Plains to Oregon in 1846," *Transactions of the Oregon Pioneer Association* (1928): 57–64, cited in Schlissel, 51.

124. Luchetti, 113–116.

125. Jeffrey, 142–146.

126. Luchetti, 66.

127. Elizabeth Le Breton Bunn to Family in Philadelphia, February 29, 1851, Records of a California family; journals and letters of Lewis C. Gunn and Elizabeth Le Breton Gunn, ed. Anna Lee Marston (San Diego, CA, 1929); available online at "California as I Saw It: First Person Narratives of California's Early Years, 1849–1900," http://memory.loc.gov/ammem/cbhtml/cbhome.html (accessed August 25, 2005).

128. Luchetti, 63–64.

129. Root and de Rochemont, 177, 349.

130. Elizabeth LeBreton Gunn to her family in Philadelphia, August 24, 1851. Records of a California family; journals and letters of Lewis C. Gunn and Elizabeth Le Breton Gunn, edited by Anna Lee Marston (San Diego, CA, 1929); available online at "California as I Saw It: First Person Narratives of California's Early Years, 1849–1900," http://memory.loc.gov/ammem/cbhtml/cbhome.html (accessed August 25, 2005).

131. Croly, 149.

132. Fieldwork Diary of Alice Cunningham Fletcher, October 13 and 24, 1881. Web site: "Camping with the Sioux: Fieldwork Diary of Alice Cunningham Fletcher," National Anthropological Archives, Smithsonian Institution, http://www.nmnh.si.edu/naa/fletcher/fletcher.htm (accessed September 30, 2005).

CHAPTER 5
EATING HABITS

"A Simple Company Dinner," offered as a menu to the readers of *The Successful Housekeeper*, in 1883, began with a first course of oysters on the half shell, followed by *Soup à la Reine*. For a fish course, the authors proposed salmon, accompanied by green peas or sliced cucumbers, and sherry. *Filet de Boeuf* and mushrooms, the main course, included a side of fried potatoes, as well as white wine. A salad of lettuce or tomatoes, champagne, then cold chicken and olives with Madeira, and a dessert of ices and jellies, cheese, fruits, and more sherry followed this. Coffee and cordials completed this "simple" menu.[1]

Clearly, this meal, with its layers of courses, rich menu items, French recipes, multiple wines, and colorful desserts, was designed for maximum social impact. Dinner, for Victorian Americans, implied a great deal more than the mere ingestion of good food. In a world where older means of defining social relations—deference, hierarchy, and religious orthodoxy—were declining in the face of social, geographic, and occupational mobility, urbanization, and industrial capitalism, dining rituals helped to define and maintain notions of civility. For a rapidly growing American middle class, the meal structure, food served, presentation, and dining rituals all reinforced new standards of gentility. Armed with a new awareness of the power of visual presentation through behavior, dress, and goods—including those associated with the consumption of food—middle-class families worked hard to conform to those modes that would set them apart from those whom they perceived to be of lesser station. As one writer put it, "Show me the way people dine and I will tell you their rank among civilized beings. It is a duty we owe ourselves and one another to glorify and

The frontispiece of *The Successful Housekeeper* offered an array of food delicacies worthy of any Victorian table. The featured items included turkey "garnished with flowers," sandwiches, tongue, two different molded jellies, a game pie on aspic jelly, lobster, and ham. On the center of the table, a glass epergne presided, filled with flowers and surrounded by fruits, sweetmeats, and tiny cups of punch. (M. W. Ellsworth and F. B. Dickerson, *The Successful Housekeeper* [Detroit, MI: M. W. Ellsworth and Co., 1882].)

refine eating and drinking, so as to place an infinite distance between ourselves and the brutes, even at the moment when we are enjoying a pleasure which we have in common with them."[2]

During the nineteenth century, the way people dined was literally reshaped by a modern market economy that transformed the processing and distribution of foodstuffs. Once American consumers could choose between locally grown and locally processed fruits, vegetables, meats, and comestibles and those grown and processed in faraway places, their options for menu planning and food service increased dramatically. The availability of seafood, for example, shipped by rail from both coasts, or fruits and vegetables grown in California or Florida and transported to New York or New England, greatly expanded the options open for elaboration and specialization within food rituals. Genteel dining required an elevated level of skill and performance, whether in the kitchen or in the dining room. Food and its presentation offered an important way to demonstrate one's command of the fundamentals of high-style culture. Because public performance was such an integral part of dining rituals, middle-class dinners became imbued with a new theatricality, complete with props, costumes, acts, and dramatic narrative.

The economic expansion of the Victorian era, especially after 1840, enabled much higher levels of consumer participation in these new food and dining rituals, both inside the home and out. At home, dining rooms became regular features of modern house designs, complete with an established kit of accessories and furnishings—in the manner of the European bourgeoisie about whom middle-class Americans could read in newly published books and magazines. As newspapers reported on the doings of the elites, ordinary Americans learned the details of their behaviors and began to emulate them in their own dining rooms. Moreover, Americans traveled with greater frequency, consuming their meals in railroad and steamship dining cars, hotels, and restaurants. In these new settings, they encountered wealthier Americans—who had highly developed modes of refined public eating and drinking.

Among the Victorian middle class, women in particular served as the arbiters of good manners and taste in the dining room, as well as elsewhere in the household. As the nation shifted from an agrarian to a more cosmopolitan urban economy and culture, women's importance as domestic producers in the family economy declined. No longer required to spin and weave, to make butter and cheese, or to grow a significant portion of their family's food, many American women moved into a new sphere, one charged with the maintenance of the moral character of the family. Their new worth, as "homemakers" and "domestic engineers," was expressed in terms of their ability to create household environments that would inculcate their children and husbands with the Protestant values of thriftiness, industry, and sobriety. According to Sarah Josepha Hale, editor of *Godey's Lady's Book*, "The taste and management of the mistress are always displayed in the general conduct of the table."[3] In this sense, the dinner table, a scene of daily socialization, acquired even more importance. Another etiquette writer expanded the reach of the dinner table to well beyond the perimeter of the dining room, stating, "If the truth must be known, all affectations and pretense aside, the dinner, the world over, is the symbol of a people's civilization. A coarse and meanly cooked and raggedly served dinner," he continued, "expresses the thought and perhaps the spiritual perception of a nation or family. A well-cooked and a prettily served dinner will indicate the refinement and taste of a nation or family."[4]

Dinner, then, had tremendous cultural power, shaping not only individuals but also the nation at large. Within the realm of the dining room, middle-class women aspired to nurture gentility, to counter the deleterious effects of the outside world, as well as to educate family members in the arts of gracious living, self-restraint, and refined behavior. Hale reminded her readers about the importance of dining well on a daily basis, whether or not guests were expected. The household management practices of a genteel lady were to be so well ingrained that she would never be caught unprepared:

> Perhaps there are a few occasions on which the respectability of a man is more immediately felt, than the style of dinner to which he may accidentally bring home a visitor . . . If merely two or three dishes be well served, with the proper accompaniments, the table-linen clean, the small sideboard neatly laid, and all that is necessary be at hand, the expectation of both the husband and friend will be gratified.[5]

The rules of etiquette played a key role in this process. Etiquette, an established behavioral code that unified a group and distinguished its members from those unfamiliar with the rules, had its origins in European courtly relations. By the 1840s, an American publishing industry that served a growing demand for "how-to" books of all sorts was publishing etiquette books at a rate of about three a year. That pace quickened to five or six a year after the Civil War.[6] The topics covered by these new etiquette books ranged widely, in an attempt to prepare readers for any social eventuality. Eliza Leslie, whose book, *The Ladies' Guide to True Politeness and Perfect Manners*, appeared in 1864, offered advice on "Conversation, Manners, Dress; Introductions; Entrée to Society; Shopping; Conduct in the Street; At Places of Amusement; In Traveling." She also covered situations "At the Table, Either at Home, In Company, or At Hotels," as well as "Deportment in Gentlemen's Society," and concluded with grooming advice about "Lips, Complexion, Teeth, Hands, and The Hair."[7]

Part of the impetus for the growth of etiquette literature may have stemmed from a widely held perception, especially common among Europeans, that Americans were not very well mannered. Mrs. Frances Trollope, an English traveler to the United States in the late 1820s, noted that Americans "rarely dine in society, except in taverns and boarding houses," suggesting that they were unexposed to the niceties of more genteel social settings. Moreover, she continued, "They eat with the greatest rapidity and in total silence."[8] Bolting down their food was a frequent complaint about American eaters, as was eating with their knives instead of forks, or even worse, using their fingers. In Europe, eating with one's fingers had been considered ungentle by the middle of the seventeenth century, as suggested by verses from a song by the Marquis de Coulanges:

> In times past, people ate from the common dish and dipped their bread and fingers in the sauce.
>
> Today everyone eats with a spoon and fork from his own plate, and a valet washes the cutlery from time to time at the buffet.[9]

By the Victorian era, touching food that was going to be consumed by others was socially taboo. "Always keep your own knife, fork, and spoon out of the dishes," Eliza Leslie reminded her readers. "It is an insult to the company, and a disgrace to yourself, to dip into a dish anything that has been even for a moment in your mouth."[10] New flatware forms helped to buffer diners from the food on the table, especially in public or company settings. For example, when dining in hotels, "To take butter or salt with your own knife is an abomination. There is always a butter knife or salt spoon. It is nearly as bad to take a lump of sugar with your fingers."[11]

The proper procedure for using one's personal utensils was also fraught with pitfalls. Until the mid-nineteenth century, forks often had only two tines—which made it difficult to eat certain foods easily, especially peas. The normal solution had been to use a round-bladed knife as an auxiliary eating implement. By 1853, however, "An American Lady" was reminding her readers to "Always feed yourself with the fork; a knife is only used as a divider." Furthermore, she noted, "silver forks are now met with in almost every respectable house. Steel forks," those presumably with two tines, "are now seldom placed upon the dinner table."[12]

Eliza Leslie was even more explicit in her fork-eating instructions. "Many persons hold silver forks awkwardly, as if not accustomed to them," she began. "It is fashionable to use your knife only while cutting up the food small enough to be eaten with the fork alone. While cutting, keep the fork in your left hand, the hollow or concave side downward, the fork in a very slanting position, and your forefinger extended far down upon its handle." After cutting, Leslie advised her readers to put down the knife, switch the fork to the right hand, and pick up a piece of bread with the left hand, to use as a pusher. By forcing Americans to put down their knives after cutting their food, Leslie hoped to obliterate the older custom of "knife eating" in favor of the newly fashionable fork eating.

A spoon completed the trio of personal utensils essential for refined eating. Spoons had been available long before forks, but by the mid-nineteenth century, spoons had become increasingly differentiated, both by size and by intended function. The largest spoon, a tablespoon, was used mainly for soup and dessert. In its incarnation as a "dessert spoon," it was to be used "in eating tarts, puddings, curries, etc., etc.," according to the author of *True Politeness*.[13] The probate inventory of George C. Latta, who died in 1856 in Charlotte, New York, reflected the beginnings of this functional differentiation. His china cupboard contained six silver tablespoons, six new tablespoons, six silver teaspoons, six German teaspoons, four old tablespoons, three salt spoons, and a mustard spoon. The inventory team found seven more teaspoons and five tablespoons in the kitchen, probably used for cooking or for setting a table for the household help. All of these assorted spoons represented roughly only three size categories: large (tablespoons), smaller (teaspoons), and very small (salt and mustard spoons). In addition to the spoons, Latta owned two dozen tea knives, a dozen table knives (larger than tea knives), and only six silver forks, suggesting the forks were not anywhere near as important a part of his dining kit as were knives and spoons.[14]

By 1880, however, eating styles had changed dramatically, with specialized implements readily available for eating and serving many different types of foods. Tiffany and Company, an important New York silver manufacturer, listed forks in a variety of sizes and shapes, for consuming specific types of foods at specific meal settings. In setting the table, a woman could choose between a breakfast, dinner, fish, dessert, or salad fork. Spoons—the traditional workhorses of the

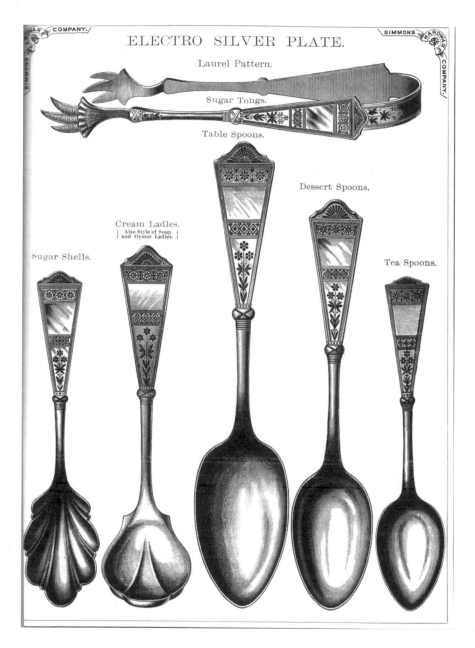

ELECTRO SILVER PLATE.

Laurel Pattern.

Sugar Tongs.

Table Spoons.

Dessert Spoons.

Cream Ladles.
Also Style of Soup
and Oyster Ladles.

Sugar Shells.

Tea Spoons.

By the late nineteenth century, table flatware was characterized by specificity of function. The "Laurel" pattern, made by Meriden Britannia Company and featured by the Simmons Hardware Company of St. Louis, Missouri, in their 1881 catalog, included tea, table, and dessert spoons, as well as coffee, egg or ice cream, mustard, salt, berry, macaroni, salad, and sugar spoons. (Courtesy of Dover Publications.)

tabletop—customized the serving and eating of berries, eggs, grape-fruit, bonbons, jelly, mustard, nuts, olives, oranges, preserves, sherbet, ice, tea, toddies, sugar, and salad.[15] Tiffany's competitor, Reed and Barton, offered a similar array of goods in their less expensive line of silver-plated flatware, including twenty varieties of spoons, as well as twelve types of forks and ten different knives—fifty-seven items in all.[16]

With this array of options for eating, there was no need to eat with one's fingers ever again. "No lady looks worse than when gnawing a bone," wrote Eliza Leslie, "even of game or poultry. Few *ladies* do it," she concluded, "In fact, nothing should be sucked or gnawed in public," not even "corn bitten off the cob" or "melon nibbled from the rind."[17] Certain foods, however, were either exempt from the rules about finger eating or, more commonly, the subject of mixed messages about it. Chief on the list of approved finger foods were bread, peeled and quartered apples, olives, celery, asparagus (but only if the stalks were not too tender), as well as hard cheese, oranges (if eaten in sections), firm bananas, and green corn. With regard to green corn, Agnes Morton commented, "a good set of natural teeth" was "the prime requisite."[18]

In addition to specialized flatware tools and especially when they had to use their fingers, diners could rely on other table accessories to help them maintain standards of gentility. Napkins, an important part of a woman's dowry of household textiles, facilitated tidiness while eating. Whiteness and smoothness were important napkin virtues, denoting a diligent housewife. Maintenance of table linens, however, was an onerous task—one which women lessened by using napkin rings for family and boardinghouse meals. A napkin ring enabled diners to reuse their napkins over the course of several meals, while ensuring that each diner always found his or her personal napkin laid across the plate at dinner—and not someone else's. For company occasions, however, napkin rings—with their implication that the linens might be recycled to or (even worse) from another meal—were taboo. "Fold your napkin when you are done with it and place it in your ring, when at home," advised John Ruth, author of *Decorum*. "If you are visiting, leave your napkin unfolded beside your plate." Whether at home or among company, however, the napkin should never be used as a handkerchief, Ruth noted, "by wiping the forehead or blowing the nose with it."[19]

The finger bowl, something middle-class diners might encounter more commonly at a hotel than at home, was another tool used for personal hygiene while eating. It allowed diners to clean their hands between courses. Specifically, the finger bowls were brought to the table before the fruit and dessert courses. The glass bowl of water, often garnished with a slice of lemon or a fragrant blossom, came to the table on an underplate, with a colored doily in between bowl and plate. While eating fruit, diners could remove the bowl from the underplate, which they could use for their fruit course, wiping their fingers on the doily as needed. Because the doily was colored, rather than white, it was less likely to show fruit stains after laundering. The rituals surrounding finger bowls, while elegant, must have seemed rather pretentious to many Americans, based on the amount of commentary about their use in the etiquette literature. Etiquette writers constantly reminded their readers that when the finger bowls arrived, they were never under any circumstances to *drink* the water in the bowl. Instead, they were to dip their fingers lightly into the water, one hand at a time, and then wipe them dry with the doily or napkin. Eliza Leslie advised her readers pointedly to "omit the disgusting foreign fashion of taking water into your mouth, rinsing and gurgling it round, and then spitting it back into the glass."[20]

Efforts to enforce new standards of gentility and self-restraint at the table extended beyond the polite consumption of food, into the realm of conversation. Diners were to avoid "all discussions of sicknesses, sores, surgical operations, dreadful accidents, shocking cruelties, or horrible punishments."[21] In 1864, when Eliza Leslie wrote those words, however, such topics and others, including "political and sectarian controversies," must have been hard to avoid. The entire country had been laboring for three years under the burden of a bloody Civil War.

In the midst of such turmoil, ordinary routines helped preserve some measure of normalcy, at least for those on the home front. Every day, families gathered to celebrate their ordinariness by breaking bread together, sharing their triumphs and difficulties, and partaking of the basic rituals of family life. These rituals divided their days into predictable segments, at home and at work. Breakfast began the day, with various members departing for scattered destinations, some carrying lunch or dinner pails, some intending to eat their midday meal "out," and some engaging in morning marketing or social calls, returning for "luncheon." The family dinner in the middle of the day, once the norm for most American families, was quickly becoming a sentimental memory, especially for those families living in towns and cities.

For upwardly mobile women, whose days were filled with leisure, "tea" offered the possibility of a mid-afternoon social event. Tea parties, large and small, offered green or black tea, freshly brewed, along with tea's traditional accompaniments, milk or cream, sugar or honey, or lemon. In addition, hostesses generally offered some form of carbohydrate to accompany the tea—cakes, cookies, tarts, biscuits, toast, or simply bread, butter, and preserves. More elaborate offerings could include coffee, sweet wines, cordials, and assorted sweetmeats, relishes, and delicacies. While these parties were most often women-only events, men sometimes joined the group after their workday concluded. The following recipe for tea cakes, which were quick and easy to make and would have been a staple offering at an afternoon tea, appeared in *Buckeye Cookery* (1880).

Tea Cake

One quart flour, one cup sour milk, one tea-spoon soda, one-half pound lard, one-half pound chopped raisins or currants; roll two inches thick and bake in a quick oven; split open, butter, and eat while hot.[22]

End-of-day meals were defined by class. Working-class Americans, especially those of Northern European origin, came home to "tea"— which was not a party but rather a meal of tea with milk and sugar, plus cold meat, bread, or whatever other leftovers or simple dishes might be available. A more hearty working-class meal, called "supper," could have included soup, stew, or any of a wide variety of "made" dishes. By the Victorian period, for the middle class, "dinner" had shifted from its traditional place at midday to evening. Besides class, however, geographic location factored in as a mealtime or meal-type determinant, and rural families continued to follow an eighteenth-century meal schedule long after urban Americans had shifted to a more modern system.

Ordinary family dinners by the 1870s were normally divided into two or possibly three courses. Jane Cunningham Croly provided a set of menus to her readers for an entire year. Most of her normal dinners began with meat or fish, accompanied by vegetables and possibly a relish, and dessert. For February, she proposed a dinner of baked pork and beans, with boiled codfish, mashed potatoes, pickles, applesauce, and apple fritters for dessert. A "Sunday Dinner" involved a slightly elevated array, as in a menu she proposed for April of roast chickens, stewed tomatoes, new or "Bermuda" potatoes, spinach, canned corn, and, for dessert, lemon meringue pie. A "Company Dinner" listed for January was even more elaborate, beginning with vermicelli soup. This was followed by boiled turkey with oyster stuffing, as well as "roast chicken, boiled ham, cranberry jelly, celery, fried potatoes, canned corn, tomatoes, stewed parsnips, cauliflower, macaroni, plum pudding, nuts, oranges, and raisins."[23]

Parties formed the final food events of any day. They might have included dinner, but more festive events began later in the evening and included drinking, dancing, card playing, conversing, and sometimes a late supper. Eliza Leslie described a fashionable dinner party *à l'anglaise*. The table was set with a large plateau in the center, surrounded by candles and flowers. The hostess had arranged bowls or compotes of fruits and entremets down the center of the table. The meal began with two soups, one white and one brown, as well as two fish dishes (salmon and turbot), accompanied by appropriate sauces and wines. For the meat course, the guests could choose between mutton or boiled turkey (breast meat only), four vegetable dishes, and two game dishes. Sweets followed, including charlottes, jellies, frozen fruit (molded in red isinglass jelly), along with lobster salad, and two cheeses (stilton and cream cheese). Both champagne and port were served with this course. Dessert consisted of ice cream and flavored ices, as well as fruit. For the dessert course, the hostess provided her guests with doilies and two different plates, one of ground glass, the other a porcelain dessert plate. Although Leslie did not explicitly state so, the meal doubtless ended with *café français*, brandy, and liqueurs.[24]

By the 1850s, many of these mealtime events occurred in the dining room, a relatively new architectural space for the Victorian middle class. Formal dining parlors had begun to appear in the homes of the wealthy by the late eighteenth century. These were multipurpose rooms, equipped with sets of tables and chairs that could be set up in the center of the room for a dinner party or banquet or broken down and arranged around the perimeter of the room for large stand-up parties or smaller collations. Architectural plan books demonstrate that the custom of a separate space dedicated to eating and drinking had filtered down to the middle class by mid-century. The kitchen table, however, remained the customary place for family dining among those of lesser means, as well as in the country.

Furnishings for dining rooms evolved along with the social spaces. Drop-leaf tables persisted among families who owned them. They could be lengthened by the addition of semicircular "D-end" tables at each end. Many families preferred the newly conceived extension tables available in a wide range of wood choices and finishes, which could be expanded to accommodate company through the insertion of leaves. Manufacturers of mass-produced furniture offered fashionable seating to surround these dining tables, typically reflecting the historical styles of the European aristocracy, but practically finished with leather or cane seating for ease of cleaning. A sideboard and perhaps a china cabinet or serving table completed the Victorian dining-room furniture ensemble. Sideboards, which had first appeared in the shops of English cabinetmakers during the 1790s, had evolved into elegant wooden cabinets surmounted with a pedimented shelving unit. As was the case with dining tables and chairs, sideboards expressed the wealth and taste of their owners. They ranged in complexity and ornamentation from simple pine or grain-painted cabinets with applied machine-made ornaments, to heavily carved oak or lavishly veneered forms with marquetry or painted porcelain panels. Many of these Victorian sideboards had mirrored shelves to better display the items arrayed on them.

An illustration of the "Method of Setting Out a Table in America," published in *Godey's Lady's Book* in 1859, demonstrated vividly why families needed sideboards.[25] Increasingly, the social expectation that families have large sets of matching table furnishings, supplemented with an array of specialized serving implements, defined daily rituals for presenting and serving food. The arrangement of the dining-room tabletop presumed the each person at the table would have a set of cutlery and an array of plates, cups, saucers, glasses, and other individual eating implements. The more traditional style of dining that had characterized the colonial period, whereby food was served from large communal vessels on the center of the table and almost no one had individual tools for cutting or consuming food, had given way to modern notions of privacy and personal space—even at the table.

Two basic methods for setting the table prevailed throughout the Victorian era. The first, known as the "English" or "family" style, involved arranging all food on the table at the outset of each course, using tureens, platters, entrée dishes, serving bowls, and other silver or, more commonly, ceramic vessels. If ceramic, whether transfer-printed English earthenware, relief-molded white ironstone or "granite ware," or elegantly painted French or English porcelain, the serving pieces typically matched the individual place-setting items. The overall effect created was one of balance, complexity, and visual unity—a lingering reference to the functional community of earlier times.

Family and guests seated themselves around the table according to a strict protocol: heads of household at each end and honored guests and other family members arranged by rank down the sides of the table. Food service under the English system was an obligation shared among the participants. At one end of the table, the hostess ladled soup from a large tureen onto soup plates, which were then passed down the table hand over hand. At the other end of the table, the host

By the 1850s, elaborate sideboards like this one, which stood over six feet tall, were becoming fixtures in middle-class dining rooms. Made of expensive woods—walnut or sometimes even rosewood—they were designed with locking cabinets below and open storage above for silver, china, and fancy bric-a-brac. The marble serving shelf offered a convenient staging area during a dinner party and the sumptuously carved decoration confirmed the artistic sensibilities of the hosts and their guests. Currier Museum of Art, Manchester, New Hampshire. Gift of Frances MacKay, 1981.56.

METHOD OF SETTING OUT A TABLE IN AMERICA.

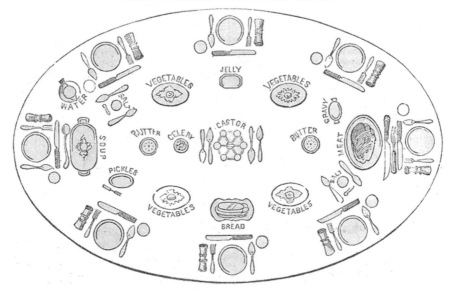

Diagram showing the proper way to set a table in 1859, published in *Godey's Lady's Book* and entitled "Method of Setting Out a Table in America."

carved and served the roast, passing plates in a similar manner. Lesser items on the table—entrées, vegetables, birds, or smaller dishes that needed carving—were attended to by those seated near them. The dining experience, then, whether the meal was a simple family supper or a fancy dinner party, was participatory, and a person's ability to perform serving and carving tasks reflected new standards for genteel accomplishment.

"Service à la russe," the alternative style of table setting and food presentation, was far more courtly and required servants to pass and dish out the menu items. Under this system, all food was staged in the kitchen and then brought into the dining room and presented to each diner, either on large trays and platters or on individual plates. Food writer Mary Henderson described this for her readers in 1877:

> In this style the dishes are brought to the table already carved, and ready for serving, thus depriving the cook of the power to display his decorative art, and the host of his skill in carving. Each dish is served as a separate course, only one vegetable being allowed for a course, unless used merely for the purpose of garnishing.[26]

This table was set for a tea or evening party to be served *à la russe*. On the center of the table is an elaborate arrangement of fruit, surrounded by smaller baskets of fruit and sweetmeats, as well as a caster set, a covered butter dish, and tea and coffee service at the far end. During the party, the sideboard was used by the servants as a staging area for wine and cordials, as well as additional plates and serving utensils. (Courtesy of Dover Publications.)

This style of service had several distinct advantages. First, the food could be kept warm in the kitchen up to the moment of service, instead of sitting on the table while diners consumed prior courses. Second, because the serving vessels remained either in the kitchen or on the sideboard, the center of the table remained free as a platform for decorative elements—elaborate arrangements of flowers or fruits, sugar sculptures, silver plateaus, candelabra, and other ornaments. According to Henderson, when serving dinner "*à la Russe*, the table is decorated by placing the dessert in a tasteful manner around a centre-piece of flowers. This furnishes a happy mode of gratifying other senses than that of taste; for while the appetite is being satisfied, the flowers exhale their fragrance, and give to the eye what never fails to please the refined and cultivated guest."[27] As a final benefit of this style, the act of serving oneself gracefully with one hand while twisting around to the left afforded yet another opportunity to demonstrate one's gentility.

The sets of tablewares required for either of these two forms of service included a standardized array of constituent parts. Etiquette writer Elizabeth Ellet recommended an inventory of ceramic tablewares that included one full dinner service, one common set for the kitchen, a good tea service, as well as a common one, a breakfast service, and a dessert service. The complete dinner service required several different sizes of plates, as well as dishes (platters), bakers, nappies, covered dishes, casseroles, a soup tureen, sauce tureens, sauce boats, pickle dishes, one or two covered butter dishes, footed compotes, salad bowls, and perhaps a custard or fruit stand with matching custard cups. Dessert services tended to be more elegantly decorated than dinner sets, often painted with fruits or flowers and trimmed with gold. Breakfast sets reflected the reduced menu of that meal—the plates were smaller and often made of more durable ceramic materials. Specialized items for the breakfast table might have included a covered butter dish, a jam or preserve pot, eggcups, large coffee cups, and a toast rack.

Glass, strictly a luxury material until the advent of mass-production techniques in the 1820s and 1830s, became increasingly popular for serving beverages, as well as richly colored condiments and sweetmeats. By the end of the century, household arbiter Maria Parloa wrote in the *Ladies' Home Journal*, "glass has largely taken the place of silver on some of the most elegant tables." "The woman of moderate means," she continued, "will find it possible to set her table with a plain, clear glass of dainty and elegant shapes." Parloa believed that glass would enhance the appearance and brilliancy of the entire table.[28] According to Elizabeth Ellet, an adequate inventory of table glass included three dozen wine glasses, two dozen champagne glasses, two dozen claret glasses, and three dozen goblets, as well as six water carafes, six decanters, a liqueur stand and a dozen liqueur glasses, two glass pitchers, a celery glass, trifle bowl, and eight dessert dishes.[29] This, of course, represented an ideal quantity. A more realistic appraisal is suggested by the inventory of glass in George Latta's estate. He died in 1856, leaving behind two cut glass decanters, six goblets, one glass preserve dish, two round glass dishes in two sizes, two covered glass jars, five wine glasses, and a spoon tumbler (to hold teaspoons on the tea tray). In addition, he owned ten "old" tumblers and four "good" ones, as well as assorted glass bottles, jars, and flasks.[30]

No. 1878, . . $10.00 (PERTAIN).   No. 1880, . . $10.50 (PERTINENT).   No. 1881, . . $11.50 (PERUKE).

No. 1874, Satin, Engraved, $10.50 (PICA).   No. 1877, . . $12.00 (PICTURE).   No. 1875, . . $10.50 (PICKET).

SARDINE TONGS, $1.50 each (see Flat Ware) (PICNIC).

(281)

The Meriden Britannia Company catalogue of 1886–1887 offered a variety of sardine serving dishes, all made of glass of different colors and styles, with silver-plated lids and frames. (Courtesy of Dover Publications.)

Often, table glass was combined with silver in some way as a means of enhancement. By the 1870s, the American silver industry was producing large quantities of silver hollow wares, much of it frames, stands, or baskets that held glass components. This trend greatly expanded the serving capacities of silver objects—which sometimes had the problem of negative chemical interactions with foods. Fashionable tea tables might have been graced, for example, with a silver sardine serving dish, with an engraved or cut nonreactive glass liner. The widespread substitution of electroplated silver for sterling made it possible for people of ordinary means to acquire silver tea sets, trays, breadbaskets, cake stands, cruet sets, coffee urns, and numerous other items, once out-of-reach luxuries. Despite Ellet's warning that silverplated wares were pretentious and represented a false economy, the abundance of such wares produced during the last quarter of the nineteenth century suggested that glitter held a powerful appeal for those seeking to present an elegant table.[31]

Popular ideas about what constituted a proper table were shaped, for many people, by table presentations and dining customs that they witnessed in public places. Urban Americans, in particular, were exposed to an increasing variety of culinary experiences in the burgeoning array of restaurants, tearooms, hotels, boarding houses, railroad dining cars, steam ships, and other public dining arenas. In New York City, for example, those wishing to dine out could choose from numerous French and German restaurants, as well as local English chop houses, seafood restaurants, and oyster bars. One commentator, C. W. Gesner, writing about New York's restaurants for *Harper's New Monthly Magazine* in 1866 remarked, "So far as one can judge, there are about ten varieties of restaurants in New York; and by restaurants we mean places with tables and chairs and plate and knives, not counter eating-houses."[32]

Gesner described a French restaurant in the cellar of a building in the theater district. "You descend steep cellar stairs," he began, "and enter a low and not nice smelling room, with sanded floor, hard chairs, and a little bar tended usually by a woman."

> There is an alcove at one end, under the sidewalk, formed of oyster-shells and bits of tinsel, and sometimes a boy with a violin will seem to afford music to the feast. Before "gold went up" the *diner des jour* at this place, consisting of soup, one entree, and cut of roast meat with one vegetable, and cheese with bread at discretion, would be had for 25 cents, with a pint of red wine at 12 1/2 cents extra. Now, however, the price for the "diner" is 35 cents, and the wine 20 cents—55 cents in all, and a very cheap and good dinner it is with no fried dishes and no pies. The wine is good. Hungry people, who are generally cross, become amiable after the second glass.[33]

Surviving menus, photographs, guidebooks, literary fiction, and traveler's accounts offer a picture of restaurant dining in Victorian America. Charles Dickens made an American tour in 1842 and recorded his impressions of dining aboard a canal boat, en route to Cincinnati. "There are three meals a day," he wrote. "Breakfast at seven, dinner at half-past twelve, supper about six. At each, there are a great many small dishes and plates upon the table, with very little in them." Breakfast on board consisted of tea, coffee, bread and butter, accompanied by salmon, shad, liver, steak, potatoes, pickles, ham, chops, black puddings, and sausages—from which the passengers were expected to make a selection. Dickens went on to complain that other meals consisted typically of "a joint" of roast pig, accompanied by "fancy slices of beet-root, shreds of dried beef, complicated entanglements of yellow pickle, maize, Indian corn, apple sauce, and pumpkin." Hot corn bread was another table staple, as were pitchers of water. Dickens, like many other British travelers, was not impressed by the manners of his fellow passengers. They ate too quickly, used their own forks and knives to serve themselves from the dishes and platters on the table, and seemed incapable of polite conversation. "Nobody says anything, at any meal, to anybody."[34]

Eliza Leslie explained to her readers what to expect for breakfast at a hotel. She urged them to arrive before 9:00 a.m. and noted that the menu items would be served after the coffee or tea and bread and butter. "To each person is allowed a separate dish or plate of the articles selected," she continued, "and it is understood to be for yourself alone, and that no other person has a right to partake of it." She reminded travelers not to use their own fork or knife for helping themselves to food from common dishes and to use the butter knife to take butter from the butter dish. "Carefully avoid cutting bread with your own knife, or taking salt with it from the salt cellar," she admonished. "It looks as though you had not been accustomed to butter-knives and salt spoons."[35]

Isabella Byrd, an Englishwoman traveling in America in 1858, described her experience in a hotel among travelers who were obviously not familiar with Eliza Leslie's advice:

> We went down to dinner, and only the fact of not having tasted food for many hours could have made me touch it in such a room. We were in a long apartment, with one table down the middle, with plates laid for one hundred people. Every seat was occupied, these seats being benches of somewhat uncouth workmanship. . . . At one side was a large fireplace, where, in spite of the heat of the day, sundry manipulations were going on, coming under the general name of cookery. At the end of the room was a long leaden trough or sink, where three greasy scullery-boys without shoes, were perpetually engaged in washing plates, which they wiped upon their aprons. The plates, however, were not washed, only superficially rinsed.

In terms of the food offered, Bird mentioned boiled leg of mutton ("nearly raw"), some "antiquated fowls, whose legs were the consistence of guitar-strings," pork with "onion fixings" (swimming in grease), and three vegetables: yams, corn on the cob, and squash. Because there were no carving knives on the table, diners were forced to use their own and some people "carved them dexterously with bowie-knives taken out of their belts." People also contaminated the communal saltcellar, using the tips of their own ("greasy") knives to extract a bit of salt. Pumpkin pie concluded the menu, but Bird was so disgusted by the waiters that she was unable to eat any.[36]

A Boston restaurant described by Bartley Hubbard, a fictional character in William Dean Howell's novel, *A Modern Instance* (1882), seemed a bit more upscale. The marble-top tables were set with a silverplated caster set in the center of each. Other condiments on the table included a salt shaker and a bottle of "Leicestershire" sauce. At each person's place, the plates were jauntily embellished with a red "doyley," folded into the shape of a cocked hat. Hubbard commented that the red doiley "does not betray use like the indiscreet white napkin," perhaps implying that the doiley was not freshly laundered.[37] A city the size of Boston would have offered eating facilities for a wide range of people, visitors and residents alike. B. F. Brightman's French Coffee Rooms at No. 12 Court Square offered a discreet spot to relax and converse during a busy workday. Crawford House, an elegant hotel housed in a grand mansard structure at Scolley Square, had dining rooms for both men and women, as did most other public eating facilities.[38]

Restaurant menus from the Victorian era reveal a fairly consistent menu structure, beginning with soup and then moving through courses of fish, oysters, and game. The main courses paralleled family meals, featuring hot meats, boiled or roasted, and accompanied by vegetables and sauces. An 1855 menu from the Gentlemen's Ordinary at Franklin House in Philadelphia offered boiled "Quaker City Ham," tongue, corned beer, leg of mutton with pickle sauce, chicken with egg sauce, corned pork with sauerkraut, and calf's head with mustard sauce. In the "Roast" category, diners at Franklin House could choose from beef, lamb, veal, breast of pork, chicken, wild duck, turkey with cranberry sauce, and goose with apple sauce.

"Side Dishes" or "Entrees" opened up possibilities for a restaurant chef to excel, producing exotic dishes with elaborate preparation methods and rich sauces. The International Hotel in Niagara Falls, New York, presented five entrees, all with European pedigrees. If "Liver Fried with *Fine Herbs*" or "Turkey Wings *ala Creole*" did not appeal, then perhaps "*Fricandeau d'Agneau à la Jardiniere*," or "Calves Feet *al'Italienne*" might. If all else failed to please, that old standby, "*Macaroni au Fromage à la Holand*" (macaroni and cheese) would have satisfied even the most finicky palate.[39] For Americans who aspired to sophistication, France seemed the pinnacle of elegance. Following the publication of Brillat-Savarin's *Physiologie du Goût* in 1825, French culinary terms—fondue, bonbon, fricassee, and countless others—as well as French recipes, ingredients, salads, ices, and other fashions in food and drink began to enter the mainstream American vocabulary and diet.[40] One fictional cultural commentator in 1875 (humorously named "Mrs. Nouveau Riche"), exclaimed about French food, "Such heavenly garnishes, and flowers everywhere, and the lovliest side-dishes, and everything so exquisitely served!"

Restaurant meals typically concluded with "Pastry," or sometimes "Puddings," which, at the Wyoming Valley Hotel in Wilkes-Barre, Pennsylvania, included whortleberry pie, Washington pudding with brandy sauce, ginger snaps, wafer jumbles, gingerbread, sponge cake, grape drops, lemon pie, pound cake, jelly cake, and Boston cream pie. Dessert followed, a course of fruit, nuts, ice cream, and coffee.[41]

Most upscale restaurant menus also featured extensive wine lists, which would have appealed strongly to America's growing merchant class after the Civil War. In 1872, the dinner menu of Philadelphia's Merchants' Hotel listed champagne, sherry, Madeira, and port, as well as French, Moselle, and Rhenish wines. The Merchants' Hotel, Philadelphia's largest, was originally constructed in 1837 as the Washington Hotel. It was considered to be quite luxurious, with "soft carpets, stuffed furniture, and heavy curtains, and was looked upon as a kind of palace hotel."[42] In such an environment, prosperous gentlemen and ladies could choose from ten different champagnes, including selections from Mumm & Company, Moet & Chandon, and Heidsieck & Company. The hotel's wine cellar also held fine vintages from the Medoc, including wines from St. Estephe, Chateau Margaux, Chateau Lafitte, and Chateau St. Julienne, from the highly regarded Bordeaux importer, Barton et Guestier. Brandies, whiskies, gin, malt, and mineral water rounded out the offerings.[43]

American restaurants in the latter half of the nineteenth century served clientele from all classes, not just the champagne crowd. In Fitchburg, Massachusetts, "eating houses" was a business new category in the 1880 City Directory. Thirteen of these establishments were listed that year, including the Old City Bakery, which offered "meals at all hours," as well as "Board and Lodgings by the Day or Week."[44] Menus from this type of eatery tended to have an extensive array of *a la carte* offerings. Diners could eat as much (or as little) as they could afford—or as time permitted. As the new industrial cities of the North and Midwest filled up with newcomers, boarding houses and residential hotels provided a convenient temporary, or even relatively permanent home. Many of these restaurants and hotels were located near the railroad station—increasingly an important urban hub in many American cities. Early railroad travel began in the 1830s, exposing those who partook of the chance to travel to a wealth of new cultural experiences, including new foods. During the trip, dining opportunities were at first limited to what was available at the stations since there was no food service on the train. According to one commentator, when the train pulled into a station,

> All the doors are thrown open and out rush all, the passengers like boys out of school, and crowd round the tables to solace themselves with pies, patties, cakes, hard-boiled eggs, hams, custards, and a variety of railroad luxuries too numerous to mention.[45]

Forty years later, train stations had evolved as eating places, although travelers still complained about the haste with which they had to eat and the poor quality of the food offered. The editors of the *New York Times* criticized the railroad companies for not having a higher regard for the stomachs of their passengers, apparently believing "that eating and drinking are not at all necessary to human beings bound on long journeys, and that nothing more is required than to put them through their misery in as brief a time as possible." Passengers, according to the editors, were herded into "a dismal long room," and given a fifteen-minute meal of breakfast, dinner, or supper.[46] The St. Charles Hotel in downtown Syracuse, New York, served train passengers. A printed menu from October 23, 1863, informed travelers, "This Train Stops for Dinner, 20 Minutes." Those wishing to partake of the hotel's *Table d'Hote* were instructed to exit from the left side of the car for the restaurant and that the dining room was "in full view of the cars." Once inside, diners could choose from a full menu, including macaroni soup, baked whitefish with port wine sauce, a variety of roasted and boiled meats, baked chicken pie, giblet stew, hashed liver with poached eggs, lamb "harricut"—a stew made from lamb neck meat and white haricot beans, or baked macaroni and cheese, as well as a selection of cold meats. Worcestershire sauce, horseradish, onions, cheese, cucumbers, pickles, and "Cold Slaw" accompanied these offerings. The vegetables offered reflected the time of year and were limited to those seasonally available: potatoes, beets, squash, turnips, onions, and cabbage. Those passengers with time to spare could finish off their meals with a pastry course (baked custard pudding, orange fritters with brandy sauce, or apple, berry, and pumpkin pie), as well as dessert (lemon ice cream, blancmange with cream, wine jelly, preserved apples, or sponge cake).[47]

Eating conditions while traveling via train improved significantly because of two innovations. The first came about when entrepreneur

Fred Harvey realized the potential of trackside eateries that would offer well-prepared, quick, clean, easy meals for travelers. Beginning in the 1870s, he established a series of "Harvey Houses" along the route of the Atchinson, Topeka & Santa Fe railroad line. These were enormously successful, staffed by a well-trained crew of "Harvey Girls," who made sure that all diners were served promptly and with finesse.[48]

The second innovation in railroad dining came with the invention of the dining car—which was, at first, merely a retrofitted baggage car. Railroad entrepreneur George Pullman, however, turned his attention to problem of food service, introducing a luxury Pullman dining car in 1868. Pullman dining cars were outfitted with chandeliers, banks of tables on either side of a center aisle, and an efficient kitchen where "every variety of meats, vegetables and pastry may be cooked in the car, according to the best style of culinary art."[49] Charles Nordhoff, author of *California: A Book for Travellers and Settlers*, described the dining car in detail. He was particularly impressed by the efficient design of the kitchen:

> The Pullman hotel-car is one of the most ingenious as well as one of the most convenient of all modern arrangements for travel. It can seat forty persons at the tables; it contains not only a kitchen—which is a marvel of compactness, having a sink, with hot and cold water faucets, and every "modern convenience"—but a wine closet, a china closet, a linen closet, and provision lockers so spacious as to contain supplies for thirty people all the way from Chicago to the Pacific if necessary; its commissary list contains, as I ascertained by actual count, 133 different articles of food; it carries 1000 napkins, 150 tablecloths, 300 hand-towels, and 30 or 40 roller-towels, besides sheets, pillow-cases, etc., etc. And unless you are of an investigating turn, you would never know that the car contained even a kitchen.[50]

PICNICS AND DINING OUT OF DOORS

Dining away from home did not always involve railroad travel, or even long distances. During fine weather, families enjoyed carrying tables and chairs out of doors onto the lawn or into the garden for a simple tea or a more elaborate party. In 1831, English traveler God-frey Vigne recorded such an event, which took place outside of the city of Baltimore. "The environs of Baltimore are exceedingly pretty: almost every eminence is crowned with a country house," he wrote, "surrounded by gardens and pleasure grounds richly wooded, and laid out to the best advantage, so as generally to afford a peep through the

The Pullman Dining Car, introduced in 1868, transformed the experience of eating while traveling by railroad. (Courtesy of Cornell University Library, Making of America Digital Collection, Charles Nordhoff, "California," *Harper's New Monthly Magazine* 44: 264 [May 1872]: 871.)

trees at some part of the Patapsco, or the Chesapeake." Because of this romantic location,

They are admirably adapted for a fete *champêtre*, or a strawberry party, as it is called at Baltimore. I had the honour of an invitation to the only one that was given during my stay in that city. The company assembled about six o'clock. Quadrilles and waltzes were kept up with great spirit, first on the lawn, and then in the house till about eleven. In the mean time strawberries and cream, ices, pineapples, and champagne, were served up in the greatest profusion.[51]

The opportunity to be outside in the fresh air appealed not only to Baltimore's gentry—ordinary people relished the idea of packing up a meal in a wicker hamper or even a simple shopping basket and finding a spot to relax and perhaps even frolic in the open air. English cookbook author, Isabella Beeton, whose *Book of Household Management*, published in 1859, was an international runaway success, offered advice about "Things not to be forgotten at a picnic:"

> A stick of horseradish, a bottle of mint-sauce well corked, a bottle of salad dressing, a bottle of vinegar, mae mustard, pepper, salt, good oil, and pounded sugar. If it can be managed, take a little ice. It is scarcely necessary to say that places, tumblers, wine-glasses, knives, forks, and spoons, must not be forgotten; as also teacups and saucers, 3 or 4 teapots, some lump sugar, and milk, if this last-named article cannot be obtained in the neighborhood.[52]

Excursions into nature, by means of a picnic, became increasingly popular during the nineteenth century, as the population of the United States began to move from country to city. Urban dwellers regarded the picnic as a sort of antidote to the debilitating effects of city living. Urban planners responded to this growing perception by creating green spaces where citizens could relax out-of-doors. Central Park in New York City, designed by Calvert Vaux and Frederick Law Olmstead in 1858, represents only one of many examples of this phenomenon. Even before then, however, American city dwellers used the newly created rural cemeteries—Mount Auburn in Cambridge, Massachusetts, for example—as places to gather and enjoy nature, as well as commune with their departed loved ones over an *al fresco* meal. Still others saw picnicking as a way to avoid scrutiny. Young people were not held to the same constraints as they were in their parents' parlors. A picnic was an ideal opportunity for a romantic tryst. It also afforded friends a chance to share a memorable experience, as described in a fictional account, published in *Putnam's Monthly Magazine* in 1856:

> It was a pleasant thing, after we had secured the bent by an iron grapple, to pick our way over the sharp rocks—now holding by a lithe cedar, now swinging around a jutting crag by a pendulous wild grape-vine, anon stepping from block to block, with a fine river view in front and below; and then coming suddenly upon the little nook where lay the flat stone we were in quest of, and then come the great cloth-spreading, and opening of the basket. And we took from the

basket: first, a box of matches and a bundle of choice cigars of delicate flavor; next, two side bottles of claret; then we lifted out carefully a white napkin, containing only one fowl, and that not fat; then two pies, much the worse for the voyage; then two more bottles of claret; then another centre-piece—ham sandwiches; then a bundle of knives and forks, a couple of cork-screws, a tier of plates, six apples, and a half bottle of olives; then twenty- seven hickory nuts, and a half dozen nut-crackers; and then came the cheese and the manuscript.[53]

HOLIDAY MEALS AND CELEBRATIONS

New Year's Day

Victorian Americans rang in the New Year by making the rounds of their friends' open houses and sharing a glass of eggnog or other alcoholic punch and perhaps some cake or cookies. This custom had originated with the Dutch in New Amsterdam and persisted among other Americans into the nineteenth century. Typically, women remained at home to receive the visitors, and men made the calls. Elizabeth Sedgwick, sister-in-law to novelist Catherine Maria Sedgwick, wrote to her father proudly that "about 70 gentlemen" had visited her home on New Year's Day in 1834.[54] The sheer numbers of visitors required that the ladies prepare refreshments that would be quick and easy to consume. A perusal of cookery books reveals a number of recipes associated with New Year's. Catharine Beecher published a "Recipe for New Year's Cookies" in 1846. Her cookies, as did Jane Cunningham Croly's "New Year's Cake" in 1870, included caraway seeds as a flavoring ingredient, perhaps a reference to the Dutch origins of the calling custom. Other cooks produced shaped cookies, including Croly (whose cookbook included three different recipes for New Year's baked goods). In describing her "New Year's Biscuits," made of butter, grated lemon rind, milk, soda, and eggs, Croly noted, "The proper way to shape these biscuits is by wooden blocks having pineapples, leaves, and other devices carved on them." Eliza Leslie, too, described stamped butter cookies for New Year's Day. The use of cake prints or cake boards to decorate the surface of these cookies differentiated them from other, more ordinary tea cakes.[55]

Jennie June's American Cookery Book, published in 1870, devoted an entire chapter to "New Year's Tables, Parties, Etc." The author, New Yorker Jane Cunningham Croly assumed that the tradition of calling on New Year's Day had become widespread. "The custom of receiving calls is becoming so very general out of New York city," she wrote, "that a few hints on the method of setting the table for the occasion may not come amiss." She reminded her readers "that as it is the taste of *gentlemen*, and not of ladies that are to be consulted on this day, sweets, cake and the like, should be subordinated to chicken salad, pickled oysters, potted salmon, sardines, and the like, which gentlemen generally greatly prefer." She went on to describe the table setting, which had a "handsomely ornamented cake, raised high on a china, glass, or silver *plateau*" on the center, surrounded by vases of flowers. The food was all cold and could be decorated with flowers, lemon slices, or "with little bits of evergreen." In addition to the above-mentioned pickled oysters, sardines, and cold salads, the table should offer small sandwiches made from biscuits enclosing tongue, ham, or potted veal. Other recommended table items included fruit ("A dish of oranges ornamented with tufts of green moss, and sprigs of scarlet geranium looks very nice"), jellies, and baskets of mixed cakes or cookies. "It would be much better if no wines were offered New Year's day," Croly concluded, although if desired "cherry, old Bourbon, and claret punch are in great demand."[56]

Passover

In 1871, Mrs. Esther Levy published the first American Jewish cookbook. One of her primary concerns was to ensure that the important food rituals be passed along to successive generations of Jewish housekeepers. Passover, one of the most important religious holidays, required strict adherence to protocols. According to Levy, "In preparing for the Passover, which generally commences in the middle of spring and lasts eight days, every particle of leaven must be out of the house by ten o'clock of the preceding morning. On the same day," she continued, "14th of Nisan, or on the previous eve, the house must be thoroughly cleaned from dirt, and everything be in perfect order." Once that was accomplished, the religious rituals could proceed, many of which revolved around food.

It is customary, when the synagogue service is over, for the master of the house to sit down to a table prepared with Passover cakes, parsley, chervil, horseradish, a lamb bone, and baked eggs, as well as wine, usually made in this country with raisins. The Passover cakes are placed between napkins. The herbs are placed upon a plate, together with a glass of salt water or vinegar, prepared for Passover, and a mixture made of chopped apples and raisins, and almonds rolled in cinnamon balls; all of these being symbolical of events of the past, in the history of our people. The humblest Jewish servant must sit at the table during the prayers, which occupy three-quarters of an hour before supper. When ready for this, everything there was on the table, during the reciting of the prayers, must be removed. The supper generally consists of some well-prepared fish, etc. It is not usual to partake of anything roasted on that eve or the next day.[57]

Easter

In early America, Easter was not widely celebrated. Puritans regarded it as popish, and the population of Catholics and others, for whom it was an important religious festival, was small. By the later nineteenth century, however, Easter had become an important celebration of spring, the end of Lent, and the Christian resurrection. Easter church services were supplemented with Easter parades, where families displayed their new springtime finery. For children, the Easter Bunny—a descendant of the German *Oschter Haws*, or Easter Hare, who delivered colored eggs—emerged to fill their Easter baskets with specially produced confections.[58] Coloring eggs persisted as an Easter tradition. "Jennie June" instructed readers to use a tallow candle to inscribe names or dates on the eggs before dyeing. "The parts over which the tallow has passed being impervious to the dye," she explains, made "the eggs come out presenting white inscriptions on colored grounds." Eggs could also be painted or decorated by etching with a steel pen and India ink. For color, Croly suggested using traditional dye agents (onion skin for brown, indigo for blue).[59]

Molded chocolate eggs, as well as bunnies, chicks, and lambs, began to appear in the 1870s. All of these forms were strongly associated not only with Easter but also with the themes of rebirth and Spring. The English firm of Cadbury & Company produced their first cream-filled chocolate Easter egg in 1875.[60] The American chocolate industry grew tremendously during this period as well, facilitated, in part, by the arrival of immigrants from Europe who brought with them the skills for producing chocolate confections and the molds to make them.

A recipe for "Easter Jelly," included in *Buckeye Cookery* (1880), further suggests the links between Easter food rituals and traditional pagan springtime rites of fertility, and rebirth.[61]

Easter Jelly

Color calf's-foot jelly a bright yellow by steeping a small quantity of dried saffron leaves in the water. Pare lemons in long strips about the width of a straw, boil in water until tender, throw them into a rich syrup, and boil until clear. Make a blanc-mange of cream, color one-third pink with poke-berry syrup, one-third green with spinach, and leave the other white. Pour out eggs from a hole a half inch in diameter in the large end, wash and drain the shells carefully, set them in a basin of salt to fill, and pour in the blanc-mange slowly through a funnel, and place the dish in a refrigerator for several hours. When ready to serve, select a round, shallow dish about as large as a hen's nest, form the jelly in it as a lining, scatter the strips of lemon peel over the edge like straws, remove the egg-shells carefully from the blanc-mange, and fill the nest with them.—Mrs. C. M. Coates, Philadelphia[62]

Fourth of July

The celebration of American independence, the Fourth of July, assumed increasing importance in an era more characterized by sectional divisiveness than unity. On Independence Day, families, neighbors, and even whole communities got together to share food, drink, and patriotic spirit. In small towns across the country, citizens gathered to listen to public readings of the Declaration of Independence and political speeches, and then to partake of community picnics, clambakes, dances, fireworks, and other festivities. In the city of Boston, in 1854, the day was filled with parades, floral displays, speeches, and, in the evening, fireworks on the Common. The same year, in Cincinnati, Ohio, the day was celebrated "with great spirit," including a parade, which was "very long, occupying an hour and a half to pass a given point."[63] The ladies of Sutter Creek, California, arranged festivities for their town's Fourth of July celebration in 1880. The day began with a splendid parade, led by a the "Car of Liberty," drawn by four white horses. On this float, children in white robes, representing the States and Territories, surrounded the Goddess of Liberty. Following the parade, everyone gathered to hear a reading of the Declaration of Independence, a choir singing patriotic songs, prayers, and even a speech that advocated women's rights. The day concluded with a grand ball in the evening.[64] Large-scale celebrations, such as the Sutter Creek Grand Ball, required elaborate food preparations suitable to commemorate the importance of the day. Jane Croly's "Independence Cake," embellished with sprigs of box and garnished with rose petals, would have let a suitably impressive air to any Fourth of July festivity.

Independence Cake

Twenty pounds of flour, fifteen pounds of sugar, ten pounds of butter, four dozen of eggs, one quart of wine, one quart of brandy, once ounce of nutmegs, three ounces each of cinnamon, cloves, and mace, two pounds of citron, five pounds each of currants and raisins, and one quart of yeast. Frost it, and dress it with box and rose leaf.[65]

For many families, however, the day was marked by a picnic, where they enjoyed such cold favorites as fried chicken, accompanied by fresh strawberries, or whatever other fruit was in season. The family of Katherine Bragdon, in Rochester, New York, took a boat excursion in the early part of the day, and then returned home to feast on chicken and strawberry shortcake.[66] In 1878, the *New York Times* offered its readers suggestions for "enjoyable short trips" for the Fourth of July holiday. These included places close enough to the city so that travelers could make the journey in one day and be able to enjoy the sea or perhaps "meditate upon the restful pleasure to be had in some pastoral or mountain retreat, where cool brooks ripple and splash over rocky beds, and no sounds but those of the woodland are likely to salute their ears." At Sea Cliff, a popular summer resort reachable by the Long Island Railroad, visitors could enjoy a clambake "on the Rhode Island plan."[67] The reference to Rhode Island offered visitors the prospect of authenticity. Rocky Point, near Providence, became a destination for a "genuine Rhode Island shore dinner" during the 1850s and set the standard for clambakes up and down the East Coast.[68]

Thanksgiving

Thanksgiving, which had begun as a local or regional harvest festival and day of religious obligation, turned into a national, highly commercialized, family-centered holiday during the nineteenth century. The transformation of Thanksgiving began in 1820, when interest in the event was revived by the two-hundredth anniversary of the landing of the Pilgrims. For the next twenty years, the event was fairly predictable: church services in the morning and a large family dinner in the afternoon, held, if possible, at the old family homestead. In this incarnation, Thanksgiving affirmed family continuity, in an era of increasing family instability, as well as national spirit and religious values. The menu for this event had also become codified by the 1840s, consisting of turkey, stuffing, squash, and pie—mince, apple, or pumpkin. The tone of the event was self-consciously "old fashioned," as families tried to retain the values of community and persistence that were under threat in a rapidly changing world.

It was at this point that Sarah Josepha Hale, editor of *Godey's Lady's Book*, was lobbying to make Thanksgiving a national holiday. Through her writings, both editorial and fictional, Hale had helped shape national ideas of what constituted a proper Thanksgiving dinner. Her fictional tables were set abundantly with a roast turkey, stuffing, roast sirloin of beef, a leg of pork, loin of mutton, gravy for all meats,

vegetables, ducklings, goose, chicken pie, pickles, preserves, butter, wheat bread, plum pudding, custards, cake, sweetmeats, and, of
course, pumpkin pie.[69] Hale published this recipe for pumpkin pie in
The Good Housekeeper in 1839.

Pumpkin Pie

Stew the pumpkin dry, and make it like squash pie [with milk, sugar, and five
eggs per quart of milk], only season rather higher. In the country, where this
real yankee pie is prepared in perfection, ginger is almost always used with other
spices. There too, part cream instead of milk is mixed with the pumpkin, which
gives it a richer flavor.

Roll the paste rather thicker than for fruit pies, as there is only one crust. If the
pie is large and deep it will require to bake an hour in a brisk oven.[70]

An analysis of a Thanksgiving menu from 1870 reveals some important
continuities, as well as the changing times in post–Civil War America.
The meal began with oyster soup, cod with egg sauce, lobster salad,
roast turkey, cranberry sauce, mixed pickles, mangoes, pickles peaches,
coleslaw, and celery. This menu presumed a transportation network
that would overcome the old problems of seasonality as well as the
availability of canned goods. Oysters had to be moved by refrigerated
rail car. The lobster salad was probably made from canned lobster.
The celery was grown in hothouses on the outskirts of major cities and
then transported to the market for the holiday. In its structure, this
course, as does the next, reflects a new complexity of offerings at American Thanksgiving tables. The second course, the "removes," or items
brought on to replace the initial courses, consisted of boiled ham,
chicken pie jelly, mashed potatoes, tomatoes, boiled onion, canned
corn, sweet potatoes, and roasted broccoli. Here, too, the menu included a far wider variety of vegetables than would have been found
on a Thanksgiving table in 1835. Americans, who had been exposed
to the French fashion for cooking and eating diverse vegetables, had
embraced this new fashion in their most traditional yearly ritual. Tomatoes might have been canned, or grown under glass. The broccoli, an
Italian culinary import, was possibly also fresh, grown in a hothouse.
Only the potatoes and onions would have seemed familiar to earlier
generations.

Following this course, the table would have been cleared again, to
make way for a pastry course of mince and pumpkin pie, apple tarts,
and Indian pudding. This course seems consciously "old fashioned,"
especially the inclusion of Indian pudding—with its early American
associations. For dessert, the menu concluded with apples, nuts, and
raisins.[71] Once again, this menu seems consciously upwardly mobile in

its conception, including a dessert course that one would have found on a restaurant menu but less commonly on a normal family dinner menu. This menu was, of course, prescriptive rather than "real." It reflected the ambitions of its author, Jane Cunningham Croly, a member of New York's upper crust. Croly's readers, however, especially those who actually purchased her cookbook, would have learned from her prescriptions and perhaps integrated some of her ideas into their own family traditions, transforming the celebration as they did. In reality, however, most American families fell somewhat short of Croly's expectations. Julia Holmes Cook noted in her diary for 1881 that for Thanksgiving, "we have our customary chicken and are *thankful* it is as well with us as it is."[72]

The Thanksgiving dinner required a feverish amount of planning and preparation. In 1870, Almira MacDonald of Victory, New York, wrote in her diary that she "prepared mincemeat for pies and made gold and silver cake" on Tuesday, November 22. The next day, she made four mince pies and prepared stuffing for the turkey. Stuffing may or may not have included chestnuts, but the other ingredients for a good stuffing included onion, bread, sage, butter, pepper, salt, egg, minced pork, and chopped celery, according to cookbook author Mary Henderson.[73] On Thanksgiving Day, her family went to church in the morning and dined at 3 o'clock (despite the absence of Mr. MacDonald, a lawyer, who was busy with a murder case all day and could not attend). The intensity of the preparations varied little from year to year for MacDonald. In 1882, she wrote, "Thanksgiving Day—12 to dinner and no hired girl, but was able with mother and Anne's help to get a good dinner of roast turkey, chicken salad, onions, potatoes, cranberry sauce, lemon pie, mince pie, and cider."[74]

Mince pie, a staple of the Thanksgiving table, had to be started early so that it could age, according to cookbook writer Maria Parloa. "Make it as early in the month as possible. When making the Thanksgiving Pies, add to every two quarts of the prepared mince-meat one pound of candied fruit—cherries, apricots, and pineapple, all cut fine; also a tumbler of crab-apple or quince jelly. Bake the pies five or six days before Thanksgiving and warm them before using, reserving one for such guests as may prefer it cold."[75]

Christmas

The food year for most Victorian Americans culminated with Christmas. In a short story published in *Gleason's Pictorial Drawing-Room Companion* in December 1853, the characters Lizzy and Sam decided to have Christmas dinner at their house, a total of thirteen guests. Lizzy said, "We must have a turkey, of course, and a pair of chickens, a sirloin of beef, and you may get me a half gallon of oysters. Let's see again—we shall want all kinds of vegetables, and we are about out. You'd better get a new lot, and some celery and cauliflowers; some cranberries too. I must have some squashes for pies, and tell the butcher to send some mince-meat. That makes me think I must have a new box of raisins." Later, Lizzy remembered that she also needed almonds and other nuts, Malaga grapes, oranges, and teacake.[76]

The story would have been of great interest to a society that was only beginning to celebrate Christmas. The Puritans had outlawed Christmas celebrations, and the taboo did not disappear until the 1850s. *Gleason's* commented for the benefit of those readers who might not know, "The Church of England celebrates this feast, as do most of the European protestants. All over the world, Christmas is heralded as an occasion for mutual good feeling, reunions, family gatherings, and the exercise of those charities so blessed in the sight of heaven."[77] As late as 1857, however, author Caroline Cowles Richards wrote in her memoir, *Village Life in America*, "Grandmother and Grandfather do not care much about making Christmas presents. They say, when they were young no one observed Christmas or New Years." The only holiday Richards' Puritan grandparents celebrated consistently was Thanksgiving.[78]

The American acceptance of Christmas coincided with the arrival of large numbers of immigrants from countries where Christmas was actively celebrated, in particular Germany. Americans witnessed the British royal family gathered around a Christmas tree (Prince Albert, Queen Victoria's husband, was German) and quickly followed suit. Popular magazines, including *Harper's New Monthly Magazine*, published articles with tantalizing details about how Christmas was celebrated elsewhere, especially in Germany.[79]

Charles Dickens's story *A Christmas Carol*, written in 1843, provided Americans with another source of information about Christmas customs. They could have heard Dickens read from his text in person during his 1867–1868 tour of the United States. The Cratchit's Christmas dinner, with its goose (courtesy of Mr. Scrooge) and steaming plum pudding surely helped to convey both the fabric and the romance of English Christmas dining rituals across the Atlantic, to complement those acquired from Germany. The front page of *Harper's Weekly* on December 29, 1860, was emblazoned with a Dickensian image of a Christmas dinner, complete with the plum pudding making a grand entrance.[80]

Popular literature, women's magazines in particular, offered constant annual advice about Christmas preparations from the 1850s on. The December 1871 issue of *Godey's Lady's Book* addressed the topic of Christmas cookery—as have generations of women's magazines before and since. That year, *Godey's* offered instructions for preparing a suitable array of "Holiday Sweets." The article showed readers how to make Christmas plum pudding in five different ways, as well as Christmas fruit or plum cake, lemon pudding, gingerbread, tea cakes, lemon cheesecake, lemon cream, marble cake, raisin pudding, suet pudding, vanilla toffey, almond hard-bake, rich mincemeat, and cranberry tart. In addition to Christmas sweets, *Godey's* explained how to stuff and roast a turkey, goose, duck, and capon and, finally, how to make croquettes from the leftovers.[81] An illustration published in the same issue, entitled "Preparing for Christmas," depicted a child making battle with a variety of Christmas food. The caption beneath read, "Turkey, Goose, Duck, Fish, Turtle, Celery, Plum Cake, Plum-Pudding, Cornucopias, Champagne, etc., etc."[82]

By the 1870s, Christmas was widely celebrated in the United States and had become a holiday that centered on family celebration, gift giving, the indulgence of children, and excessive eating (and often excessive drinking as well). Food permeated all of the Victorian Christmas rituals. Even the Christmas tree decorations were typically edible. In the 1830s, English traveler Harriet Martineau described a Christmas tree decorated, "as dictated by the mistress' German maid" with cherries, plums, strawberries, and peaches attached to the boughs of the tree, as well as gilded egg cups filled with "comfits, lozenges, and barley sugar."[83] Thirty years later, families still used fruit to decorate their Christmas trees, as indicated by a diarist in 1867, who noted on December 26, "Had our Christmas tree taken down and the last fruit taken from it."[84]

The food served on Christmas day, as indicated by numerous prescriptive sources, was to be rich, varied, frivolous, delicious, and appealing to the tastes of children and adults alike. The Bragdon family's Christmas menu in 1867 followed this pattern. The offerings consisted of oyster soup, fried and raw oysters, chickens, fried cakes, coffee, tea, apple, raspberry, cherry, and squash pies, pickles, peaches, chestnuts, walnuts, apples, and cider.[85] This sounds more like a party menu than a formal sit-down dinner—although it could have been the latter. Catherine Bragdon did not indicate courses; she merely listed everything as she remembered it. With some rearrangement, this menu makes much more sense as a traditional meal structure.

Plum pudding, the grand finale of any Victorian Christmas table, had a history that dated back at least to the early eighteenth century. The earliest description, published in 1711, described plum pudding as "a boiled pudding now composed of flour, bread crumbs, suet, raisins, currants, and other fruits, with eggs, spices, etc., sometimes flavoured with brandy or other spirit, eaten at Christmas."[86] Originally, the pudding would have been boiled in the stomach or entrails of a pig or sheep. By the nineteenth century, a cloth pudding bag was more commonly used, and by 1878, when Mary Henderson published her recipe for plum pudding, she recommended using a buttered tin pudding mold. This recipe appeared in Henderson's *Practical Cooking and Dinner Giving*.

Plum Pudding, with Rum or Brandy

Take three-quarters of a pound of chopped suet, three-quarters of a pound of stoned raisins, three-quarters of a pound of currants, quarter of a pound of citron, three-quarters of a pound of sugar, three-quarters of a pound of bread-crumbs, two apples cut into small dice, and the grated peel of a lemon; mix the while in a basin, with three pounded cloves, a pinch of salt, six eggs, and half a gill of rum or brandy. Butter a pudding-mold, fill it with the mixture, and tie a cloth over the top. Place a plate at the bottom of a kettle which is three-parts full of boiling water. Put the pudding in, and boil for four hours, keeping the pot replenished with boiling water. Turn out the pudding on a hot dish; sprinkle over it sugar. Pour over half a pint of warm rum or brandy, and light it when putting the pudding on the table.[87]

NOTES

1. M. W. Ellsworth and B. B. Dickerson, *The Successful Housekeeper* (Detroit: M. W. Ellsworth & Co., 1883), 472.

2. "Silver and Silver Plate," *Harper's New Monthly Magazine* 37 (September 1868), 434.

3. Sarah Josepha Hale, *The New Household Receipt Book* (New York: H. Long & Bro., 1853), 210.

4. Robert Laird Collier, *English Home Life* (Boston: Tickenor & Co., 1885), 71. Collier, an American who had spent seven years living in England, was commenting on the universal importance of civilized dining during the Victorian era.

5. Hale, 210.

6. John F. Kasson, *Rudeness and Civility: Manners in Nineteenth-Century Urban America* (New York: Hill and Wang, 1990), 44.

7. Eliza Leslie, *The Ladies' Guide to True Politeness and Perfect Manners* (Philadelphia: T. B. Peterson & Bros., 1864), title page.

8. Frances Milton Trollope, *Domestic Manners of the Americans*, 4th ed. (London; New York: Whittaker, Treacher, & Co, 1832), 58.

9. Norbert Elias, *The History of Manners: The Civilizing Process* (originally published in Switzerland, 1939; New York: Pantheon Books, 1982), 92.

10. Leslie, 127.

11. Ibid., 127.

12. An American Lady, *True Politeness: A Handbook for Ladies* (New York: George A. Leavitt, 1853), 48–49.

13. *True Politeness*, 49.

14. George C. Latta, Household Inventory, Charlotte, New York, 1856.

15. Charles H. Carpenter, Jr., and Mary Grace Carpenter, *Tiffany Silver* (New York: Dodd, Mead & Co., 1978), 92.

16. George S. Gibbs, *The Whitesmiths of Taunton* (New York: Harper & Row, 1943), 255–256.

17. Leslie, 128.

18. Agnes Morton, *Etiquette* (Philadelphia: Penn Publishing, 1894), 88.

19. John A. Ruth, *Decorum* (New York: Union Publishing House, 1883), 214, 103.

20. Leslie, 135.

21. Ibid., 132.

22. Estelle Woods Wilcox, ed., *Buckeye Cookery and Practical Housekeeping* (1880; reprint St. Paul, MN: Minnesota Historical Society Press, 1988), 39.

23. Jane C. Croly, *Jennie June's American Cookery Book* (New York: American News Company, 1870), 256–259; digital edition available at "Feeding America: The Historic American Cookbook Project," Michigan State University Library, http://digital.lib.msu.edu/collections/ (accessed January 11, 2005).

24. Leslie, 327–339.

25. "Method of Setting Out a Table in America," illustration in *Godey's Lady's Book* 58 (March 1859): 267.

26. Mary F. Henderson, *Practical Cooking and Dinner Giving* (New York: Harper & Brothers, 1877), 13.

27. Henderson, 13.

28. Maria Parloa, *Ladies' Home Journal* 8 (November 1891): 29.

29. Elizabeth F. Ellet, ed., *The New Cyclopedia of Domestic Economy, and Practical Housekeeper* (Norwich, CT: Henry Bill Publishing Co., 1873), 25.

30. George C. Latta, Probate Inventory, Charlotte, NY, 1956.

31. Ellet, 24.

32. C. W. Gesner, "Concerning Restaurants," *Harper's New Monthly Magazine* 32, no. 191 (April 1866): 592.

33. Gesner, 593.

34. Michael Slater, *Dickens on America and the Americans* (Sussex: Harvester Press, 1979), 154–155; Charles Dickens and John Lance Griffith, "American Notes," *American Notes, by Charles Dickens*, e-Text,

November 12, 2004, available at http://www.people.virginia.edu/~jlg4p/dickens/dkswhole.html (accessed December 29, 2005), 173.

35. Leslie, 103.

36. Isabella L. Bird, *Englishwoman in America* (1856; London: John Murray, 1856), 149–150; digital edition available at "American Memory," Library of Congress, Washington, D.C., http://memory.loc.gov/ (accessed May 22, 2004).

37. William Dean Howells, *A Modern Instance* (1882; New York: Library of America, 1982), 312.

38. *The Fitchburg Directory* (Fitchburg, MA: Price, Lee & Co., 1880), 5.

39. Menu, International Hotel, Niagara Falls, NY, October 24, 1863, Menu Collection, Library Company of Philadelphia (5763 F 25).

40. Root Waverley and Richard de Rochemont, *Eating in America: A History* (1976; New York: Ecco Press, 1981), 103.

41. Menu, Wyoming Valley Hotel, Wilkes-Barre, PA, August 24, 1868, Menu Collection, Library Company of Philadelphia (5763K79).

42. Joseph Jackson, *America's Most Historic Highway: Market Street, Philadelphia* (Philadelphia: John Wanamaker, 1926), 120–122.

43. Menu, Merchants' Hotel, Philadelphia, February 8, 1872, Menu Collection, Library Company of Philadelphia (5763 F37).

44. *The Fitchburg Directory* (Fitchburg, MA: Price, Lee & Co., 1880), 144.

45. Captain Frederick Marryat, 1839; quoted in Root and de Rochemont, 318. For a more extensive discussion of food possibilities during early train travel, see Barbara Haber, "The Harvey Girls," chapter 4 in *From Hardtack to Home Fries: An Uncommon History of American Cooks and Meals* (New York: Free Press, 2002), especially 88–91.

46. Root and de Rochemont, 319.

47. Menu, St. Charles Hotel, Syracuse, NY, October 23, 1863, Menu Collection, Library Company of Philadelphia (5763 F27).

48. Haber, "Harvey Girls," 92–104.

49. Reported by the Detroit *Commercial Advertiser* in 1867; quoted in Root and de Rochemont, 319–320.

50. Charles Nordhoff, *California: A Book for Travellers and Settlers* (New York: Harper & Brothers, 1874), 30.

51. Godfrey Vigne, 1831, quoted by Mary Hanlon, "Music, Literature, Balls, and Entertainments," *Women in America, 1820–1842*, American Studies at the University of Virginia, May 22, 2004, available at http://xroads.virginia.edu/~HYPER/DETOC/FEM/entertain.htm (accessed May 23, 2004).

52. Isabella Beeton, *Mrs. Beeton's Book of Household Management, 1859–1861*, quoted in Susan Williams, *Savory Suppers and Fashionable Feasts: Dining in Victorian America* (1985; Knoxville, TN: University of Tennessee Press, 1996), 202.

53. "Living in the Country," *Putnam's Monthly Magazine of American Literature, Science and Art* 7, no. 39 (March 1856): 296.

54. See Stephen Nissenbaum's discussion of New Year's Day customs and the transformation of holiday celebrations during the Victorian era in *The Battle for Christmas* (New York: Alfred A. Knopf, 1996), 190, 348, n. 25.

55. Search for "New Year's" as recipe title in *Feeding America* Digital Archive recipe database, http://digital.lib.msu.edu/projects/cookbooks/index.html (accessed January 3, 2006); Catharine Esther Beecher, *Miss Beecher's Domestic Receipt Book: Designed as a Supplement to Her Treatise on Domestic Economy* (1846; New York: Harper, 1850), 142; Croly, 196–197, 208.

56. Croly, 309–310.

57. Esther Jacobs Levy, *Jewish Cookery Book* (Philadelphia, 1871; reprint Cambridge: Applewood Books, 1988), 7–8.

58. *Oxford Encyclopedia of Food and Drink in America*, s.v. "Easter" (by Cathy K. Kaufman).

59. Croly, 294–295.

60. Cadbury Trebor Bassett, "Cadbury Milestones," *Cadbury Trebor Bassett: Chocolate and Sweets*, company Web site, 2005, available at http://www.cadbury.co.uk (accessed January 4, 2006).

61. Wilcox, 184–185.

62. Ibid., 184.

63. "Celebration of the Fourth of July at Boston," *New York Times* (July 6, 1854): 8.

64. "A Ladies' Celebration," *New York Times* (July 19, 1880): 3.

65. Croly, 195.

66. Katherine Bradgon Diary, July 4, 1861, Bragdon Family Papers, Department of Rare Books and Special Collections, Rush Rees Library, University of Rochester.

67. "Fourth of July Excursions," *New York Times* (June 30, 1878): 7.

68. Kathy Neustadt, *Clambake: A History and Celebration of an American Tradition* (Amherst: University of Massachusetts Press, 1992), 55.

69. See curator Jan Longone's discussion of Hale at "Feeding America" Web site, http://digital.lib.msu.edu/projects/cookbooks/html/intro_essay.html (accessed January 11, 2005).

70. Sarah Josepha Buell Hale, *The Good Housekeeper, or The Way to Live Well and Be Well While We Live* (Boston: Weeks, Jordon & Co., 1839), 71.

71. Croly, 263.

72. Julia Holmes Cook Diary, Cook Papers, Department of Rare Books and Special Collections, Rush Rees Library, University of Rochester.

73. Henderson, 167.

74. Almira MacDonald Diary, Osborne Family Papers, Strong Museum Library, Rochester, NY.

75. Maria Parloa, "Everything About the House," *Ladies' Home Journal* 8: 12 (November 1891): 29.

76. Miss. P. Hamilton, "Keeping Christmas," *Gleason's Pictorial Drawing-Room Companion* 5 (December 24, 1853): 411.

77. Hamilton, 416.

78. Caroline Cowles Richards, *Village Life in America, 1852–1872*; digital edition, available at http://www.wordowner.com/richards/ (accessed January 4, 2006).

79. See, for example, "Christmas in Germany," *Harper's New Monthly Magazine* 4 (March 1852): 499–500.

80. "Christmas-Day, 1860," illustration in *Harper's Weekly* 4 (December 29, 1860): 1.

81. "Receipts, Etc.," *Godey's Lady's Book* 83 (December 1871): 564–566.

82. "Preparing for Christmas," illustration in *Godey's Lady's Book* 83 (December 1871): 515.

83. *Yuletide at Winterthur* (Winterthur, DE: Winterthur Museum, 1980), 19, 55.

84. Louisa Coleman Hayes Diary, December 26, 1867, Coleman-Hayes Diaries, Ontario County Historical Society, Geneva, NY.

85. Catherine Bragdon Diary, December 25, 1862, Bragdon Family Papers, Department of Rare Books and Special Collections, Rush Rees Library, University of Rochester.

86. *Oxford English Dictionary*, s.v. "Plum Pudding."

87. Henderson, 269.

CHAPTER 6
CONCEPTS OF DIET AND NUTRITION

In a majority of the works extant on the subject of preparing food for the table, the strong point of authorship seems to have been, to mix and mingle the greatest possible amount of seasonings, saltings, spicings, and greasings into a single dish.... No wonder the patrons and admirers of such cook-books are full of dyspepsia, and constipation, and hemorrhoids, and biliousness of every degree, and nervousness of every kind.

R. T. Trall, *The New Hydropathic Cook-Book*, 1853

The relationship between Americans and their food was sorely tested during the nineteenth century. As the passage above from medical theorist and dietary reformer R. T. Trall suggests, the notion of what was a proper, adequate, and healthful diet had become a matter of serious debate. As the nation changed in response to industrialization, urbanization, and social and ethnic diversification, many feared that the Republic was at risk, that Americans were becoming "soft." The pace of American life seemed problematically fast, threatening the health of the nation. The success of the national experiment seemed to have a darker side, and many feared that the excesses generated by the market revolution were undermining the virtue of the Republic. According to Amherst College professor, Edward Hitchcock, "No nation becomes rich and prosperous, without becoming also luxurious and debilitated." Likewise, Andrew Bigelow, a worried Boston clergyman noted, "We see luxury, the bane of all republics, spreading its infection and eating as a gangrene into the vitals of the state."[1] Bigelow's metaphor, which linked illness and food with the body of the nation, was carefully chosen and reflected prevailing notions of the day. For some, dietary reform offered a cure; for others, food served to buttress existing institutional structures that offered conservative options to the current frenzy of progress. Finally, for many American families, ideas of food and diet were closely linked to religious beliefs and rituals, as well as to their hopes for health, prosperity, and a better future for their children.

DIETARY REFORM AND THE HEALTH OF THE NATION

For nineteenth-century reformers of all sorts, the words "stimulation" and "excitement" had negative connotations. Moral reformers believed that too much excitement compromised stability and reason, leading to a national insanity—which seemed to be visible all around them. City streets abounded with ragged beggars, drunkards, prostitutes, petty thieves, and orphaned children; Western states and territories venerated lawlessness over religious piety; and Southerners colluded in the transportation and exploitation of human flesh. These widespread fears carried over to health and dietary reformers, beginning in the 1830s. Mary Mann, author of *The Physiological Cookery Book* (1858) and wife of education reformer Horace Mann, expressed the connection between food and morality succinctly: "There is no more prolific, indeed, there is no such prolific cause of bad morals as abuses of diet."[2]

The relentless movement of people from the countryside into the burgeoning cities, and accompanying occupational mobility, also led to dietary adjustments. No longer limited in their food choices to what was locally available, or to what was traditionally acceptable, urban Americans, particularly those in the rising middle classes, began to experiment with their food choices. Catharine Beecher, a notable domestic reformer, addressed this phenomenon, making an explicit comparison between the vitality of the early republic and her world of 1856. "In the palmy days of our early Republic," she wrote, "all classes rose with the sun, and all the hours of labor, even for the highest, were by daylight. And their social gatherings," she continued, "were ordinarily ended when the 'nine o'clock bell' gave warning that all well-ordered families should retire to rest."[3] In the civilized world of the modern age, however, Beecher felt it natural that tastes and habits would progress to a higher plane, at the table as elsewhere.

The farther man advances from childhood and in social life from the savage state, the more do refined and intellectual pleasures take the place of merely animal. In the lower states of society, the chief attractions to social gatherings were *eating and drinking*. But just in proportion as man becomes elevated, this lowest species of enjoyment gives place to higher and more refined pleasures.[4]

This theory of progress presented Beecher with a dilemma, however, because what she saw around her was not "higher and more refined pleasures," but increasing levels of gluttony, decadence, and ill health. She urged her readers to rethink their culinary pleasures, suggesting that an overemphasis on eating and drinking would lead to decline rather than progress.

Beecher and many other reformers of the Victorian era believed fervently that the "cure" lay with Americans themselves. In her world, perfection was possible through human intervention, discipline, and self-will. "Animals, having no reason to guide them," Beecher reasoned, "are formed so that they usually have an instinct to warn them from those kinds of food that would harm them. But man, having reason bestowed for his guidance, is expected to from habits of virtue and self-control, so that when experience shows any practice to be pernicious it will be avoided."[5] Whether through temperance, vegetarianism, avoidance of stimulants, bodybuilding and fitness activities, water cures, or participation in institutional reform activities, American could apply dietary ideologies to restore their own health and vigor, as well as that of the nation.

Sylvester Graham and the Rise of Vegetarianism

Sylvester Graham, another prominent leader in the dietary reform movement, would have agreed. Graham's early history set his course for a preoccupation with health issues. He was born at the end of the eighteenth century, the seventeenth child of a father who was in his seventies. Graham's father died two years after his son's birth, and as a result, his mother lost her mind. Graham himself contracted tuberculosis in 1810, when he was sixteen years old. He recovered and subsequently entered Amherst College in 1823, but had a nervous breakdown and dropped out after one term. In 1828, Graham became a minister and a Temperance activist; within two years, he had become General Agent for the Pennsylvania Temperance Society.[6]

Graham's own health problems doubtless inspired him to explore the causes of disease, but the outbreak of cholera in New York City in 1832 stimulated him to reconsider traditional explanations and treatments for illness. The type of "heroic" medicine practiced widely in the United States relied on purging the body of disease, through blood letting and the use of dangerous purgatives, including arsenic, calomel, and mercury. Graham argued that cholera was linked to over-stimulation of the intestines by too much liquor, too many spices, fats, and other stimulants. He had noticed that the disease had intestinal symptoms—diarrhea and stomach cramps, in particular—and believed that dietary methods could successfully treat a mild case of cholera. He devised a new dietary approach, prescribing "Indian meal gruel, or rice-water, or coarse unbolted wheatmeal gruel, or wheat-bran tea . . . in moderate quantities."[7]

Cholera made Graham's career. Upon studying those who got cholera and those who did not, he discovered that those who led healthy, temperate lives did not contract the disease (for the most part). His dietary theories, which came to be known as "Grahamism," were widely embraced, following the epidemic. He recommended that bread be made only from whole grain flour. By the 1830s, millers were beginning to "bolt" flour to make it white. Bolting removed the bran, or outer casing from the grains, but, in doing so, also removed many of the nutritive elements. Whiteness—a value associated with luxury—was perceived to be debilitating by Graham. The bread that would most benefit Americans, thought Graham, was the bread made in "those blessed days of New England's prosperity and happiness when our good mothers used to make the family bread." This association with bread and a golden age, when women made the family bread, continued in a full-blown critique of modern women's deficiencies:

> Could good wives and mothers fully comprehend the importance of good bread, in relation to all the bodily and intellectual and moral interests of their husbands and children, and in relation to the domestic and social and civil welfare of mankind, and to their religious prosperity, for both time and eternity, they would estimate the art and duty of bread-making far, very far more highly than they now do.[8]

Graham believed food should be simple, plain, and natural. "Simple" meant "not compounded and complicated by culinary processes." "Plain" meant "not dressed with pungent seasonings and condiments," and "natural" required that food be "as created by God for man's most efficient use."[9] Graham's diet supplemented crusty (stale) bread with raw fruit and vegetables. According to Graham, "food should not be robbed of its most important values in the course of preparation."[10] Chewing, or "mastication," was as important as the nutritional makeup of a food. Graham criticized commercial bakers as well for using additives in their bread to both soften and whiten, stirring up a controversy as he did so. As late as 1880, *Godey's Lady's Book* was still carrying on his crusade about the problem of adulteration by commercial bakers. "The introduction of alum in flour, for various purposes, has been a trick of the baker for the past 100 years," *Godey's* wrote. "There has been too much indifference on this subject—indifference that has resulted in Americans earning the title of 'a race of dyspeptics.'"[11]

John Harvey Kellogg, another important dietary reformer, described the impact of bolting and its social impact: "By removing from the kernel of wheat the outer layers, called bran, ... the grain is deprived of its most nutrient portions, which are fed to hogs or other domestic animals, who thrive upon the best portion of the wheat while man contents himself with the impoverished residue." Moreover, according to Kellogg, "in the center of the grain is found almost nothing but pure starch, which is so incapable of sustaining life that even a dog will starve to death in a short time if fed upon it exclusively."[12] Kellogg's comparisons of human beings with animals were conscious; he knew that in the wake of Darwinian ideas about evolution, those comparisons would tap into a cultural nerve among class-conscious Americans.

Catharine Beecher, in a statement clearly shaped by Graham's notions about bread, argued that stale bread was preferable to bread fresh from the oven. She offered a chemical explanation for her assertion:

> Universal experience has shown that unmixed and simple food digests more easily than rich and complicated articles. New bread is far more difficult of digestion than stale, because mastication changes it to a compact dough form, which does not readily unite with the gastric juice. It is quite the reverse with stale bread.[13]

Graham's ideas about diet were widely embraced for most of the Victorian period, albeit often in a more moderate format, as was reflected in numerous cookbooks of the era. Cooks could choose from Graham cake, Graham biscuits (4), Graham bread (21), Graham breakfast rolls, Graham Christmas pudding, Graham crackers, Graham fig biscuit, Graham gems (18), Graham griddle cakes (5), Graham muffins (11), Graham mush (3), Graham paste, Graham popovers, Graham porridge, Graham pudding (8), Graham wafers (2), Graham wheatlets, Graham rolls, and Graham pancakes (2). Graham crackers, as described by Kellogg, seemed suitably austere for a Grahamist diet. His recipe involved mixing graham flour with cold water, then rolling the ensuing unleavened dough into a thin sheet, cutting it into cracker forms, pricking the dough all over to prevent the surface from blistering, and baking the crackers in a hot oven for twenty minutes. The ensuing crackers would have been dry, relatively tasteless, and lacking in any sort of gustatory stimulation.[14]

"Graham Christmas Pudding," seems contrary to the spirit of Grahamism; the recipe below, however, was prefaced by a testimonial from its contributor, Mrs. Rollin A. Edgerton of Arkansas: "The Christmas pudding which I add was served up this Christmas on my table and pronounced delicious. Dyspeptics need not fear this 'Plum Pudding,' and it is rich enough to please the most fastidious."[15] Upon a closer examination of the recipe, Graham flour represented only a third of the total amount of flour called for. The other two cups of flour were not specified but were presumably white. Although molasses was substituted for sugar, sweetness itself was considered a stimulant by the strictest dietary reformers. Spices prevailed in the recipe, despite their prohibition by Beecher, Kellogg, and others, and the pudding itself, although not flamed with rum or brandy, was served with a rich buttery hard sauce.

Graham Christmas Pudding

Beat two eggs; take one-half cup of sweet milk; one-half cup of molasses, in which dissolve one-half teaspoon of soda; a lump of butter the size of an egg; one cup of Graham flour (don't sift); two cups of flour, in which a cup of stoned raisins are well rubbed; one small teaspoon of salt; spice with cinnamon, cloves and nutmeg, one teaspoonful all together. Then steam two hours and serve with a hard sauce of butter and fine sugar creamed together, with one well beaten egg and grated nutmeg as a finish. Wholesome, delicious, and extremely simple to prepare.[16]

Raising Healthy Children

Graham's influence was widespread. The creation of Graham Societies, Graham hotels and boardinghouses—where guests could partake of a Graham diet—and Graham food products introduced his ideas to a large population of Americans during the 1840s and beyond. A contemporary of Graham, Dr. William Andrus Alcott, shared much of his dietary philosophy. Alcott had been converted to vegetarianism around 1820 by a Swedenborgian minister named William Metcalfe. Metcalf had come to America in 1817 and began preaching abstinence from meat shortly after his arrival. Alcott heard one of Metcalf's sermons and renounced meat. In 1838, he wrote his vegetarian tract, *A Vegetarian Diet*. His role as a physician lent credibility to his dietary advice, and his book gained popularity among intellectuals and radicals, including his cousin, Bronson Alcott, who founded Fruitlands, a vegetarian utopian community in Harvard, Massachusetts.[17]

Alcott's household manual and cookbook, *The Young Housekeeper*, articulated his philosophy about diet and its relationship to health. "The grand question, in short," he asked, "is, What are the kinds of food which are best for healthy persons—best for their whole being, here and hereafter?"[18] Alcott, like Catharine Beecher, imbued housekeeping with an important degree of national significance. In his first chapter, "The Dignity of the House-Keeper," Alcott quoted Dr. Benjamin Rush's statement that "Mothers and teachers . . . sow the seeds of nearly all the good and evil in our world."[19] Alcott believed women had the moral power and moral responsibility to shape their families, and especially their children, into productive, responsible, healthy human beings. "They educate us not only intellectually and morally, but physically," he wrote. "It is mothers who operate on our whole nature." Alcott aimed to educate the educators. He dismissed most published cookbooks as "little more than large bundles of recipes for fashionable cookery." Through his cookbook, he aimed to provide women something more: the principles that could guide them in their profession, especially those principles related to food, cookery, and physical education.[20] To that end, he offered forty-something chapters on specific foods and how to use them most beneficially. He also included a chapter titled "Summary of Leading Principles," in which he encouraged women to cook simply, to respect the importance of mastication, to avoid serving foods too hot, to keep a regular meal schedule, and to pay attention to drinking, the proper combination of foods, and the differing effects of food with regard to age. While taste, or "gustatory pleasure" was perfectly acceptable to Alcott, he decried the superfluous labor and waste of materials involved in preparing elaborate recipes. He used the example of a potato, arguing,

> To boil, steam, roast or bake a potatoe, is a useful process. If it does not increase the quantity of the nutriment, it certainly improves its quality. But how few house-keepers stop here! Salt must certainly be added, and probably butter. Nay, this is but common-place; and does not bring into view the skill of the cook at all. By no means. A simple boiled potatoe is surely unfit to be eaten; and to eat a cold potatoe—one I mean which is not smoking—would be horrid. How heavy it would lie on the stomach! And does not this prove it to be unwholesome? Yes, just as much as the fact that simple cool water is at first too heavy for the stomachs of those who have been accustomed twenty, thirty, or fifty years to hot tea or coffee, or to cider, beer, or spirits, proves that cool water is unwholesome. And when house-keepers can prove cold potatoes to be, in their nature, unwholesome, I will be ready to prove that cold water is so.[21]

Ultimately, Alcott asserted that serving food cold slows down the eating process, forcing people to eat less food—and improving their overall health. In the same manner, "compound" dishes, those sweetened or highly seasoned, he believed encourage faster eating and, thus, should be avoided. Alcott's goal was to transform people's conceptions of taste in food and to teach them to be satisfied with simple meals, limited options on the table, and plain cookery.

Vegetarianism Institutionalized

R. T. Trall, another dietary reformer of the same era, criticized other cookbook writers for recipes that he considered excessive. He cited Sarah Josepha Hale, esteemed editor of *Godey's Lady's Book*, for a recipe for "Head Cheese" in her *New Book of Cookery*. He was disgusted by the slaughter of meat required to produce the dish. Moreover, the dish was "highly seasoned with pepper, cayenne, and salt," which Trall considered excessive, and he further condemned Hale's recommendation that it be "eaten with vinegar and mustard, and served for luncheon or supper."[22] He even criticized fellow reformer Catharine Beecher for using wine and brandy in the recipes in her *Domestic Receipt Book*. "The wine and brandy she commends in her cakes, and pies, and pudding sauces are better calculated to make men drunkards, than to make them wise in choosing."[23]

Trall was particularly concerned with the relationship between food intake and excretory output. "Nutrition," he wrote, "is the replenishment of the tissue, not the accumulation of fat," a notion that he believed should guide people in their daily intake. "The latter is a disease, and a fattened animal, be it a hog or an alderman, is a diseased animal . . . Fat men, fat women, fat children, and fat pigs, are not examples of excessive nutrition so much as of deficient excretion."[24]

These dietary theories helped formalize the growing interest in vegetarianism. In 1850, Sylvester Graham, William Metcalf, William Alcott, and R. T. Trall founded the American Vegetarian Society.[25] Trall, whose *New Hydropathic Cook-Book* appeared in 1853, commented on the impact of vegetarianism. "Under the auspices of the vegetarian reform movement, many improvements have taken place in the manner of preparing a great variety of dishes for the Table," he began. He added that vegetarian cookbooks offered "improvements on the ordinary plan of mixed diet, mainly in excluding 'flesh, fish, and fowl,' and substituting butter for lard." He was concerned, however, that the movement did not have a clear consensus about its philosophy. While some vegetarians concerned themselves about the slaughter of animals, others saw vegetarianism as a means of saving people and, by inference, society.[26] Catharine Beecher pointed out that working people from cultures around the world eat vegetarian diets, summoning social as well as ecological justifications for vegetarianism. "The working people in almost every nation are obliged to live almost entirely on vegetable diet, because it is so much cheaper," she wrote, "for it takes fifteen times as much land to provide animal food as it does to supply a vegetable diet." Beecher also invoked history in her provegetarian argument: "The brave and vigorous Spartans never ate meat." What she referred to as "animal food," she regarded as a source of stimulation rather than nourishment, finding distinctly less virtue in the former than in the latter.[27]

The Crusade Against Condiments

Beecher and other dietary reformers were particularly concerned about the use of what they termed "condiments." According to Beecher, "There is a class of articles called condiments, that stimulate the appetite to an unnatural degree. Pepper, mustard, and spices, are those most commonly used." She viewed these items as problematic because they "tend to create a false appetite."[28] Dr. John Harvey Kellogg, of Battle Creek, Michigan, agreed. "Every day a hundred thousand dyspeptics sigh and groan in consequence of condiments," wrote Kellogg. "Pepper, spice, salt, vinegar, mustard, and all kinds of fats belong to the list of dyspepsia-producing articles known as condiments. . . . Whether the food does taste better or not does not depend upon the condiment, but upon the taste of the eater. If his taste is unperverted, he likes food best without condiments." Kellogg, a physician, offered a scientific explanation for the effect of condiments on the process of digestion: "Condiments are innutritious and irritating. They induce a heated condition of the system which is very unfavorable to health. They clog the liver, imposing upon it a great addition to its rightful task. Worst of all, they irritate the digestive organs, impairing their tone and deranging their function."[29]

Kellogg, a Seventh-Day Adventist, was the final star in the dietary reform constellation. He became head of the Western Health Reform Institute in Battle Creek, Michigan in 1876, and from there, he crusaded for vegetarianism and health reform for the next sixty-two years.[30] "The world abounds with books that teach how to use salt, soda, saleratus, butter, etc.;" wrote Kellogg in *The Hygienic Cook Book* in 1876, "our object is to teach people how to cook without the use of these disease-producing agents." A hygienic diet, according to Kellogg, was one that discarded spices, vinegar, pickles, mustard, pepper sauce, aged cheese, pork, fine flour, tea, and coffee. Butter, salt, and meat could be used, but only in moderation, and sweet fruits were to be substituted for sugar. He believed that "tea, coffee, chocolate, and cocoa differ somewhat in their poisonous qualities, but the difference is primarily in degree, not in kind, since the element which gives them their peculiar properties is essentially the same in each." Meat was a problem because of its propensity to carry trichinae and tapeworms; fish were also subject to disease and "less nutritious than beef." But it was for pork that Kellogg reserved special venom, terming hogs "those scrofulous scavengers which supply our citics with ham and sausage."[31] "As a man eateth, so is he," wrote Kellogg. "A loaf of bread, eaten, digested, assimilated, becomes flesh. A pound of pork, treated in the same way, also becomes flesh. The first becomes pure, healthy flesh; the second becomes gross, diseased flesh."[32]

The editors of *Godey's* concurred. In 1876, the centennial anniversary of American independence, the magazine published an article entitled "The Art of Cookery," which took aim at the state of the American diet. The article began with the assertion that "the prevalence of dyspepsia among Americans is simply the result of a century of bad cookery." The argument continued, drawing explicit historical parallels. "Our forefathers came here from Europe healthy and hearty, from an equable temperature, out-of-door work, and meals which, though coarse enough, were well cooked and nutritious." As generations progressed, and Americans began "following sedentary occupations," bad eating habits became the norm. "The stomach is the centre of life. When it is sick, the whole body suffers in sympathy." Women, in particular, seemed to have been afflicted by lack of exercise, household worries, and improper diet. What would save them? According to *Godey's*, ventilation, exercise, good cookery, all principles with which Graham, Alcott, Beecher, Trall, and Kellogg would have heartily agreed. *Godey's* cited the recent establishment of cooking schools as a helpful antidote to the problem of dyspepsia among women, as well as the scientific studies of food and diet. As a final note, the editors saw redemption from ill health and poor diet in the ignorance of the serving class. "Above all," they noted, "the pest of ignorant servants has forced ladies to go down into their own kitchens to superintend, if not to execute."[33]

TEMPERANCE REFORMERS AND THE ELEVATION OF WATER

In addition to dietary issues, the persistence of the drunkenness problem caught the attention of many early reformers. Once people realized that this was not a problem inflicted by God, but rather by men and women themselves, reformers set about to correct it by persuading the offenders to either moderate their intake or totally abstain from strong drink. The stated goal of the American Temperance Society, founded in 1826, was total abstinence. The movement grew rapidly, in a world where the annual per capita consumption of alcohol was 5.2 gallons of ninety-proof spirits and 15 gallons of twenty-proof cider per person.[34] The annual Fitchburg, Massachusetts, Directory for 1876 listed seven different groups under the heading "Temperance Organizations." The mission of these temperance organizations complemented the goals of other dietary reformers, who proscribed not only spirituous drink, and later wine, beer, and ale, but also coffee, tea, chocolate, and anything else deemed too "stimulating." By 1860, alcohol consumption in the United States had dropped considerably, to about two gallons per person.

Not all families embraced temperance. Although a temperance society had been formed in Amherst, Massachusetts, in 1846, the family of Emily Dickinson chose not to participate. Their brick wine cellar in the basement stored rye, sherry, port, and sweet Malmsey wine—which Mrs. Dickinson served to her afternoon callers. Emily herself made currant wine, which she sometimes gave to her friends as gifts, as well as wine jelly, made in a rose or sheaf of wheat mold.[35] Wealthier Americans considered drinking a class problem that they did not share, regarding temperance as an ideology for those who needed it—not themselves. Bromfield Carey, a fictional Boston Brahmin in William Dean Howells' *The Rise of Silas Lapham* (1885), spoke condescendingly about the Laphams, whom he considered beneath him socially. "I don't believe they have the habit of wine at table," he said. "I suspect that when they don't drink tea and coffee with their dinner, they drink ice-water," which Carey deemed "Horrible!"[36]

The elevation of water as a beverage of choice, as well as root beer, ginger ale, and other "soft" drinks, was a direct result of the temperance movement. The medicinal qualities of certain spring waters had been known since the eighteenth century. William Penn had reported on the availability of "purging mineral waters...as good as Epson," as early as 1683. By the early nineteenth century, Ballston and Saragota, New York, had become fashionable spa towns, where visitors came to bathe in the waters as well as drink them. One visitor described the Saratoga waters as "emetic, cathartic, and diuretic," as well as "good in scrofulous and rheumatic afflictions; likewise in venereal complaints."[37] By 1815, the waters of Saratoga's Congress Spring were being bottled and sold off-site; by the late 1820s, the demand for bottled Saratoga water had generated a thriving industry.

Water from a number of springs in the Saratoga area was marketed to the consuming public in artfully molded glass bottles, like this spring water bottle from Congress Spring, Saratoga Springs, New York, 1865–1889. These bottles were excavated at the site of the tannery dam, Charles Barrett Sr. House, New Ipswich, New Hampshire. (Courtesy of Greg Hanselman.)

In 1880, J. F. Bruce, a Fitchburg grocer advertised that he offered "Saratoga Spring Water on Draught and in Bottles." By then, however, the natural spring waters—and Saratoga was one of many—were being challenged in the market by artificially produced mineral waters and soda water. These were consumed less for their therapeutic effect than for their nonalcoholic character. Mineral and soda waters were often sold by the glass at "fountains," which later transformed into ice cream parlors.[38]

Filtering water was another option that became widespread during the nineteenth century. The scientific understanding of waterborne germs and the role that they played in spreading disease coincided with the increasing use of water filters. According to Dr. J. H. Hanaford, writing in the popular woman's magazine, *The Household*, tap water carried the risk of "many, many ills," including typhus, diarrhea, and indigestion. The problem, as Hannaford described it, was caused by runoff from sink drains and cesspools into the water supply.[39] Household water filters were typically in the form of a large cylindrical crock, with a charcoal filter insert, a lid, and a spigot for dispensing the water.

On the table, as Bromfield Carey had suggested, water was served iced, from a large insulated ice water pitcher or in decorative glass carafes. Either of these items on a dinner table gave tangible evidence to a family's political and moral standards with regard to excess and alcohol. Even water had its pitfalls, however: J. H. Kellogg would have disapproved of ice water, which he felt was "injurious" in large amounts. "In the summer time especially iced water is harmful on account of the sudden cooling of the internal organs which it induces. If drank at all," he argued, "it should be only in small sips and very slowly."[40]

Women, as cooks for their families, had a particular role to play in the Temperance Movement. Dr. E. G. Cook, writing in a popular magazine, *Demorest's Monthly*, challenged women to recognize the potential damage that their cooking could render, as well as to share the blame for drunkenness should they choose to ignore her warning:

> It is one of women's rights to help cure intemperance in drinking by removing excitants from the food. By constantly stimulating, in early life, an unnatural appetite for condiments and dainties, the foundation of intemperance is often laid. Seasoning, therefore, should never be excessive.[41]

Cookery literature reflected women's concerns about alcoholism and their understanding of the relationship between eating habits and drinking patterns. Ann H. Allen, an "Old Housekeeper" and author of *The Housekeeper's Assistant, Composed Upon Temperance Principles* (1845), had been influenced by the early temperance beliefs of Dr. Benjamin Rush. Allen, in her introduction to her cookbook, explained why she had written this book: "I have been anxiously waiting to see, in the numerous publications on temperance, some allusion

No. 236. GOBLET, GOLD LINED.
Satin, Applied, $4.00 (POINTED).
Crystal, Chased,   4.75 (POETIZE).

PATENT FOUNTAIN PITCHER.

Patented April 28, 1885.

New, durable, simple in construction, works
easily, will not get out of order, and keep ice
longer than any other Ice Pitcher manufactured.

No. 241. FOUNTAIN PITCHER.
Porcelain Lined.
Satin, $28.00 (POET).   Satin, Engraved, $30.00 (POLAR).   Hammered, $30.00 (POLE).
Metal Lined, $3.00 less.

(268)

In its 1886–1887 catalog, the Meriden Britannia Company presented ninety different water pitchers, including this innovative
form with its patented serving handle. Part of the appeal lay in
the symbolic importance of water during the Temperance movement, but the ability to keep drinks cold at the table was equally
important. (Courtesy of Dover Publications.)

made to the use of liquors in the preparation of viands, but thus far, I
have not met with even a remark on the subject; this consideration,"
she concluded, "first induced me to get up this little volume."[42] Allen
used no intoxicating liquors in any of her recipes.

RELIGIOUS IDEOLOGY AND FOOD RITUALS

Perfection Through Diet

Prevailing religious ideologies contributed to the transformation of
American ideas about health and diet. The Second Great Awakening,
a series of religious revivals that swept across the United States during
the late eighteenth and early nineteenth centuries, made Evangelical
Protestantism a powerful force in antebellum America. During the

1820s and 1830s, the revivals were particularly strong, drawing thousands of people at a time to hear such charismatic preachers as Charles Grandison Finney. Finney gave his audience a potent antidote to the uncertainty of the times. "Any man can be saved if he will," preached Finney, offering the possibility of salvation through individual action, rather than the uncertainty of waiting for God to reveal one's fate. Evangelical Protestants assumed the imminence of the Second Coming of Christ, and many believed that the United States was destined to be the place where that would happen. Their task, then, was to make the country ready for the millennium by cleaning up problems wherever they saw them. In the minds of many, the restoration of physical health was closely linked to the restoration of moral and spiritual health. If the ills that plagued the nation could be cured, then the millennium would come.[43]

These religious enthusiasms and the camp revivals that they generated had their own sets of foodways. The camp meetings—held out-of-doors where followers camped out for several days in tents—attracted large crowds, sometimes several thousand people. A high level of organization was required to stage an event of this scale—and churchwomen and men developed set procedures, using a committee structure to make it happen. Churchwomen were the main food providers, led by the charitable example of the minister's wife. A typical menu for a tent revival, according to one scholar of historic foodways, might have included a "spit roasted half steer, gallons of coffee, and even candies and confections for the attendees," or perhaps, "boiled dinner, salt fish, and pie."[44] A commentator in California, H. C. Bailey, described the preparations for a Baptist meeting in 1857, beginning with hiring the labor to cook, wash dishes, maintain the stoves and bake ovens, and do whatever was necessary to feed the expected eight hundred to one thousand participants. "Come one, come all, free grub, free provender, and free salvation," she proclaimed. In order to cook for such a crowd, "a large brick baker's oven was provided, with two hundred pounds of bread capacity or double as much beef." She noted that the food committee "generally exchanged donated flour for bread," but this was not always the case. "On one occasion, I mixed, worked, and set to rise two hundred pounds of flour from one o'clock Saturday night till ten o'clock Sunday morning." For meat, the committee looked to donations from local stockmen. According to Bailey, "If we wanted meat, all the committee had to do was butcher it. Stockmen would say, 'You know my brand, go get what you want.'"[45]

Keturah Penton Belknap offered a similar description of a camp meeting that she attended in June 1850. "But here we are in sight and hearing of the Camp meeting, just at the time when the afternoon service was dismissed and Oh, what tumult it was Friday afternoon," she wrote. "A large circle of tents were already up and many more on the way and long tables that would seat twenty or more and Beef hanging in the trees all around. Verily, it did look like feeding the multitude," she exclaimed. Like Bailey, Belknap was involved with the food preparations. "Saturday is preparation day," she explained. "We must cook up for the Sabbath and it all has to be done by stick fire." This was because they did not have any stoves; the women did all of their baking for the encampment at home, baking enough "to last over Sunday." Because cooking was prohibited on the Sabbath, the women's strategy was to get everything done in advance so they would not have to cook on Sunday: "Will cook a lot of meat and roast some chickens in the Dutch oven by the fire and cook dried fruit and make a couple of nice puddings, so all we will have to do is make coffee and tea."[46]

Setting a Religious Table

Other religious events had their own particular sets of food rituals, in particular the days of celebration or fasting that were defined by religious doctrine. For Jews, Passover required an elaborate meal-based ceremony, the Seder. Church laws required Christians to fast during the period of Lent. Nineteenth-century cookbooks reflected these religious traditions, often including recipes and menus specifically related to those events. The following recipe for "Lent Potatoes" called for crushed biscuit and almonds, bound together by eggs and rosewater, rolled into balls, and then deep-fried in boiling lard. What made this "Lenten" was the omission of actual potatoes from the dish, as well as the omission of sugar—although the author, temperance reformer Ann Allen, called for them to be served with a sweet sauce. This recipe came in her cookbook, *The Housekeeper's Assistant, Composed Upon Temperance Principles* (1845).

Lent Potatoes

4 oz. of almonds, and a few bitter,

4 eggs,

3 Savoy biscuit,

1 glass of orange-flower water,

1/2 lb. of lard,

1/2 lb. of butter.

Blanch the almonds with the orange-flower water, then add the butter and the eggs well beaten and strained, a little rose-water, and sweeten to taste. Beat all quite smooth, and grate the biscuit. Make balls with a little flour, the size of a chestnut; have the lard boiling, and throw them in; boil them a fine yellow brown, drain, and serve with sweet sauce in a boat.[47]

Allen also included a recipe for "Cross Buns," a traditional Good Friday pastry. Both of these inclusions suggest that Allen's dietary philosophy was closely linked to a deeply religious worldview. Many reformers, like Allen, crossed over the boundaries between movements, embracing temperance, Grahamism, vegetarianism, and other forms of dietary purification that, they believed, would lead to purification of the nation as a whole.

Cross Buns

2 1/2 lbs. of flour,
1/2 lb. of sifted sugar,
1/2 lb. of butter,
1/2 pint of milk,
1 cup yeast.

Warm the milk and butter together, have the flour sifted and warm by the fire; then put coriander seeds, cinnamon, and mace, all in powder, a table spoonful of each with some salt, then add the milk and butter, and then the yeast; mix in a paste, and set to rise before the fire; when light, mix, make in buns, put them on tins, cover with flannel and set them to rise for one quarter of an hour, then brush them with very hot milk, and bake a nice brown in a moderate oven.[48]

Cookery literature also respected the more generalized religious strictures related to food and diet. Jews, who had been in America since the earliest European migration era, were required to abide by *Kashrut*, the Jewish dietary laws. These laws prohibited the ingestion of certain forbidden animals, or those that had not been killed in accordance with Jewish law. Esther Levy's *Jewish Cookery Book*, published in 1871, clarified these laws for her readers. "We must observe to have the meat coshered and porged by a butcher, that is, to take out the veins and sinews, which are prohibited. Then lay the meat in cold water for an hour," she continued,

afterwards on a perforated board, sprinkling salt on all sides, for about an hour. It must remain there in order to draw out the blood forbidden to our people, after which it must be rinsed under the hydrant, and wiped with a cloth; likewise all the utensils used for that purpose must be well rinsed.

Levy also reminded her readers that food for the Sabbath (Saturday) was to be prepared on Friday and that "it is customary to break off a piece of the dough of two loaves, which are made in commemoration of an ancient offering, and burn it, accompanying the action with a blessing."[49] The menus and recipes offered by Levy reflected the dietary laws as well. For Friday night, or "Sabbath Supper," she proposed "Coffee with hot milk, tea and ice water; white or brown stewed fish as in directions, cold fish fried in oil, or hot, fried in butter, German puffs, hot or cold, some lady finger cakes, salads, horseradish with the white stewed fish." Dessert for this meal consisted of fruits, or possibly ice cream (for which Levy provided two recipes, one made with cream, one without).[50] For breakfast the following morning, Levy commented, "We are not allowed to cook fresh viands on the Sabbath, so we can have the fish that was cooked on Friday, the same as for the Friday supper." For Saturday dinner, she recommended Frimsel soup for a first course, "as that will keep best over night; vegetable soup would be likely to spoil." For the second course, a selection of cold roast fowl or turkey with mashed potatoes and warmed over spinach had to suffice.[51]

For American Catholics—a population that grew dramatically during the nineteenth century with the arrival of immigrants from Ireland, German, Italy, and other European Catholic cultures—this meant meatless Fridays. Friday was fish day. In the Catholic calendar, Friday (the day of the Crucifixion) was a traditional day of fasting. Eating fish was a common alternative to meat, which was prohibited during the fast. As the Catholic population increased, the fish industry responded by bringing fresh fish to market for Friday. According to one commentator, "The retail fish business is peculiar; in fact, it is all retail to the consumer for the reason that it is largely used only on certain days. That practice has come to use from Europe. With all Catholics over here Friday is fish-day, and there is always some kind of fish on the table."[52]

Food and Religious Community

Food provided one of the strongest bonds for religious communities, outside of faith. Sharing food affirmed the strength of the religious community, on a daily basis. Moreover, many religious groups used food as a means of outreach. Sunday suppers, organized and executed by churchwomen, confirmed group values of industry and charity, as did the bake sales, strawberry socials, and other events organized to raise funds, both for charities and for upkeep of the church. This kind of public cooking and sale of food not only benefited the charity but also offered the women a means of female empowerment through a degree of financial independence.[53] The women of the First Congregational Church in Marysville, Ohio, published a cookbook in 1876. Their primary objective, to raise money to build a parsonage, was supplemented by their desire to offer recipes that would help stave off economic hard times by teaching families to cook frugally. In the original edition, entitled *The Centennial Buckeye Cook Book*, the ladies stated that "housekeepers are really finding it a pleasant pastime to search out and stop wastes in household expenses, and to exercise the thousand little economies which thoughtful and careful women understand so readily and practice with such grace."[54]

The Ladies of Marysville had been preceded by the Ladies of Dayton: in 1872, the Ladies Society of the First Presbyterian Church of Dayton, Ohio, had published "a small collection of recipes for plain household cooking." The initial edition of five hundred cookbooks sold out, and the Society published a revised and expanded edition in 1873. In their introduction to the volume, the authors offered the following description of their intentions:

> The present book is much larger than its predecessor, and the recipes it contains have been selected with great care. Many of them were sent voluntarily by parties who were willing to hold themselves responsible for their excellence, while others were solicited, often at the cost of much time and pains—a corn bread here, a pudding there, a salad from some one else—from ladies who had gained a reputation for preparing this or that particular dish.
>
> Our subject is an inexhaustible one, and this book does not venture into the mystical realm of fancy cookery; but is a collection of safe and reliable recipes for the preparation of plain food.[55]

Church cookery, especially within the African-American community, often served political as well as financial objectives. During the antebellum era, the African Methodist Episcopal Church held church suppers, bake sales, and pie raisings to raise funds to support the antislavery cause. According to one participant, "Such coffee, cake, succotash, and fried chicken I have never tasted before."[56]

Other religious communities had distinctive culinary traditions that corresponded to their group ideology. During the late eighteenth and nineteenth centuries, many European religious utopian societies planted their roots and flourished in American soil, including the Amana Colonies in the Midwest, the Amish and the Mennonites in Pennsylvania, and the Shakers, who began in England in 1774.

"Mother Ann" Lee led a group of Shakers to America in 1779 and established the first Shaker community at Watervliet, New York. During the next century, Shaker communities spread out across the United States; by 1850, there were eighteen Shaker communities with around five thousand members.

Under the guidance of Dr. Thomas Corbett, the Shaker community at Canterbury, New Hampshire, dedicated itself to herbal healing. Corbett planted the first herb garden at Canterbury in 1816, which ultimately led to extensive business dealings in medicinal herbs with the outside world. Corbett published the Canterbury community's first herb catalogue in 1835; within two years, annual sales in herbal medicines exceeded one thousand dollars.[57]

The Shakers embraced simple cookery to reflect their ideals of simplicity and absence of ornamentation. As with other religious communities, the Shakers came to see cookery as a form of religious outreach, opening their kitchens and dining rooms to the "World People," offering them meals, and selling pots of "Shaker Beans" and other foodstuffs to the public.[58] Nathaniel Hawthorne visited the Canterbury Shaker community in 1831 and described the experience:

> I walked to the shaker village yesterday, and was shown over the establishment and dined there with a squire and a doctor, also of the "world's people." On my arrival, the first thing I saw was a jolly old shaker carrying an immense decanter, full of their superb cider, and as soon as I told my business, he turned out a tumbler full and gave me. It was as much as a common head could cleverly carry. Our dining room was well furnished, the dinner excellent, and the table was attended by a middle aged shaker lady, good-looking and cheerful, and not to be distinguished either in manners or conversation from other well-educated women in the country.[59]

Initially, the Shakers retained their English foodways, eating a traditional diet that would have been familiar to most rural Americans, combining meats, grains, vegetables, and homemade pastries. After 1837, a period of intense religious revivals within the Shaker communities, however, the Shakers began to embrace dietary reforms. In particular, all Shakers under fifty were required to abstain from drinking imported Chinese tea and coffee, as well as from eating "swine flesh." Those over fifty could exercise "free will."[60] All were encouraged to consume only those foodstuffs produced by the local community. Even though they were separated from the world, Shakers coped with the turmoil and encroachments of modern life in a manner similar to that of the rest of the American public—by embracing forms of self-discipline that

Stereoscopic view of a Shaker dining room at Christmas, set for sixty people. Despite their reputation for austerity, this dining room seems quite festive, with its paper chains, greenery, and vases of hothouse flowers. Most interesting are the caster sets that line the tables, each suspended from the ceiling by a chain to save room on the tabletop as well as facilitate passing. (Courtesy of the Canterbury Shaker Museum.)

would ideally prove to be a hedge against the deteriorating effects of a new age.

NOTES

1. Edward Hitchcock, *Dyspepsy Forstalled and Resisted, or Lectures on Diet, Regimen, and Employment* (Amherst, Massachusetts: J. S. & C. Adams, 1831), 328; Andrew Bigelow, *God's Charge unto Israel: A Sermon Preached . . . at the Annual Election, on Wednesday,* January 6, 1836

(Boston: Dutton and Wentworth, 1836), 22. Quoted in Harvey Green, *Fit for America: Health, Fitness, Sport, and American Society* (New York: Pantheon Books, 1986), 15–16.

2. Quoted in William Woys Weaver, ed., *A Quaker Woman's Cookbook: The Domestic Cookery of Elizabeth Ellicott Lea* (Philadelphia: University of Pennsylvania Press, 1982), xxvii.

3. Catharine Beecher, *Physiology and Calisthenics for Schools and Families* (New York: Harper & Brothers, 1856), 188.

4. Ibid., 102.

5. Ibid., 102.

6. For a more extended commentary on Graham and his significance, see *Oxford Encyclopedia of Food and Drink in America*, s.v. "Sylvester Graham" (by Bonnie J. Slotnick). Stephen Nissenbaum has written a thorough study of Graham and his world, *Sex, Diet, and Debility in Jacksonian America: Sylvester Graham and Health Reform* (Westport, CT: Greenwood Press, 1980). See also, Green, "Spices and the Social Order," in *Fit for America*, especially 45–53.

7. Sylvester Graham, *Lecture on Epidemic Diseases Generally, & Particularly the Spasmodic Cholera* (New York: Mahlon Day 1833).

8. Sylvester Graham, *Lectures on the Science of Human Life*, vol. 2 (Boston: Marsh, Capen, Lyon and Webb, 1839): 448, 455–456; quoted in James Whorton, *Crusaders for Fitness* (Princeton: Princeton University Press, 1982), 47–48.

9. R. O. Cummings, *The American and His Food: A History of Food Habits in the United States* (Chicago: University of Chicago Press, 1940), 44–45.

10. Quoted in Siegfried Giedion, *Mechanization Takes Command* (New York: W. W. Norton & Co., 1969), 206.

11. "Results of Vivisection: Interesting Experiments," *Godey's Lady's Book* 100 (May 1880): 473.

12. John Harvey Kellogg, *The Hygienic Cook Book* (Battle Creek, MI: The Office of the Health Reformer, 1876), 13; ibid., *Household Manual of Domestic Hygiene, Food, and Diet* (Battle Creek, MI: Good Health Publishing, 1882), 51.

13. Beecher, 95.

14. Search for "Graham" as a recipe title in "Feeding America: The Historic American Cookbook Project," Michigan State University Library, http://digital.lib.msu.edu/collections/ (accessed January 9, 2006); Kellogg, *Hygienic Cook Book*, 43.

15. Carrie V. Shuman, *Favorite Dishes: A Columbian Autograph Souvenir Cookery Book* (Chicago: R. R. Donnelley & Sons, 1893), 134; digital edition available at "Feeding America" Web site (accessed January 12, 2006).

16. Ibid., 134.

17. On Alcott, see *Oxford Encyclopedia of Food and Drink in America*, vol. 2, s.v. "Vegetarianism" (Rynn Berry).

18. William Andrus Alcott, *The Young House-Keeper, or Thoughts on Food and Cookery* (Boston: Waite, Pierce, and Co., 1838, 1846); digital edition available at "Feeding America" Web site. See also Jan Longone's excellent scholarly introduction to Alcott's life and work, also on this Web page (accessed January 12, 2006).

19. Ibid., 25. Rush was a Philadelphia physician and early advocate of temperance and dietary reform.

20. Ibid., 18.

21. Ibid., 308.

22. R. T. Trall, *The New Hydropathic Cook-Book* (New York: Fowlers and Wells, 1853), viii.

23. Ibid., ix.

24. Ibid., 146.

25. *Oxford Encyclopedia of Food and Drink in America*, s.v. "Vegetarianism" (by Rynn Berry).

26. Trall, xi.

27. Beecher, 91–92.

28. Ibid., 97.

29. John Harvey Kellogg, *Household Manual of Domestic Hygiene, Food and Diet* (Battle Creek, MI: Good Health Publishing Co., 1882), 51–52.

30. *Oxford Encyclopedia of Food and Drink in America*, s.v. "Vegetarianism" (by Rynn Berry).

31. Kellogg, *Hygienic Cook Book*, iv, 22–23, 18, 8.

32. Ibid., *Household Manual*, 47.

33. "The Art of Cookery," *Godey's Lady's Book* (1876): 91.

34. William J. Rorabaugh, "Estimated U.S. Alcoholic Beverage Consumption, 1790–1860," *Journal of Studies on Alcohol* 37 (March 1976): 360–361. These figures are for 1830.

35. Nancy Harris Brose, Juliana McGovern Dupre, Wendy Tocher Kohler, and Jean McClure Mudge, *Emily Dickinson: Profile of the Poet as Cook, with Selected Recipes* (1976; reprint Amherst, MA: Dickinson Homestead, 1981), 9.

36. William Dean Howells, *The Rise of Silas Lapham* (1885; reprint New York: Library of America, 1982), 988.

37. Helen McKearin and Kenneth M. Wilson, *American Bottles & Flasks and Their Ancestry* (New York: Crown Publishers, 1978), 233. Scotsman J. B. Dunlop, touring Saratoga in 1811, quoted in McKearin and Wilson, 233.

38. Ibid., 237.

39. See Green, *Fit for America*, 108ff., for a discussion of germs and the use of water filters; J. H. Hanaford, "Pure Water," *The Household* 12 (April 1879): 201.

40. Kellogg, *Household Manual*, 66.

41. Mrs. E. G. Cook, M.D., "Sanitarian," *Demorest's Monthly Magazine* 23 (September 1887): 716.

42. Ann H. Allen, Dedication to *The Housekeeper's Assistant, Composed Upon Temperance Principles* (Boston: James Munroe and Co., 1845); digital edition available at "Feeding America" Web site (accessed January 9, 2006).

43. For a more comprehensive discussion of millennialism, see Green, *Fit for America*, 10–12.

44. Cathy Luchetti, *Home on the Range: A Culinary History of the American West* (New York: Villard Books, 1993), 169.

45. Quoted in Luchetti, 170–173.

46. Luchetti, 175–176.

47. Allen, 20.

48. Ibid., 19–20.

49. Esther Levy, *Jewish Cookery Book* (Philadelphia, 1871; reprint Cambridge: Applewood Books, 1988), 5–6.

50. Ibid., 176.

51. Ibid., 177.

52. Thomas A. Rich, *Testimony to Senate Committee on Foreign Relations*, 1885, quoted in Sandra L. Oliver, *Saltwater Foodways: New Englanders and Their Food at Sea and Ashore in the Nineteenth Century* (Mystic, CT: Mystic Seaport, 1995), 338.

53. See Cathy Luchetti's discussion of church cookery and fundraising in *Home on the Range*, 170.

54. See Virginia Westbrook's "Introduction to the Reprint Edition of Buckeye Cookery," in Estelle Woods Wilcox, ed., *Buckeye Cookery and Practical Housekeeping* (1880; reprint St. Paul, MN: Minnesota Historical Society Press, 1988), vii.

55. The Ladies of the First Presbyterian Church, Dayton, OH, *Presbyterian Cook Book* (Dayton, OH: Oliver Crook, & Co, 1873), 7–8; digital edition available at "Feeding America" Web site (accessed January 9, 2006).

56. Luchetti, 168.

57. Scott T. Swank, *Shaker Life, Art, and Architecture: Hands to Work, Hearts to God* (New York: Abbeville Press, 1999), 220.

58. Luchetti, 170. See also Amy Bess Miller and Persis Fuller, *The Best of Shaker Cooking* (1970; reprint New York: Macmillan, 1985). The Canterbury Shakers had begun commercial dairy and cider production in 1801, making butter, cheese, and cider to sell to the public market. Swank, 220.

59. Norman Holmes Pearson, "Hawthorne and the Mannings, *Essex Institute Historical Collections* (July 1958), 185; quoted in Swank, 20.

60. Swank, 84, 221.

GLOSSARY

Apple parer. A mechanical device, table mounted, with a cutting blade and rotary gearing, enabling the apple skin to be removed as the handle was turned. The same principle was used for peeling potatoes.

Bain-marie. A rectangular tin vessel with inserts for food; the pan could be filled with hot water to keep foods in the inserts warm until serving time.

Bolted flour. Flour made white by removing the bran, or outer layer, from the grains of wheat before milling. Health reformers, especially Sylvester Graham and John Harvey Kellogg, were troubled by the ensuing loss of nutritional value.

Bouillabaisse. A Creole fish stew, made with onions, garlic, fish, tomatoes, wine, and herbs. Served with toasted bread.

Burgoo. A thick stew, composed of various meats and vegetables, often cooked outdoors in a large kettle; a Kentucky speciality.

Butter print. A round wooden mold with a carved disk, used for stamping a unique design onto the surface of a round of butter.

Cake board. A carved wooden board used to stamp a design onto the surface of cookies or cakes. Required for New Year's cakes.

Charlotte Russe. A fancy French dessert, popular during the Victorian era; made with custard encased in sponge cake or lady fingers.

Chocolate. A traditional hot drink made by dissolving solid chocolate in hot water or milk, often further flavored with sugar, vanilla, nutmeg, or sometimes wine.

Chowder. A traditional fish-based soup, often flavored with salt pork, potatoes, corn, and onions; sometimes milk-based.

Chutney. A spicy condiment or relish made from fruits, tomatoes or other vegetables, nuts, vinegar, and sugar; originally from India.

Condiment. A flavoring for food; may include salt, pepper, vinegar, ketchup, chutney, or other made or bottled sauces. Considered unhealthy by dietary reformers because "too stimulating."

Confectioner. Someone who makes and sells sweets, candy, chocolate, cakes, and the like.

Cookstove. A cast-iron cooking appliance, generally in a box form, that enclosed a cooking fire; usually equipped with an oven and cooking surface on top. Introduced in the early nineteenth century; common by the 1850s.

Cordial. A liqueur or other alcohol-based stimulant; sometimes used for medical or restorative purposes.

Croquette. A French term for chopped meat and vegetables, formed into a small roll, coated with bread crumbs, and fried.

Deviled. A recipe term to indicate spiciness, through the use of mustard, cayenne, Tabasco Sauce, or other such additives.

Dutch oven. A heavy, iron cooking pot, usually on legs and lidded. The legs allowed cooks to put coals beneath the pot for cooking; the lid was often recessed, so that hot coals could also be put onto it. Widely used as a multipurpose vessel for hearth and open-air cooking and baking.

Dyspepsia. Indigestion, caused by eating excessive amounts of rich foods, especially those prepared with fats and spices. A widespread gastronomic affliction during the nineteenth century.

Eggbeater. A mechanical device, invented in the nineteenth century, for beating air into eggs. The usual form included a gearing mechanism, turned by a handle, that drove wire paddles (which agitated the eggs).

Escalloped. A mode of preparation whereby the main ingredients (for example, oysters, asparagus tips, or minced chicken) are baked in a buttered dish, topped with crushed crackers or bread crumbs.

Fricassee. A French term for stewlike preparation, but unlike stews, the chicken, meat, or shellfish are first sauteed in butter before adding other ingredients and cooking liquid.

Ginger beer. A popular beverage made at home from sugar, ginger, water, and yeast. Typically decanted into small stoneware bottles for storage prior to consumption. Low alcohol content.

Graham flour. Whole wheat flour, advocated by dietary reformer Sylvester Graham as being more healthful. Used to make "Graham bread," "Graham crackers," etc.

Graniteware. Cookware made of porcelain-coated metal; an alternative to tinware. Also refers to white, porcelainlike tablewares with molded decorations. Introduced around 1850.

Griddle cake. A term that encompasses many different forms of flat, round cake, made from a batter of flour or meal, leavening, milk, and eggs, and fried in butter or grease.

Gumbo. A Creole stew, typically made with poultry and/or oysters, crab, or shrimp, and thickened with okra or pounded sassafras leaves (filé). Served with rice.

Hominy grits. Dried, hulled, white grains of corn (hominy), usually ground into a fine meal (grits), soaked and cooked into a mush. Sometimes served at breakfast with sugar and milk, or chilled, sliced, and fried in fat. Grits also mixed with meat, fish, or cheese to produce popular Southern dishes.

Hoppin' John. A traditional African-influenced Southern dish, made with ham hocks, black-eyed peas, and rice.

Icebox. An insulated cabinet, usually found in or near the kitchen, where food could be kept cool with blocks of ice. In urban areas, ice wagons delivered ice to families on a regular basis.

Icehouse. A separate building, room in a house or barn, or subterranean chamber; used to store blocks of ice packed in sawdust so as to keep foods cool during warm weather.

Indian meal. Cornmeal.

Indian pudding. A traditional New England dish, made from cornmeal mixed with milk, molasses, spices, and fat—baked or boiled in a pudding bag or cloth.

Jambalaya. A traditional Creole stew, made with chicken, rice, tomatoes, and ham or smoked sausage.

Lager beer. A clear, light brew produced through a bottom fermenting process (as opposed to ales, porters, and stouts, which were top-fermented). Introduced to Americans by Bavarian brewers in Philadelphia in 1840.

Lard. Rendered and clarified pork fat; used for frying or as an ingredient in pastry, pudding, or other baked goods.

Leavening. Various substances added to dough to make it rise. Yeast was most common, but pearlash, saleratus, baking soda, and later baking powder were also used.

Mason jar. A glass canning vessel with a zinc screw cap; introduced in 1858 by John Mason for preserving fruit.

Mincemeat. A combination of ground meat, suet, nuts, fruits, spices, sugar, lemon peel, and rum, brandy, or cider; the basis for mince pie.

Patty pan. A small tin mold for baking tarts and small cakes; often formed into hearts, stars, rosettes, or other fancy shapes.

Pearlash. Carbonate of potash, commonly used as a leavening agent before baking soda; baking powder.

Pepper pot. A Southern dish, from the West Indies. A tripe-based stew.

Pilau. A traditional Carolina dish, made from chicken, bacon, and rice. Generally known as pilaf elsewhere.

Saleratus. Sodium bicarbonate (baking soda). Widely used as a leavening in the nineteenth century.

Sanitary Fair. Fund-raising events organized by women to raise money for the Civil War effort, specifically to support the work of the Sanitary Commission in Union Army field hospitals and camps. Often revolved around cookery.

Saratoga potatoes. Thin slices of potato, fried until crisp; also known as Saratoga chips—the forerunner of the modern potato chip. Introduced in Saratoga Springs, NY, in the early 1850s.

Scrapple. A Pennsylvania specialty made grinding leftover pork scraps with herbs and spices, cornmeal, and buckwheat flour; cooked as a pudding until thick.

Service à la russe. A fashionable alternative to family-style food service; all food brought to the table by servants, either on individual plates or on platters and dishes. Introduced in the 1840s.

Shrub. A cold beverage made by mixing sweetened fruit juice with brandy, rum, or sweetened fruit vinegar with soda water, as in raspberry shrub.

Souse. A jellied sausage made from the head, feet, ears, and other remaining bits of pig, seasoned with salt, pepper, cayenne, green onion, and parsley. Served cold in slices.

Succotash. A traditional New England dish, made from corn and lima beans.

Sweetmeats. A term used for jellies, jams, preserves, candied fruits, and other delicacies sweetened with sugar syrup. Commonly on the tea or dessert table. Superseded by canned fruit in the 1870s.

Syllabub. An elegant dessert, made with whipped cream flavored with sherry or white wine. Generally served in individual syllabub cups or glasses, often further embellished with jelly.

Temperance. A widespread reform movement in the United States during the nineteenth century, advocating abstinence from alcoholic beverages.

Tin kitchen (aka reflector oven). Widely used for hearth roasting before the advent of cast-iron cookstoves. A rounded tin box containing a spit for roasting meat. Tin kitchens had a door on one side for basting and tending the roast, and open face on the other. The oven's metal surface reflected the heat of the fire back on the roast.

Tureen. A large, covered vessel for serving soup or stew. Part of a dinner service.

SELECTED BIBLIOGRAPHY

Many of the nineteenth-century cookbooks in this bibliography are avail-able as digital reprints on the "Feeding America" Web site (http://digital.lib.msu.edu/projects/cookbooks/). These are indicated with an asterisk (*). In some cases, the edition listed here may differ slightly from that available at "Feeding America."

*A Practical Housekeeper. *The American Practical Cookery Book.* Philadelphia: G. G. Evans, 1860.

Albala, Ken. *Food in Early Modern Europe.* Westport, CT: Greenwood Press, 2003.

*Alcott, William Andrus. *The Young Housekeeper, or, Thoughts on Food and Cookery.* Boston: Waite, Peirce & Co., 1846.

*Allen, Ann H. *The Housekeeper's Assistant, Composed Upon Temperance Principles.* Boston: James Munroe & Co., 1845.

An American Lady. *True Politeness: A Handbook for Ladies.* New York: George A. Leavitt, 1853.

Anderson, Oscar Edward. *Refrigeration in America: A History of a New Technology and Its Impact.* Princeton: Princeton University Press, 1953.

Barlow, Ronald S., ed. *Victorian Houseware, Hardware and Kitchenware: A Pictorial Archive with Over 2000 Illustrations.* Mineola, NY: Dover Publications, Inc., 1992.

Beecher, Catharine E. *Physiology and Calisthenics for Schools and Families.* New York: Harper & Brothers, 1856.

*Beecher, Catharine E., and Harriet Beecher Stowe. *The American Woman's Home.* New York: J. B. Ford and Co., 1869.

*Beecher, Catharine Esther. *Miss Beecher's Domestic Receipt Book: Designed as a Supplement to Her Treatise on Domestic Economy.* 1846. New York: Harper, 1850.

Bird, Isabella L. *Englishwoman in America*. 1856. London: John Murray, 1856.

Brewer, Priscilla J. "Home Fires: Cookstoves in American Culture, 1815–1900." In *House and Home: The Dublin Seminar for New England Folklife Annual Proceedings 16–17 July 1988*. Ed. Peter Benes, pp. 68–88. Boston: Boston University, 1990.

Brillat-Savarin, Jean Anthelme. *The Physiology of Taste*. 1826. Trans. M. F. K. Fisher. San Francisco: North Point Press, 1986.

Brose, Nancy Harvis, Juliana McGovern Dupre, Wendy Tocher Kohler, and Jean McClure Mudge. *Emily Dickinson, Profile of the Poet as Cook, with Selected Recipes*. 1976. Amherst, MA: Dickinson Homestead, 1981.

Brown, Dona. *Inventing New England: Regional Tourism in the Nineteenth Century*. Washington, DC: Smithsonian Institution Press, 1995.

Brown, William J. *The Life of William J. Brown, of Providence, R.I., with Personal Recollections of Incidents in Rhode Island*. 1883. Freeport, New York: Books for Libraries Press, 1971.

Bushman, Claudia. *"A Good Poor Man's Wife": Being a Chronicle of Harriet Hanson Robinson and Her Family in Nineteenth Century New England*. Hanover, NH: University Press of New England, 1981.

Carlo, Joyce W. *Trammels, Trenchers, & Tartlets: A Definitive Tour of the Colonial Kitchen*. Old Saybrook, CT: Peregrine Press, 1982.

Carpenter, Charles H., Jr., and Mary Grace. *Tiffany Silver*. New York: Dodd, Mead & Co., 1978.

Child, Lydia Maria. *The American Frugal Housewife*, reprint 1832. Worthington, OH: Worthington Historical Society, 1965.

Christmas in Germany. *Harper's New Monthly Magazine* 4 (March 1852): 499–500.

Collier, Robert Laird. *English Home Life*. Boston: Tickenor & Co., 1885.

*Collins, Angelina Maria. *The Great Western Cook Book*. New York: A. S. Barnes & Co., 1857.

*Cornelius, Mary Hooker. *The Young Housekeeper's Friend*. Revised ed. Boston: Brown, Taggard, and Chase, 1859.

Corson, Juliet. *Cooking School Text Book and Housekeeper's Guide*, 4th ed. 1877. New York: Orange Judd Co., 1881.

*Corson, Juliet. *Miss Corson's Practical American Cookery*. New York: Dodd, Mead & Co., 1886.

Cowan, Ruth Schwartz. *More Work for Mother: The Ironies of Household Technology from the Open Hearth to the Microwave*. New York: Basic Books, 1983.

Croly, Jane Cunningham. *Jennie June's American Cookery Book*. New York: American News Company, 1870.

Cronon, William. *Nature's Metropolis: Chicago and the Great West*. New York: W. W. Norton & Co., 1991.

Cummings, R. O. *The American and His Food: A History of Food Habits in the United States*. Chicago: University of Chicago Press, 1940.

Davidson, Alan. *The Oxford Companion to Food*. New York: Oxford University Press, 1999.

*De Voe, Thomas F. *The Market Assistant*. New York: Hurd and Houghton, 1867.

Douglas, Mary, and Baron Isherwood. *The World of Goods: Towards an Anthropology of Consumption*. New York: Basic Books, 1979.

Dover Stamping Company. *Dover Stamping Company 1869 Illustrated Catalogue*, reprint 1869. Mendham, NJ: Astragal Press, 1994.

Dublin, Thomas, "Women and Outwork in a Nineteenth-Century New England Town: Fitzwilliam, New Hampshire, 1830–1850." In *The Countryside in the Age of Capitalist Transformation: Essays in the Social History of Rural America*. Ed. Steven Hahn & Jonathan Prude, pp.51–69. Chapel Hill: University of North Carolina Press, 1985.

Earle, Alice Morse. *Customs and Fashions in Old New England*. New York: Charles Scribner's Sons, 1893.

Edge, John T. *A Gracious Plenty: Recipes and Recollections from the American South*. New York: G. P. Putnam's Sons, 1999.

Elias, Norbert. *The History of Manners: The Civilizing Process*. 1939. New York: Pantheon Books, 1982.

Ellet, Elizabeth F., ed. *The New Cyclopaedia of Domestic Economy, and Practical Housekeeper*. Norwich, CT: Henry Bill Publishing Co., 1873.

Faragher, John Mack. *Sugar Creek: Life on the Illinois Prairie*. New Haven: Yale University Press, 1986.

*Farmer, Fannie Merritt. *The Original Boston Cooking School Cookbook, 1896*, Facsimile 1896. New York: Weathervane Books, n.d.

"Feeding America: The Historic American Cookbook Project." *Feeding America: The Historic American Cookbook Project*. Digital Archive, May 21, 2004. Available at http://digital.lib.msu.edu/projects/cookbooks/html/intro_essay.html.

*Fisher, Mrs. Abby. *What Mrs. Fisher Knows about Old Southern Cooking*. San Francisco: Co-op Printing Office, 1881.

Franklin, Linda Campbell. *300 Years of Kitchen Collectibles*, 4th ed. Iola, WI: Krause Publications, 1997; 5th ed. Iola, WI: Krause Publications, 2003.

Funderburg, Anne Cooper. *Chocolate, Strawberry, and Vanilla: A History of American Ice Cream*. Bowling Green, OH: Bowling Green State University Popular Press, 1995.

Fussell, Betty. *The Story of Corn*. New York: Alfred A. Knopf, 1992.

Gabaccia, Donna R. "As American as Budweiser and Pickles?" In *Food Nations: Selling Taste in Consumer Societies*. Ed. Warren Belasco and Philip Scranton, pp. 175–193. New York and London: Routledge, 2002.

Gabaccia, Donna R. *We Are What We Eat: Ethnic Food and the Making of Americans*. Cambridge: Harvard University Press, 1998.

Gesner, C. W. "Concerning Restaurants." *Harper's New Monthly Magazine*, 32(191) (April 1866): 591–592.

Giedion, Siegfried. *Mechanization Takes Command.* New York: W. W. Norton & Co., 1969.

*Gillette, Fanny Lemira. *The White House Cook Book: A Selection of Choice Recipes Original and Selected, During a Period of Forty Years' Practical Housekeeping.* Chicago: R. S. Peale & Co., 1887.

Glasse, Hannah. *The Art of Cookery Made Plain and Easy,* reprint 1805. Bedford, MA: Applewood Books, 1997.

Green, Harvey. *Fit for America: Health, Fitness, Sport, and American Society.* New York: Pantheon Books, 1986.

Haber, Barbara. "The Harvey Girls." In *From Hardtack to Home Fries: An Uncommon History of American Cooks and Meals.* New York: Free Press, 2002.

*Hale, Sarah Josepha. *The Good Housekeeper, or The Way to Live Well and To Be Well While We Live.* Boston: Weeks, Jordon and Co., 1839.

Hale, Sarah Josepha. *The New Household Receipt Book.* New York: H. Long & Brother, 1853.

Hamilton, Dr. Alexander. "Itinerarium." 1744. In *Colonial American Travel Narratives.* Ed. Wendy Martin. New York: Penguin Books, 1994.

Hanlon, Mary. "Music, Literature, Balls, and Entertainments." *Women in America, 1820–1842.* American Studies at the University of Virginia. Available at http://xroads.virginia.edu/~HYPER/DETOC/FEM/entertain.htm (May 23, 2004).

Hanson, Karen V. *A Very Social Time: Crafting Community in Antebellum New England.* Berkeley: University of California Press, 1994.

*Harland, Marion. *Breakfast, Luncheon, and Tea.* New York: Scribner, Armstrong, & Co., 1875.

*Harland, Marion. *Common Sense in the Household: A Manual of Practical Housewifery.* 1871. Birmingham, AL: Oxmoor House, Inc., 1985.

*Hearn, Lofcadio. *La Cuisine Creole.* New Orleans: F. F. Hansell & Bro., Ltd., 1885.

*Henderson, Mary F. *Practical Cooking and Dinner Giving,* eBook. New York: Harper & Brothers, 1877.

Hess, Karen. *The Carolina Rice Kitchen: The African Connection.* Columbia, SC: University of South Carolina Press, 1992.

Hiett, Constance B., and Sharon Butler. *Pleyn Delit: Medieval Cookery for Modern Cooks.* Toronto: University of Toronto Press, 1976.

Hindle, Brooke, and Steven Lubar. *Engines of Change: The American Industrial Revolution, 1790–1860.* Washington, DC: Smithsonian Institution Press, 1986.

Hines, Mary Ann, Gordon Marshall, and William Woys Weaver. *The Larder Invaded: Reflections on Three Centuries of Philadelphia Food and Drink.* Philadelphia: Library Company of Philadelphia and The Historical Society of Pennsylvania, 1987.

Hooker, Richard J. *Food and Drink in America: A History.* Indianapolis and New York: Bobbs-Merrill Co., Inc., 1981.

Jeffrey, Julie Roy. *Frontier Women: Civilizing the West? 1840–1880.* Revised ed. New York: Hill and Wang, 1998.

Jensen, Joan M. *Loosening the Bonds: Mid-Atlantic Farm Women, 1750–1850.* New Haven: Yale University Press, 1986.

Jordan, Terry G. *North American Cattle-Ranching Frontiers: Origins, Diffusion, and Differentiation.* Albuquerque: University of New Mexico Press, 1993.

Kaplan, Anne R., Marjorie A. Hoover, and Willard A. Moore. *The Minnesota Ethnic food Book.* St. Paul: Minnesota Historical Society Press, 1986.

Kasson, John F. *Rudeness and Civility: Manners in Nineteenth-Century Urban America.* New York: Hill & Wang, 1990.

Kellogg, John Harvey. *Household Manual of Domestic Hygiene, Food, and Diet.* Battle Creek, MI: Good Health Publishing, 1882.

Kellogg, John Harvey. *The Hygienic Cook Book.* Battle Creek, MI: The Office of the Health Reformer, 1876.

*Kramer, Bertha. *"Aunt Babette's" Cook Book.* Cincinnati: Block Publishing and Printing Co., 1889.

Kreidberg, Marjorie. *Food on the Frontier: Minnesota Cooking from 1850 to 1900, With Selected Recipes.* St. Paul: Minnesota Historical Society Press, 1975.

*Ladies of the First Presbyterian Church, Dayton, Ohio. *Presbyterian Cook Book.* Dayton, OH: Oliver, Crook & Co, 1873.

Larcom, Lucy. *A New England Girlhood, Outlined from Memory.* 1889. Available online at http://www.gutenberg.org/etext/22932004.

Leslie, Eliza. *The Ladies' Guide to True Politeness and Perfect Manners.* Philadelphia: T. B. Peterson & Bros., 1864.

*Leslie, Eliza. *Miss Leslie's Directions for Cookery: An Unabridged Reprint of the 1851 Classic.* A facsimile of the 1851 edition with an introduction by Jan Longone. Mineola, NY: Dover Publications, Inc., 1999.

*Leslie, Eliza. [A Lady of Philadelphia]. *Seventy-Five Receipts, for Pastry, Cakes, and Sweetmeats.* 1828. Cambridge: Applewood Books, 1988.

Leavitt, Sarah A. *From Catharine Beecher to Martha Stewart: A Cultural History of Domestic Advice.* Chapel Hill: University of North Carolina Press, 2002.

Levy, Esther Jacobs. *Jewish Cookery Book.* 1871. Reprint, Cambridge: Applewood Books, 1988.

Lewis, George H. "The Maine Lobster as Regional Icon: Competing Images Over Time and Social Class." In *A Taste of American Place.* Lanham, MD: Rowan & Littlefield Publishers, Inc., 1998.

*Lincoln, Mary J. *Mrs. Lincoln's Boston Cook Book.* Revised ed. 1883. Boston: Little, Brown, and Co., 1909.

Longone, Jan. "Introduction to Feeding America: The Historic American Cookbook Project." *Feeding America: The Historic American Cookbook Project.* Digital Archive, May 21, 2004. Available at http://digital.lib.msu.edu/projects/cookbooks/html/intro_essay.html.

Lowenstein, Eleanor. *Bibliography of American Cookery Books, 1742–1860.* Worcester: American Antiquarian Society, 1972.

Luchetti, Cathy. *Home on the Range: A Culinary History of the American West.* New York: Villard Books, 1993.

Markham, Gervase. *The English Housewife.* Ed. Michael R. Best. 1615. Montreal: McGill-Queen's University Press, 1994.

Marling, Karal Ann. *George Washington Slept Here: Colonial Revivals and American Culture, 1876–1986.* Cambridge: Harvard University Press, 1988.

McKearin, Helen, and Kenneth M. Wilson. *American Bottles & Flasks and Their Ancestry.* New York: Crown Publishers, 1978.

McMahon, Sarah. "A Comfortable Subsistence: the Changing Composition of Diet in Rural New England, 1620–1840." *William and Mary Quarterly,* 42(1)(January 1985): 26–65.

Miller, Amy Bess, and Persis Fuller. *The Best of Shaker Cooking.* New York: Macmillan & Co., 1985.

Mintz, Sidney W. *Sweetness and Power: The Place of Sugar in Modern History.* New York: Viking Penguin, Inc., 1985.

Morton, Agnes. *Etiquette.* Philadelphia: Penn Publishing Co., 1894.

Neustadt, Kathy. *Clambake: A History and Celebration of an American Tradition.* Amherst: University of Massachusetts Press, 1992.

Nissenbaum, Stephen. *The Battle for Christmas.* New York: Alfred A. Knopf, 1996.

Nordhoff, Charles. *California: A Book for Travellers and Settlers.* New York: Harper & Bros., 1874.

Nylander, Jane C. *Our Own Snug Fireside: Images of the New England Home, 1760–1860.* New York: Alfred A. Knopf, 1993.

Oliver, Sandra L. *Saltwater Foodways: New Englanders and Their Food at Sea and Ashore in the Nineteenth Century.* Mystic, CT: Mystic Seaport, Inc., 1995.

*Parkes, Mrs. William. *Domestic Duties; or, Instructions to Young Married Ladies on the Management of their Households,* 3rd American ed. New York: T & J. Harper, 1829.

*Parkinson, Eleanor. *The Complete Confectioner.* Philadelphia: J. B. Lippincott & Co., 1864.

Parloa, Maria. *Miss Parloa's New Cook Book, A Guide to Marketing and Cooking.* 1880. Boston: Estes and Lauriat, 1888.

Perkins, Elizabeth A. "The Consumer Frontier: Household Consumption in Early Kentucky." *Journal of American History,* 78(2) (September 1991): 486–510.

Plante, Ellen M. *The American Kitchen, 1700 to the Present: From Hearth to Highrise.* New York: Facts on File, Inc., 1995

Putnam, Elizabeth H. *Mrs. Putnam's Receipt Book, and Young Housekeeper's Assistant.* New and revised ed. 1858. New York: Sheldon & Co., 1867.

Pye, David. *The Nature and Art of Workmanship.* Cambridge: Cambridge University Press, 1968.

*Randolph, Mary. *The Virginia House-Wife.* 1824. Ed. Karen Hess. Columbia: University of South Carolina Press, 1984.

Richards, Catherine Cowles. *Village Life in America, 1852–1872.* 1911. Available online at http://www.wordowner.com/richards/.

*Roberts, Robert. *The House Servant's Directory.* 1827. Facsimile, Bedford, MA: Applewood Books, 1993.

Rogers, Sherbrooke. *Sarah Josepha Hale: A New England Pioneer, 1788–1879.* Grantham, NH: Tompson & Rutter, Inc., 1985.

Root, Waverley, and Richard de Rochemont. *Eating in America: A History.* 1976. New York: Ecco Press, 1981.

Rorabaugh, William. "Estimated U.S. Alcoholic Beverage Consumption, 1790–1860." *Journal of Studies on Alcohol,* 37 (March 1976): 360–361.

Roth, Rodris. "New England Kitchen Exhibits." In *Colonial Revival in America.* Ed. Alex Axelrod. New York: W. W. Norton & Co., 1985.

Ruth, John A. *Decorum.* New York: Union Publishing House, 1883.

*Sanderson, J. M. *The Complete Cook.* Philadelphia: J. B. Lippincott, 1864.

Schivelbusch, Wolfgang. *Tastes of Paradise: A Social History of Spices, Stimulants, and Intoxicants.* Trans. David Jacobson. New York: Vintage Books, 1993.

Schlissel, Lillian. *Women's Diaries of the Westward Journey.* New York: Schocken Books, 1982.

*Schuman, Carrie V. *Favorite Dishes: A Columbian Autograph Souvenir Cookery Book.* Chicago: R. R. Donnelley & Sons Co., 1893.

Shapiro, Laura. *Perfection Salad: Women and Cooking at the Turn of the Century.* New York: Farrar, Straus, & Giroux, 1986.

Shephard, Sue. *Pickled, Potted, and Canned: How the Art and Science of Food Preserving Changed the World.* New York: Simon & Schuster, 2000.

Shortridge, Barbara G., and James R., ed. *A Taste of American Place.* Lanham, MD: Rowan & Littlefield Publishers, Inc., 1998.

Slater, Michael. *Dickens on America and the Americans.* Sussex: Harvester Press, 1979.

Smith, Andrew F., ed. *The Oxford Encyclopedia of Food and Drink in America.* 2 vols. New York: Oxford University Press, 2004.

Smith, Andrew F., ed. *Souper Tomatoes: The Story of America's Favorite Food.* New Brunswick: Rutgers University Press, 2000.

Stansell, Christine. *City of Women: Sex and Class in New York, 1790–1860.* Urbana and Chicago: University of Illinois Press, 1987.

Stavely, Kevin, and Kathleen Fitzgerald. *America's Founding Food: The Story of New England Cooking.* Chapel Hill: University of North Carolina Press, 2004.

Strasser, Susan. *Never Done: A History of American Housework.* New York: Pantheon Books, 1982.

Strasser, Susan. *Waste and Want: A Social History of Trash.* New York: Henry Holt and Company, 1999.

Swank, Scott T. *Shaker Life, Art, and Architecture: Hands to Work, Hearts to God.* New York: Abbeville Press, 1999.

Trall, R. T. *The New Hydropathic Cook-Book.* New York: Fowlers and Wells, 1853.

Trollope, Frances Milton. *Domestic Manners of the Americans,* 4th ed. London; New York: Whittaker, Treacher, & Co, 1832.

Twain, Mark. *A Tramp Abroad.* Ed. Shelley Fisher Fishkin. 1880. New York: Oxford University Press, 1996.

Weaver, William Woys. *35 Receipts from "The Larder Invaded".* Philadelphia: Library Company of Philadelphia and The Historical Society of Pennsylvania, 1987.

Weaver, William Woys, ed. *A Quaker Woman's Cookbook: The Domestic Cookery of Elizabeth Ellicott Lea.* Philadelphia: University of Pennsylvania Press, 1982.

Whorton, James. *Crusaders for Fitness.* Princeton: Princeton University Press, 1982.

*Wilcox, Estelle Woods, ed. *Buckeye Cookery and Practical Housekeeping.* 1880. Facsimile edition with a preface by Virginia M. Westbrook. St. Paul, MN: Minnesota Historical Society Press, 1988.

*Williams, Martha McCulloch. *Dishes & Beverages of The Old South.* New York: McBride, Nast & Co., 1913.

Williams, Susan. *Savory Suppers and Fashionable Feasts: Dining in Victorian America.* 1985. Knoxville, TN: University of Tennessee Press, 1996.

Yenne, Bill. *Beers of North America.* New York: Gallery Books, 1986.

Yuletide at Winterthur. Winterthur, DE: Winterthur Museum, 1980.

Zuckerman, Larry. *The Potato: How the Humble Spud Rescued the Western World.* New York: North Point Press, 1998.

INDEX